Robin Jéquier

THE GENE DEAL

First published in paperback in 2018

1

ISBN-13: 978-1720860242
ISBN-10: 1720860246

www.robinjequier.com

For Camilla, with all my love

AUTHOR'S NOTE

The sequencing of the human genetic code, known as DNA, was a revolution in biomedicine. Many view it as the greatest achievement in the history of science, and a major step along the road to saving the lives of millions who suffer from genetically inherited diseases.

In 1996 the leaders of the Human Genome Project signed a global data-share agreement to put sequenced DNA in the public domain, without patent and free of charge for the benefit of mankind. The estimated cost of the Project was three billion dollars - roughly one dollar for each letter of the human genome.

The data was accessible at *GenBank*, a website set up by the National Institutes of Health. However, the prospect of huge financial rewards attracted private business to try sequencing the genome ahead of the others. Observers were alarmed about a possible catastrophe – would commercial owners of data hold the medical community to ransom for massive profit? What if data was obtained by criminals, a rogue state or someone like Hitler? Suppose it became possible to 'edit' DNA, would it trigger a dangerous new era of designer babies, or genetically modified bio-weapons with unimaginable destructive powers?

In 2000 the Human Genome Project produced its initial working draft of sequenced DNA, but many gaps still remained. Some seriously worried that private business would do all in its power, ethical or not, to fill those gaps first and somehow claim legal ownership. Much was at stake and it was felt that the world had a lot to gain from preventing what might become a perilous situation.

This novel is set in 2001 against the backdrop of the public/private race to finish sequencing human DNA. The plot is fictitious, as are the characters but their fears, exploits and suffering are real enough.

RJ
July, 2018

PART ONE

The Order of the Red Star
awarded for
Gallantry in Action

COMRADE MAJOR
ALEXANDER MIKHAIL GRISHIN

The Presidium of the Supreme Soviet awards the Order of the Red Star to Comrade Major Alexander Mikhail Grishin, Soviet Ground Forces, for gallantry in action against an enemy force in the Republic of Afghanistan. Comrade Major Grishin distinguished himself by his valour while he served as a Rifle Company Commander in 56th Airborne Assault Brigade, under command of the 40th Army.

On 12 May 1982 his unit was the forward element on search and destroy operations in rugged terrain in the strategically important Panjshir Valley. As the force neared its tactical objective, they came under intense small arms and rocket fire from rebels in fortified bunkers. At once Comrade Major Grishin moved to the front to direct the movement of his men and to locate the enemy positions. While his men gave cover fire, Comrade Major Grishin skirmished towards the enemy bunkers and assaulted them single-handed with grenades and small arms fire. His courageous actions destroyed two enemy positions and killed five insurgents before he was forced to return to replenish his ammunition. Laden with more grenades, Comrade Major Grishin ran through a hail of enemy gunfire to continue with his assault. With great determination and professionalism he wiped out three more enemy bunkers.

In the course of this action six of Comrade Major Grishin's men were gravely wounded by enemy gunfire. With no thought for his own safety, this gallant officer then rallied his troops to storm the last of the enemy positions, called for helicopter assistance and directed the airborne evacuation of the battle casualties.

Comrade Major Grishin's leadership and courage in close combat with a numerically superior enemy is in the highest traditions of the 56th Airborne Assault Brigade, and does great credit to himself, his unit and Soviet Ground Forces.

CHAPTER 1

Hertfordshire, England, August 2001

'Jacob Bank, guten Tag.'

'Can I speak with Herr Rudi Galler please?'

'Your code word?'

'*Soprano*,' said Raymond.

'Moment, bitte.'

Music from a Haydn string quartet came from the bank's switchboard for a few moments, then Raymond heard the familiar Teutonic voice, 'Galler speaking, may I have your second code word, please?'

'*Elizabeth.*'

'And now the first and the last digits of your ID number?'

'Four and seven.'

'Thank you, Raymond. How are you?'

'Fine thanks, Rudi. I hope the alpine luft is as good as ever?'

'It should be, I'm off to my chalet this weekend. What can I do for you?'

'I expect a very substantial deposit to arrive in my numbered account. I'm not sure exactly when, before the end of this year I hope.'

'All right. How much and in what currency?'

'One hundred million US dollars.'

After a studied silence, Herr Galler asked in a delicate tone, 'Will this... considerable sum come from one source?'

'Yes, one source, one transaction, from Banque Zarkof in Geneva.'

'Superb. And when will you instruct me how to invest it?'

'That's why I've called. I want the new funds to mirror my current portfolio, the same proportion of equities, bonds, real estate and cash, plus five percent to go into your managed fund of alternative instruments.'

'A wise decision, Raymond. Meanwhile what code word should I text to you when the money arrives?'

'Er... how about *Genome*.'

'Thank you, Raymond, we look forward to the arrival of the funds.'

'So do I.'

'You will need to sign the investment authorisations, of course. When you're next in Zurich let's have lunch and I'll get your signature at the same time.'

'Be my guest Rudi. Lunch will be on me.'

Seated at his mahogany desk Raymond put down the receiver and picked up a buff folder. It was not his usual style to wade through lengthy business papers, he preferred a crisp and succinct summary drafted by a subordinate. However, the report in his hand was different – marked *In Strict Confidence for Raymond Herron Only*, it arrived by courier from the author's solicitor. Furthermore, Raymond had attended the author's funeral earlier that year.

With a frown he leaned forward in his leather chair and peered at the front cover. The creak of the chair caused his black labrador, Penny, to prick up her ears from her sprawled position on a rug by the hearth. Behind him, from across the main lawn and through his study window, the morning sun spotlighted the title page: *Confidential Report on Capsella-Biotech, prepared by John Kent*. How strange that John had attached this private document to his Will, Raymond thought, as he looked at the signature and the broken wax seals on the envelope. When he had first opened the package he assumed no one else had read its contents, and today at the Polo Club he would be careful only to show selected extracts to his young guest.

It was the first Saturday of the month, the Queen Mother's one hundred and first birthday. One of the many rewards for owning the majority share of a highly successful private equity business was Sir Raymond Herron's Hertfordshire residence, Ashworth Manor, a medieval house with a Queen Anne façade. Set in six acres of fine trees and herbaceous borders, shrubs and roses, Raymond liked to impress his visitors with the all-weather tennis court and heated swimming pool. He was also particularly fond of a further twenty acres of pasture with a trout lake, and he enjoyed the annual apple blossom in his orchard.

Raymond was proud of his firm, despite his grandfather's unhealthy association with British aristocrats interested in fascism and the nineteen-thirties eugenics movement. The firm had financed sterilisation programmes in the USA, known as 'negative eugenics' later practised by the Nazis as part of their 'final solution'. It all happened long before Raymond's time – under his leadership and renamed Herron International LLP, the business was now an international post-war success story of investment in emerging markets, science and technology.

A tap on the study door stalled Raymond's thoughts and he looked up. His housekeeper entered.

'Your car's ready, Sir.' A scrape of paws on floorboards signalled the entry of Tuppence, a West Highland terrier whose white figure appeared from behind the housekeeper.

'Thank you, Winnie.' Tuppence trotted up to sniff at Penny's nose and lie down beside her. 'I'll be along in a moment.' He tucked John Kent's statement into his briefcase. He glanced at his correspondence, including the pink admission card from the Lord Chamberlain summoning Sir Raymond Herron to an Investiture at Buckingham Palace in October. He carried his briefcase out of the study followed by a hopeful Tuppence, through the galleried hall just as the grandfather clock struck eleven, and out into bright sunlight. His chauffeur Mike opened the rear door of the dark blue BMW and grabbed Tuppence by the collar.

'Straight to the Polo Club?' said Mike.

'That's right. Drop me off, then pick up Mr Shepherd from Hatfield station.'

'No problem.' Mike closed the rear door, handed a disappointed Tuppence to the housekeeper and slid behind the steering wheel.

As he was driven through the Hertfordshire countryside it seemed no time since John Kent's funeral. It reminded Raymond of the time his wife succumbed to Huntingdon's Disease ten years previously, so he had empathised with John Kent's grieving family. The man was a talented business colleague and a good friend.

'What a waste,' he thought, as he rested one hand on his briefcase. The post mortem recorded the cause of death as a leaking artery that slowly filled his chest with blood. There was an inquest but the coroner made no mention of any confidential document attached to the deceased's Will. The last time Raymond ever spoke with John was a spontaneous but tense conversation after a board meeting when they had a few minutes alone:

'You look worried, John.'

'That's because I am.' John frowned. 'It's that biotechnology company, to be frank I'm not comfortable.'

'Why? It should deliver spectacular financial returns. You're more than capable of writing a persuasive investment proposal.'

'Remember, I haven't got a clue about genetic science,' said John, 'yet they want us to invest in a scheme like the publicly funded programme in the USA. We already know a preliminary draft of the human genetic code was published recently, so how can this company gain market share just by filling in the remaining gaps?'

Raymond was unmoved. 'Listen, we've every reason to believe Capsella-Biotech is ahead of the pack in its bid to produce the code of life. Even if Capsella only possesses the rights to a mere five per cent of the data, they would own a product with massive sales potential.'

'I get that, but I can't square away the ethics. Should Herron International be funding a company that could charge the human race a fortune to read the entire human genome? It's like privatising mankind's genetic inheritance.' His voice was uptight. 'I'm suspicious about some of their clients, at my last meeting with Capsella's Chief Executive I happened to notice...'

Raymond cut in. 'Calm down. Follow your business instinct, collate the facts and draft your report.' He smiled reassuringly. 'I trust you.' He touched John on the shoulder and walked away.

The traffic noise increased as Raymond's car joined the dual carriageway. Although he now possessed John's draft report he would never be able to quiz the author - just as well, given that one section of the report recorded a meeting at Capsella's Berlin office when John had noticed on the Chief Executive's desk correspondence seemingly from a certain Middle East country.

'Thank Christ that's still under wraps,' thought Raymond, 'John was a fine colleague with a nose for business opportunities, but on this occasion he had strayed off-piste.'

As his car turned off the road into Eastern Counties Polo Club, Raymond asked Mike to drop him off by the main entrance so he could stretch his legs and walk over to the VIP area. As he strolled towards the hospitality marquee he recalled he still had to sign off an unpaid invoice from Stewart Spender Executive Search, the headhunters assigned to find John Kent's replacement, Guy Shepherd. As always their search fee was exorbitant, and Raymond was keen that this latest addition to the firm would be worth all that money.

CHAPTER 2

Naked and soaked, Guy Shepherd emerged through the steam of the men's showers with a bottle of Paradise body soap clutched in one hand. He wrapped a towel around his lean waist and strode swiftly back towards the lockers. Most weekdays he ran to work in the City of London, and back via the popular Vista Gym near his flat for an intense work-out. He would then savour the healthy after-glow that radiated through his six-foot frame.

An only child who never had to compete with siblings, Guy did not question where his competitive edge came from. At school he had trained hard to earn his position as fly half in the rugby first fifteen, and in his final year at university he had captained the men's first eight, powerful oarsmen who had scored notable wins over Bristol, Durham and Exeter.

He grabbed his clothes from his locker. He was about to meet up with an old friend.

'If you're still interested you can move in the week after next,' said Guy as he poured tea in the kitchen. Guy had just finished taking his visitor round his flat.

'This is just the sort of place I need,' said David, 'and a room with its own en-suite.'

'Well, if we can agree terms, I just need to tidy up some of my ex-girlfriend's stuff and get a decorator to give the spare room a lick of paint.' Guy handed him a mug of tea.

'How long's the room available ?'

'Indefinitely, now that Angela and I have split up.' Guy went to the fridge for some milk. 'I need to share the cost of this place.' He sipped his tea, paused for a moment and said, 'And besides, it's great to see you again after such a long gap, David. I hope you do decide to move in, it'll be like old times.' He smiled.

Guy and David had known each other since junior school. In the playground they looked out for each other, with Guy occasionally muscling in to protect David from bullies who mocked his skinny appearance or picked on him for his skill at mental arithmetic. In return David let Guy copy his maths homework, unprincipled but helpful. During the holidays the two pals would muck around for hours on their bikes and build camp fires, which also gave Guy freedom from domestic friction. They saw less of each other after Guy started at boarding school and David at the local grammar. At different universities they had lost touch, and Guy was not sure what David did after taking his degree except for a rumour that his long-time friend did a short stint in uniform, the police perhaps, or the military.

Guy told his friend that a few months ago he became a junior partner at Herron International, a private equity firm. David said he worked in software design near Finchley Road where his flat-share lease was about to end. To Guy he seemed evasive, changing the subject to talk about his training programme for a marathon run in September.

'What's it in aid of?'

'A charity called Nacro,' said David and he pointed at Guy, 'perhaps you'll sponsor me!'

As Guy opened the fridge to put back the milk jug, an old photograph slid down from the door. David stepped forward to pick it up. It was a faded picture that showed three people standing in front of a triumphal stone arch ornamented with a huge chariot drawn by four horses.

'This must be the Brandenburg Gate in Berlin,' David handed the photo to Guy, 'where I'll finish my marathon run in September.'

'It was taken before the last war when my grandfather, the one in the middle, was a teenager.' Guy pointed to another photograph on top of the fridge, of a Germanic grey-stone building. 'And that one was my grandfather's home. You remember? His family was German.'

'I'd forgotten that,' said David.

That was June 2001, it was now early August and David Bond was comfortably installed in Guy's spare room. Two busy men, they enjoyed each other's company when time allowed. Guy had made a good start at Herron International and was already accompanying senior partners to client meetings. Next week-end he was to have a private lunch with the Chairman - something about a biotech company in Germany.

CHAPTER 3

A loudspeaker welcomed everyone to Eastern Counties Polo Club 2001 Challenge Cup sponsored by Herron International LLP, and announced that the first chukka would start at two o'clock. Flags fluttered and large signs displayed the Herron logo. Company chairman Sir Raymond Herron stood holding a glass of whisky at the entrance to a white hospitality marquee that dwarfed everything in the lawned VIP area. Beyond the polo pitch his company BMW glided past rows of loose boxes, until it came to a halt opposite an array of upmarket clothing stalls. He watched the chauffeur nip smartly round to open the passenger door. Guy Shepherd got out of the car, strolled past groups of picnickers on a nearby lawn and through a gate in the white fence, the preserve of VIPs. He made his way past coloured umbrellas and tables colonised by panama hats and stylish sundresses while Raymond sized him up: Guy was good looking, well-dressed, and seemed to know it.

Raymond greeted his guest with a broad smile and a firm handshake, 'Good to see you again, Guy. Drink?' He signalled to a waiter.

'A cold beer please, sir.' The waiter nodded and went to the bar.

'Call me Raymond.' He smiled. 'I thought this a good opportunity to get to know you better after several months on Herron's payroll. Best done away from the office.'

'Do you live near here?'

'Ashworth village about ten miles away. I've been a Patron of this club for ages,' Raymond gestured with his left hand. The sun glinted off his engraved signet ring. 'This is Herron International's fifth year as sponsor of the club's annual Challenge Cup. Ah, here's your drink.'

Raymond had booked a table in a shaded area with a good view of the pitch. They took their seats and a waiter brought them menus. 'Have whatever you want Guy but I recommend the sea bass.'

From the pitch came the sound of 'stick-and-ball' as mounted polo players practised. When the waiter returned they placed their orders and Raymond selected a white wine before he directed his gaze at Guy.

'There's a client I need to discuss, you'll know which one, its European research laboratory is in Berlin.'

'An interesting coincidence,' said Guy and placed his wine glass on the table, 'my father's family comes from there.'

'Berlin? How come?'

'Dad's family was German.'

'But Shepherd is an English name.'

'Yes, it is. My great-grandparents lived in Berlin until the nineteen thirties when they got out of Germany with their only son, Carl, my grandfather. The rest of the family died at Auschwitz.' Raymond raised his eyebrows and paused with a piece of bread in his hands. 'The three who pitched up at Dover applied for British citizenship and changed their surname from Schäfer to...' He was suddenly interrupted.

'Hey, Pop!'

'Jessica, my dear,' said Raymond, as he was approached by a brunette in a cream sundress and large sunglasses. Both men stood. Raymond kissed the woman's tanned cheeks. 'I didn't expect to see you today.'

'I got an earlier flight so I thought I'd join you. I hope that's okay?'

'Of course. Let me introduce you to Guy Shepherd who joined the firm earlier this year.'

She removed her sunglasses from brown eyes, smiled and held out her hand to Guy. 'Good to see you again,' she said.

'You know each other?' asked Raymond.

'We met at the Herron summer bash in June,' said Jessica.

'In that case there's no need to introduce my step-daughter, Guy. I thought she would still be on a flight from New York today.' He turned to Jessica. 'It's wonderful to see you, dear, can I get you some lunch?'

'No thanks, Pop, I've already had a bite.' She placed her sunglasses on the table. 'Some of that wine would be nice, please.' Raymond noticed how she then looked back at Guy.

Guy blushed. 'How's business?'

'Busy,' she said, 'there's a major event coming up.'

'Jessica's modest,' said Raymond and nodded towards her, 'her firm's got a contract with New York Fashion Week next month.'

The waiter arrived with two plates of pan fried sea bass and wine for Jessica. Hooves thundered as ponies were driven towards the pitch boundary, followed by a loud 'thwack' as the ball hurtled towards the far goal. The crowds cheered.

When the noise subsided Raymond looked at the other two and said, 'Guy was telling me about his German family who came to Britain before the war, what was their name, Shaft…?'

'My grandfather was Carl Schäfer, who changed his name to Charles Shepherd – Schäfer is the German for shepherd. After the family arrived in this country he did his bit for the war effort, took a PhD and worked as a university professor. A passionate socialist.'

Raymond chuckled. 'So where does your capitalist DNA come from?'

'D N what?'

'DNA, Guy. Your genes.'

'Oh, Dad was an industrial accountant so perhaps I've inherited his free-market genes.'

Jessica grinned and turned to Raymond. 'Pop, will you excuse me while I look at some of the ponies and watch a few chukkas? I'll leave you both to your discussion.'

'Of course. Join us for coffee later.' They stood as Jessica got up. She kept hold of her wine glass and walked past a spectator stand towards a row of trees where strings of ponies were tethered in the shade.

'I hope you didn't mind the chat with Jessica,' said Raymond, I'm very fond of my step-daughter.'

'When did she become your step-daughter?'

'She was four when I married her mother, Elizabeth Parry.'

'Elizabeth Parry the singer?'

'That's right. When she died ten years ago I became Jessica's only so-called parent.'

'She's delightful,' said Guy.

Teams mounted on fresh ponies trotted out to the pitch like medieval jousters. Over coffee both men removed their jackets in deference to the heat and Raymond steered the conversation back to business. 'Guy, you've read an outline brief on Capsella-Biotech' He did not wait for a response and explained that several years ago Capsella had launched its quest to sequence the genetic code of human existence, known as the human genome. News of the company's activity had seeped out but nobody knew the overall extent of its progress, and there were serious concerns about what Capsella might do with the data.

Raymond described the publicly funded Human Genome Project and its 1996 data-share agreement with free access via a website, and the huge cost to US taxpayers.

'Since the initial draft of the genome was published, Capsella has developed a clear lead, and it looks like they'll complete their private sequencing programme way ahead of the public one and at a fraction of the cost. Capsella is led by a highly motivated molecular biologist, Alex Grishin, whose vision is to shortcut the whole process of gene identification.

'I presume Alex's operation can pick up the information already made public by the Human Genome Project?'

'Quite so. Think of Capsella as the gateway to a vast database of the human genome. To gain online access users would register with Capsella online, pay subscription fees and tick a box that legally binds them not to re-sell any of the data. While research scientists might view segments for free, that would be a loss-leader to tempt them to subscribe to the entire database.'

'What about other users?'

'Whether it's a pharmaceutical multi-national or a lone academic, the full data can be accessed for an annual subscription, on a sliding scale. That could be millions a year for big corporates, with smaller fees for individuals. Much of the information will be critical in research fields such as biomedicine, and Capsella would become the world's principal supplier of genomic information.'

'How do you know that governments will let it happen?'

'They can't prevent it. Patent law is international.' Raymond could see that Guy was thoughtful. 'You joined this firm to make money. Lots. Here's your chance.'

'What do you want me to do?'

'Review Capsella-Biotech and its structure, then put together a draft investment proposal. I want Herron International to finance their operations and reap the rewards.' Raymond produced a folder from his briefcase, clutched it with both hands and leaned towards Guy. 'Look, this also involves John Kent, the partner who died whom you've replaced,' and as he tapped the folder he spoke in a discreet, measured tone, 'what I'm about to tell you is in strict confidence between you and me. Understand?'

Fifteen minutes later Jessica rejoined their table. She was chatty, interested in Guy and eager for some black coffee.

CHAPTER 4

'Lufthansa flight LH 921 to Berlin Tegel Airport is now ready for boarding, passengers should proceed to gate nine.'

Guy put down the Financial Times and made his way from the departure lounge. Seated in Club Class he felt tired after his date with Jessica Parry the previous evening.

'Good to see you again, Guy,' she had pecked him on the cheek, 'this is very kind of you. I've not eaten here before, French isn't it?'

'Yes, I hope you like it,' he said, eyeing her figure.

They chatted about their earlier lives. Jessica said she graduated in Fashion PR followed by a stint at a major fashion house. Later she set up her own fashion events business with a fair portion of her time now spent in the States. She had seemed impressed by Guy's sportive prowess. 'I hope I've not kept you from your work-out this evening,' she giggled, but Guy just smiled. Jessica cut too slim and enchanting a figure to bother about weights and the rowing machine.

'How do you find Pop's firm?' she had asked.

'Fine. Early days but lots to do. I'm off to Berlin tomorrow to visit a potential client, a biotech company.'

Over a hot breakfast at thirty-two thousand feet Guy recalled Jessica's' remarks about her connection with Raymond. Her eyes had twinkled above cheeks flushed by the vintage wine when she had said, 'I was four when Pop married Mummy. After she died he and I have always supported each other.'

'Does your Pop, er, I mean Raymond, have any other family?'

'One identical twin, that's all, Ben Herron the actor. Have you heard of him?' Guy looked blank.

'Ben started out in theatre but he now does radio and television voice-overs.'

'Do they see much of each other?'

'Now and again, but they have a remarkable natural communion. Ever since childhood one has often known what the other's thinking, so-called telepathy that sometimes occurs between identical twins,' she said. 'Pop and Ben call it thought transference. It can be triggered by sudden pain, bad news or negative emotions.'

'Sounds a bit far-fetched,' said Guy.

'Not at all,' said Jessica. 'Take the founder of The Guinness Book of Records, Ross McWhirter, assassinated by the IRA in 1975. His identical twin Norris had a simultaneous reaction to his brother's sudden death. At exactly the same time as the shooting, Norris, who lived several miles away, for no apparent reason suffered a spasm and slumped into a chair as if similarly struck.'

'I don't remember that…'

'It was before your time,' Jessica touched his arm which gave him goose bumps, 'and mine. I heard about it from Uncle Ben, he's a council member of the Society for Psychical Research.'

Guy paid with a debit card and smiled. 'My flat for more coffee?'

She hesitated. 'Guy, I'm not sure if…'

'Just coffee, that's all,' he said with a boyish smile. 'Call it a simultaneous action, you'll meet my flatmate David Bond. He's an old friend.'

'That would be nice, thank you.'

At the Arrivals gate Guy was met by a driver from Capsella-Biotech. It was half an hour to Wannsee lake on the south west outskirts of Berlin. On Königstrasse, a straight highway that runs adjacent to an area of forest, the driver slowed and came off the main road in the direction of the woods. They passed an enclave of sumptuous villas whose freeholders, Guy presumed, owned the cluster of sailing yachts he had just seen moored at the water's edge where sunlight danced on ripples as the boats bobbed up and down. The car swung off the main road onto a driveway of several hundred metres flanked on both sides by woodland. Although not a keen naturalist Guy was amazed that a city like Berlin was home to vast areas of forest. As the car slowed he singled out beech trees, conifers and silver birches that towered above the shrubs on a carpet of dead leaves, until at last the car reached the main gate. The perimeter fence displayed signs at regular intervals: 'Betreten Verboten!' *No Entry!*

Beside a billboard marked *Capsella-Biotech GmbH* security guards with clipboards asked, 'Ihr Identifikation?' Guy produced his passport and the appointment letter from Alex Grishin. The barrier was raised and they were waved through. They parked opposite four parallel smoked glass buildings connected to each other by glazed walkways; it was not possible to see what went on indoors behind the reflective windows. The driver escorted him from the car to the main entrance and through a wide porch adorned by four giant letters carved in granite, A, T, G and C, which Guy later learnt represent the four base letters of DNA code.

The lobby was at the far end of a large indoor atrium, a space-age arcade covered by a glass roof supported by diagonal steel beams. To reach reception Guy first had to walk along an aisle interspersed with three water pools. Bordered by fig trees, the aisle was also criss-crossed by a raised line of flowers that curled its way above. After he was handed a visitor pass and shown upstairs to a waiting area, he looked down into the atrium and saw that the horticultural design he had just walked through imitated the DNA helix.

On display in the waiting area he saw a large high-definition colour photograph of an unusual plant, with a caption underneath that he did not understand:

Capsella Rubella oder 'Rot Schäfer'
Es begann sich selbst zu befruchten vor
circa 200,000 Jahren
Und ist ein ausgezeichnetes Modell für die
Untersuchung der Wirkung auf sein Genom

Apart from the word 'Schäfer' - his ancestral surname - the remnants of his schoolboy German were hazy and he wondered what the rest of it meant. He scribbled on a notepad for several minutes until the whiff of perfume interrupted his jottings. A woman introduced herself as Kirsten, the Chief Executive's PA. She was accompanied by two security guards, uniformed bouncers with shaved heads who followed at a discreet distance as she took Guy up a floor where they walked through a door inscribed: *Dr Alexander M. Grishin, Chief Executive*. The two heavies remained outside.

'Welcome to Capsella, Guy, nice of you to visit.' Alex spoke excellent English but with a distinct Russian accent. As they shook hands Guy felt a twinge in his stomach.

They settled into easy chairs in front of a large teak desk. Photo frames lined up on the desk faced away from the room towards Alex's leather swivel chair. Fragmented light came through the smoked glass window behind. While they exchanged courtesies Guy's thoughts accelerated, he was looking at someone who resembled his own father. Probably in his early fifties, Alex Grishin was a thoughtful looking man of slim build with grey hair, a finely cut face and bright intelligent eyes. An alcoholic? A liar? A lousy parent and beater of young boys? Unlikely, he supposed, but sound reasons for Guy to have hated his father.

'How long have you headed up this firm, Alex?'

'I became chief executive two years ago. Before that I was managing director of a genetic research company in Berlin that was bought out by Capsella-Biotech.'

'I'm going to review your company and write an investment prospectus. I've taken over from John Kent who...'

'Yes I heard. Sorry he'd passed away.'

Tea and coffee were brought in by Alex's PA. 'Tell me why Herron International should invest in your operation,' said Guy.

'In the end this is about prolonging life expectancy and cutting the long-term costs of managing illness,' Alex smiled. 'The financial benefits for health care organisations around the world will be enormous. Herron specialises in technology and has global reach. A perfect fit.'

'What about other competitors, private companies?'

'Others might claim patent rights to different genomes, but they haven't got the complete human genome. We've got great IT, but with a further four hundred million dollars we can obtain three hundred of the latest Spectra 6500 computers with enough memory to make us the largest sequencing facility in the world.'

'Where would all these computers go?'

'We've got that figured out, Guy. Look, drink up your coffee then why don't I show you round this place?'

On his tour of the premises Guy was introduced to various heads of departments whose technical functions he struggled to understand. He was not introduced to the two security men whose presence he almost felt as they tailed him and Alex like creepy shadows. One vast floor was empty save for dozens of wall sockets and sprouting electric wires. The whole of this area was designated for the hoped-for Spectra computers.

As they strolled through a walkway that connected two wings Alex said, 'You know what turns me on about this whole damn operation? It'll throw light on one of mankind's deepest concerns.'

'What's that, Alex?'

'The mystery of our own existence. Years ago, when I came out of Afghanistan, I yearned to understand the science of life, its whole meaning...' his voice tailed off and he gave his security men a meaningful glance. 'Guy, we already have six clients ready to pay twenty-five million a time for our data, and I've also got hundreds of employees whose livelihoods depend on this work. If we fail to accelerate our research, the clients will go elsewhere.' They walked through a pair of double doors into an air-conditioned space.

'Unusual,' observed Guy as he entered what was described to him as the Sequencing Room, 'what's this all about?'

'Think of us as a production pipeline,' said Alex, 'that sequences millions of DNA fragments and uses biochemists to prepare them for these machines. Computer algorithms then kick in to re-order the samples into the completed sequence.' He gave Guy a knowing look. 'When we get the new Spectra computers we'll do the same, only a great deal faster.'

'What DNA are you using?'

'We started with DNA from Drosophila, the fruit fly. We've also worked on the DNA from Capsella Rubella, a plant that originated thousands of years ago, we've used it in earlier studies. But what really excites me is we're now onto blood and sperm from a real human.'

Guy looked pensive. 'Whose?'

Alex's eyes narrowed. 'Mine.'

What do I make of him? It was Guy's thought as he took his first sip of wine on the return flight to London. Does Alex really think he has a decent business model with a mere six clients that pay twenty-five million a time, when most health organisations would wait to obtain their genetic data for free from the public database? Or perhaps the Human Genome Project is flawed and will fail to produce the complete DNA sequence? Either way, if Herron International is to risk a substantial cash injection into Capsella, more hard evidence will be needed of the potential rewards.

There had to be more to Capsella's operation than Alex seemed prepared to divulge. John Kent's report had hinted at Capsella's plans to patent its data, which in effect could hold the global genomics community to ransom. A massive money spinner, but it would stifle scientific progress – Guy speculated whether Alex Grishin wanted that to happen.

He recalled how Alex had side-stepped an earlier question about sole ownership of intellectual property – for what reason? It reminded Guy how his father often ducked awkward questions. And why was that two-man swat team following them throughout his visit? As for all that crap about Afghanistan and the meaning of life, who was this Ruski trying to impress?

Guy was also curious why Raymond did not show him the full contents of John Kent's report, although bits of it had been explained. As he finished his wine he wished he was a clairvoyant who could communicate with the deceased John Kent. A steward then appeared and topped up his wine glass. Guy wondered how much he could trust Raymond – when does a Chairman invite a young partner to a polo club for a simple business discussion? It seemed almost devious. Surely they could have talked in the office during work hours, after all they hardly knew each other. Was it really a coincidence when Jessica showed up at the polo club, or had that been stage managed to put Guy off his guard? Maybe Raymond thought him naïve, someone to be manipulated.

Guy knew he should focus. With three hundred and fifty Capsella jobs to sustain at a profit he must have information that stacked up, know what the product will do, the costs and more details of potential clients. He also wanted to find out why Raymond was holding back the John Kent report. Something was not right.

He needed to see that report. By the time his plane landed he had a pretty clear idea where he might find it.

CHAPTER 5

The buzzer sounded on Raymond's intercom. A light indicated it was the senior Managing Partner.

'Raymond I must speak with you now, please.'

'What's the matter?'

'It's that Shepherd fellow, he's in deep shit. I'll come up and explain.'

'Oh, no.' Raymond groaned, released the intercom button, leaned back with both hands clasped on the arms of his swivel chair and raised his eyes to the ceiling. Only the previous week he had called Capsella's Berlin office to ask Alex about the meeting with Guy.

'He's a good man,' Alex had said, 'and he seemed to grasp the need for our new Spectra computers.'

'Did Guy mention John Kent or Westfälische Strasse?'

'Hardly at all, Raymond. Just relax.'

'I'll ensure that Guy's written proposal convinces my senior partners.'

'Raymond, we need that money. You must get it.'

Raymond's attention was brought back to the present by the abrupt appearance of Herron's Managing Partner who marched through the office door and across the Kashmir wool carpet. William Vinson held a disk in his right hand and refused Raymond's offer of a seat.

'That runt Guy Shepherd has been with Herron International for barely two minutes.' He was seething.

'Now he gets caught filching through files when he thought nobody was looking.'

Raymond's hands held on to the edge of his desk and he asked what, precisely, had happened and he was handed the disk and urged to watch the CCTV recording right away. The first shot was of Guy as he arrived at Herron's London office over the week-end to 'catch up on work' as he later stated, but he did not take into account the building's twenty-four-seven CCTV security. In Raymond's outer office a microchip camera concealed in the face of a wall clock provided a wide-angle view of the PA's work area. With the date and time at the bottom of the picture, Guy was seen to enter and search the PA's desk for the keys to four large filing cabinets. He then sifted through every drawer.

Raymond clicked 'pause'. 'When did you find out about this?'

'This morning. I've already interviewed Guy. I didn't show him this footage to begin with, but just told him someone must have been through your PA's files over the week-end, and did he know anything about it as the porter had seen him here on Sunday morning.

'And?' Raymond lifted his eyebrows.

'Guy said yes, and claimed he wanted to look for background information on Capsella, so I told him he should have requested the files in working hours, and just who the fuck did he think he was.'

'What did he say?'

'That he required further details about Capsella's clients. Look at the rest of the footage.'

Raymond clicked the mouse and the images came back to life. Guy could be seen examining files, taking photocopies of several folios and tucking them into his briefcase.

'What's happened to those copies?' asked Raymond.

'When I asked him if he made copies of any documents, he stared at me in silence. So I showed him this security footage. He went as red as a tomato. I told him his behaviour was unprofessional and to hand back the photocopies immediately.'

'Leave this with me.' Raymond pushed his chair back from the computer screen and stood up. 'Send Guy up now. I'll find out what he's up to. It may be necessary to arrange a cooling off period.'

'Okay, but we can do without this sort of thing, I hope you give the bloody fool an imperial rocket. And what about Capsella?'

'The company has strong growth potential. I want Herron International to provide their finance.'

'I'm in. Let's do it.' William turned towards the office door. 'I'll fetch Guy.'

Raymond waited until he was alone then let out a sigh.

'Guy's here,' broke in his PA a few moments later.

'Send him in please.' He did not invite Guy to sit. The two men stood a metre apart as Raymond's gaze fixed onto those striking blue eyes, and after an awkward pause he said, 'Good morning,' his hands clasped securely behind his back.

'Good morning.' Guy took a deep breath. 'Sir, I owe you an apology.'

After awkward exchanges of 'too damn right', 'but I can explain,' and 'just what in heaven's name were you playing at?' Raymond told Guy to hand back all the material on Capsella. He asked why not put in a request for the information, and Guy said he was not sure what he was looking for, so could not really ask, in any case he would have felt embarrassed trying to identify random pieces of an unknown jigsaw.

'I bet you're bloody embarrassed now,' said Raymond. 'Look, Alex Grishin and I have told you all you need to know, so what else did you hope to find?'

'For Capsella to make squillions in profits, it needs hundreds of organisations to sign up for their data and millions of individual subscribers too. So far they have a mere dozen corporates on their client list. Where will the rest come from?'

'Once we've provided four hundred million dollars to buy the Spectra machines and Capsella spews out the rest of the human genetic code, we'll have our own marketers and business development advisors on the case. This is not short-term. Capital growth will be phenomenal once the gains come through.'

'And what about John Kent's suspicions that pointed to an unstable country not exactly a million miles from Saudi?'

Raymond braced himself as he stared wide eyed and motionless at Guy, who glared back. Raymond's lips turned up. 'Christ, you've taken a peek at John's report haven't you? What John alluded to was mere suspicion, nothing more, and what he wrote was addressed in confidence to me, do you understand? Not to you, not to some other partner in this firm, but to <u>me</u>. None of his thoughts have been verified, and I won't have my company's relationship with Capsella-Biotech stymied by his doubts or by your mistrust.'

Raymond explained that to follow due process Guy would be removed from the Capsella assignment forthwith and temporarily suspended from his job at Herron on full pay pending a disciplinary review.

'Why don't you just fire me?' asked Guy.

'I may have to.' He frowned. 'Go and clear your desk. You'll be escorted from the premises.'

Guy did not say a word, he just looked at Raymond.

'This is not personal Guy. Consider yourself lucky, as it happens I'm confident that the majority of our partners will support the Capsella contract. If we can also get over this, erm, one-off indiscretion, and provided you cooperate, we might avoid too drastic an outcome.'

An hour later Raymond strolled over to his office window and watched Guy leave the building carrying a sports bag. He wondered whether this talented man would attend his step-daughter's upcoming Fashion Preview at Somerset House. Perhaps it made no difference, the two were bound to see each other again if Jessica's recent remarks were anything to go by. He did not want to tell her what had just happened. He assumed that Guy would.

Raymond reckoned he had had enough of his office for the day, so he leaned towards his intercom and called for his car to drive him home. Puffy clouds glided across the blue sky as he climbed out of the car at Ashworth Manor. He was greeted by both dogs, their tails in overdrive.

'Penny old girl! Hello, Tuppence!' They followed him to the study and settled by the hearth. How he ached to hear her voice – he turned on the hi-fi and relished the aria sung by the renowned soprano, his beloved Dame Elizabeth Parry, and as he tried to relaxed he started to think. Churchill once described it as *Black Dog* which prompted Raymond to call it *Dark Cloud*, a name that Ben and Jessica came to understand: a stress induced glimpse of hell caused by inadequate serotonin and noradrenaline in the brain.

His thoughts turned to Alex Grishin whom he decided not to tell about Guy until the disciplinary process was out of the way. With the endorsement of Herron's senior Managing Partner the four hundred million dollars should get approved. But it was less clear how Alex planned to disguise the new sequencing machines at his other laboratory in Westfälische Strasse. With his discovery of how to edit DNA, Alex had the key to a treasure trove and Raymond fully intended to seize his share. If the plan was to stay on course he had to make sure that Alex would cover his tracks.

He reached for the telephone.

CHAPTER 6

At the Vista Gym a personal trainer looked up from behind the service counter as Guy stomped across the vinyl floor. He pounded into the locker room, slammed the door and banged his sports bag onto a bench. Mumbling obscenities he got changed. How could he have been such an idiot as to overlook the inevitable surveillance camera in the Chairman's outer office?

'So what the hell happened?' asked David as he and Guy shared a take-away that evening. Slumped on a beanbag dressed only in a frayed T-shirt and boxer shorts, his bare legs outstretched, Guy described some of his dealings with Capsella and the day's events. He also mentioned the late John Kent's misgivings.

'In strict confidence,' he gestured to David with a fork.

'Scout's honour, but why didn't you just ask to see the files you wanted?'

Guy looked uncomfortable; not wanting to reveal all his suspicions he gave David the same answer he gave Raymond earlier. Guy stood up and padded across to the kitchen counter and helped himself to another beer. 'Actually, there's one way you could help,' he opened a bottle, took a swig and gave David a steely look. 'Call it a return favour for the times I saved your ass from tight spots at school.'

Later that evening Guy phoned Jessica.

'Things are not so good. How about a drink tomorrow evening?'

'Sorry Guy, I'd love to, but I'm rehearsing for my London Preview event.'

'The next day?'

'I've a better idea. Come along to tomorrow's rehearsal, and perhaps we could nip out for a drink afterwards?'

'Sounds great. Where will you be?'

'Somerset House in the Strand. Be there for seven.'

The following evening David, intrigued by his flatmate's request to help investigate Alex Grishin, searched the internet to start building a picture of the Russian's background. David was not disappointed. The decorated Soviet Army officer Alexander Grishin featured in several archived news items and web pages that David printed out; as he did so he wondered how Guy had enjoyed the rehearsal at Somerset House.

Come to think of it, it was already one o'clock in the morning, where the heck was Guy?

Flush from the success of her final rehearsal when nobody had lost their cool, Jessica and Guy walked up the Strand towards the island church of Saint Clement Danes. Opposite, as they sat outside Lody's Wine Bar Guy described the frosty showdown with her step-father. She shrugged when he said he was taken off the Berlin client's case to spend a few days on home leave.

'That's work. It's now time to chill. Let me know any time if you need any help.'

For a while neither of them spoke until Guy said, 'You love your Pop as if he was your natural father, don't you?'

'I never knew my real father,' said Jessica.

'Who was he?'

'An artiste's agent. My mother was one of his clients. A while after my parents divorced Mummy went to an art exhibition where she met Raymond. He's always been incredibly kind. I'm lucky.'

People and night traffic passed on both sides of the church. Jessica asked what Guy had thought of the Preview dress rehearsal. He took her hand and replied that it was great, and her fashion event was destined to be a hit in New York next month.

'Did you have a good time last night?' asked David the next morning as he dropped two teabags into a pot. Guy broke into a self-conscious smile and David gave him a shrewd look, 'I'm surprised you're back here for breakfast,' he said, 'as you don't have to be in your office today.'

'Jessica had an early start, so we both caught the same docklands milk train.'

'I see,' he hesitated then poured tea. 'Guy, do you know what you're doing?'

'What do you mean?'

'The day after getting suspended from Herron International you've obviously had it off with the Chairman's daughter,' David clutched his mug with both hands, 'This is just friendly advice, but…'

'The Chairman hasn't got a daughter, he has a step-daughter and I'm incredibly fond of her. Head over heels if you must know.'

David turned pink as he put down his mug, raised both hands in a peace gesture and said, 'Sorr-ee.' He changed tack. 'Oh, I stayed up last night, your comrade Alex Grishin is no ordinary person. Look what I found.' He showed Guy an article about Dr Grishin being awarded the Order of the Red Star for personal gallantry in Afghanistan.

Guy realised there must be more to Alex than he first imagined. The man had shown leadership, bravery and physical stamina in the thick of danger.

'Where did you find this?'

'A website used by combat veterans, including Russians who fought in Afghanistan, who share their former glory. "Gory" more like.'

'What else did you learn?'

'There's a link between Alex's combat experience and his later choice of career which might interest you. I'm off to work, but take a look at these print-outs.' He pointed at documents on the kitchen counter.

'Cheers,' said Guy. 'Oh, and David?' he looked into his friend's eyes, smiled and touched his arm. 'Thanks a lot.'

David nodded. 'You're welcome.' He picked up his suit jacket and left.

Guy read more of David's research, though it was difficult to think clearly after his night in bed with Jessica.

He also asked himself what if Raymond finds out about the two of them? Unable to concentrate he went to his bedroom and picked up his sports bag. He removed a buff folder and shoved it under his mattress which would do as a hideaway for the present, and set off for a gym session. Two hours later he returned to his flat on top form and in a better mood to whip through David's research.

Guy picked up a copy of an item from the *Washington Post* in 1999 that gave a personal account of Alex Grishin. He was described as a decorated veteran, an Afghantsi with an exemplary record of military service whose experiences of combat and human torment had motivated him towards a new career in medicine. On completing active service in the mid-eighties he studied natural sciences at Moscow State University. When communism collapsed he moved to the US and enrolled at the University of Maryland to take a PhD in molecular biology. There he met his sweetheart and they later married. He was driven by the urge to accomplish cutting-edge scientific goals, so while he worked on his PhD thesis he took up a junior faculty position at the university and rapidly climbed the research ladder specialising in genomics. In due course Alex's work took him to the Max Planck Institute for Molecular Genetics in Berlin. As he turned the page Guy wondered why Alex had chosen to work in Germany, but he continued with the article.

In the late eighties Alex heard about the Human Genome Project launched by James Watson, famous for his role in the discovery of the structure of DNA. He also heard about software that sequenced DNA which would revolutionise the process to count its three billion letters. Over the next decade Alex teamed up with colleagues and applied for grants to buy several of these machines. He formed his own genetic research company, Grishin Genetics, that would combine public data from the Human Genome Project with his firm's own proprietary material. His company was later taken over by Capsella-Biotech GmbH.

Perhaps the horrors of Afghanistan transformed Alex in some way, and thanks to David's research Guy had some insight into what made this scientific entrepreneur tick. He then picked out a more recent article published in the *Wall Street Journal* in early 2001:

Press Release
$25 million Contract
for Capsella-Biotech GmbH

A contract worth $25m (€28m) was signed yesterday between the genetic science company Capsella-Biotech GmbH and Vertis Pharmaceuticals Inc. The deal includes an early access arrangement whereby Capsella will deliver sequenced human genome data to Vertis and enable the company to research mutations in genes associated with certain types of cancer. It is understood that several other pharmaceutical companies may have signed letters of intent, *in which case Capsella's annual turnover could increase significantly.*

Dr Alexander Grishin, the Berlin based Chief Executive of Capsella-Biotech commented, 'I am delighted to announce our first commercial contract to provide sequenced data on the human genome. Our ultimate goal is to unravel the code of human life itself, via a computerised technique to sequence DNA developed by Capsella's in-house research team. We expect to have a more detailed version that will cover ninety per cent of the code by the end of 2001, and to finish the entire human genome by 2003.'

None of the project leaders of the public Human Genome Project were available for comment yesterday, when Capsella-Biotech's stock price rose by twelve points.

Ends

Raymond had told Guy that Herron's marketing and business development teams would help build Capsella's customer base. Guy knew that would take time, and Capsella's clients would demand access to more than just the initial draft of the human code. They would want the complete version, unlikely to be available until 2003 at the earliest. As he mulled this over he remembered the folder under his mattress.

It seemed extraordinary to Guy that while the security guard at Herron International frisked him before he was escorted out of Adams Court into Threadneedle

Street, no more than a cursory search was made of his sports bag containing sweat-congealed running gear, a damp towel and a pair of whiffy trainers. Luckily the bottom of the bag had not been prised up, because underneath Guy had stashed the folder now hidden in his flat.

It was a risk. The folder contained photocopies of papers he gave back to the Managing Partner together with what most intrigued him: John Kent's original report which he had not had time to copy. If Raymond knows I've got this bloody report I'm as good as dead, Guy thought, but his earlier glimpse of a paragraph that mentioned a Middle East country had aroused his astonished curiosity.

He photocopied the whole report on his home printer, placed the new copy on his desk and sat in front of it armed with a yellow highlighter.

'Right,' he said to himself, 'here goes.'

CHAPTER 7

'Please hold the line while I connect you, Sir Raymond.'

'Raymond! How are you doing?'

'Fine thanks Alex. Look, I've persuaded my senior Managing Partner to back our case and secure the four hundred million. His colleagues should follow suit. I'm confident we'll get it for you.'

'Brilliant. Congratulations.'

'Don't count on the money until it's banked.'

'Be sure to thank Guy for his input.'

'Er, Guy has other urgent matters to deal with, so don't be surprised if he's not in touch over the next couple of weeks. You can always communicate with me.'

'No worries.'

'Alex, I must be certain that you won't leave any holes. Are you certain that Westfälische Strasse can do its job and not get found out?'

'Sure thing.' Alex then explained that his plans to install two hundred high speed sequencing machines at Capsella's main premises, with a further one hundred apparently in reserve at the Westfälische Strasse site, had raised no suspicions among his fellow directors. 'Trust me, Raymond.'

'Good.' Raymond put down his phone. He strolled to his outer office, leaned on the door frame and asked his PA for some coffee and the Capsella-Biotech folder.

'Thanks,' he said when both were placed in front of him. Two minutes later he leaned towards his intercom,

'Something's missing! Where's the sealed envelope from John Kent that was in this folder?'

His PA retraced her steps with a perplexed look. 'What envelope?'

'It was in this folder, for God's sake!'

'I haven't touched it.' She flushed. 'I filed away the whole bundle like you said.'

'Check the filing cabinets. Find it.' She scuttled away.

He spoke to the Managing Partner. 'Are you sure Guy Shepherd was searched when he left the other day?'

'Yes. Security frisked him and gave his bag the once-over.'

'Did they find anything?'

'I'd have told you if they had. Anyway he'd already handed those photocopies back to me earlier on... Raymond, what's the problem?'

'There may not be a problem, my PA is looking for something else on Capsella, that's all. If you find any other stuff tell me straight away.'

Half an hour later Raymond's worried PA re-entered and stepped towards his desk. 'There's nothing more on Capsella, no envelope from John Kent.' She looked uncomfortable. 'Are you sure the document you want was in that folder?'

'Of course I'm sure.' He forced a smile. 'Look, this isn't your fault, but keep looking and tell me at once if it turns up.'

'I'll check again. Oh, don't forget your lunch appointment, the car will pick you up at twelve thirty.'

'Thanks.' He leaned back in his chair as his PA tiptoed out. 'Bloody Guy Shepherd.'

When Raymond gave Jessica lunch at the Reform Club that day, she made her affection for Guy pretty obvious. Back at his office that afternoon Raymond realised how reluctant he was to drive a wedge between Guy and Jessica. He wondered how long until they would sleep together and judged that, with the amount of testosterone surging through Guy's veins at any given moment, it might not be very long at all. Perhaps they had 'done it' already, he thought, as his PA entered.

'I carried out another check of my files,' she said, 'and found nothing else from John Kent. I'm sorry.'

'That's all right,' said Raymond. He felt calmer after the lunch with Jessica, and he began to rationalise. He must regain possession of the original John Kent report, and the odds were that Guy Shepherd had either taken it or hidden it somewhere. He spoke to his PA. 'Call Guy Shepherd to make an urgent appointment with me. If he asks why, tell him you don't know.'

Raymond reminded himself that Guy had worked hard to secure the relationship between Herron International and Capsella-Biotech. He had written a convincing proposal that earned the support of Herron International's Managing Partner, ensuring the other partners would do the same. What Guy did not need to know, but John Kent must have learned, was the real purpose behind one hundred of the Spectra 6500 machines to be installed at Alex's old company, Grishin Genetics, in Berlin's Westfälische Strasse.

On his desk the Capsella-Biotech folder beckoned Raymond. He opened it and sifted through the contents, some in toughened canvass envelopes sealed by tiny coded locks. He was quite sure these had not been tampered with by Guy on his week-end snoop in the office. One envelope was labelled in black felt tip *For R. Herron ONLY* and he opened the lock, and drew out the papers from inside. The top cover was a memo from Alex:

SECURE FAX MESSAGE
Capsella-Biotech GmbH
Königstrasse
D-14109 Berlin / Wannsee
Deutschland

Date: *18 June 2001*
From: *Chief Exec, Capsella-Biotech*
To: *Chairman, Herron International*

Raymond,

This memo and attached documents have been encrypted to your private secure fax, for reasons you'll understand.

By the way, I was sorry to hear about John Kent's death. Does anyone know how he died? He was very professional. Deepest condolences.

As promised I enclose the draft terms of our arrangement with Karim Samir. Please check them and if you spot any inconsistencies let me know asap, but <u>only by secure fax</u>.

Also enclosed: an update I've shown to Karim on the DNA editing product, viz. our lawyers assure me that our international patent applications remain on track.

Karim is adamant his people must have the entire functional model of the above before any funds can be released. On delivery he will personally coordinate the payments to us.

We're on a roll, Raymond, and I'm confident we're about to make it big time!

All best,

Alex

**DR ALEXANDER M. GRISHIN
CHIEF EXECUTIVE**

P.S.   Congrats on your knighthood.
P.P.S. Not surprised Tony Blair won a second term the other week. Enjoy 5 more years of New Labour!

CHAPTER 8

Guy had spent the past hour absorbed in John Kent's report highlighting specific passages. Some of the content had already been explained by Raymond of course, but other entries shocked him. He was so engrossed that the phone rang several times before he picked up the receiver.

'Hello?'

'Dearest, it's me!'

'Jessica, hi. You okay?'

'After last night who wouldn't be! I've been thinking of nothing but you...'

'And me, of you.'

'You took ages to answer just now, are you all right?'

'Just doing a bit of, er, reading and stuff. Any chance we can meet up again soon – like, very soon?'

'That's why I'm calling. A friend of mine at the BBC has given me a couple of free tickets to the Proms at the Royal Albert Hall for tomorrow. Let's meet there after your gym session, then have supper at my apartment.'

'Thanks, I'd love it.'

With love very much on Guy's mind it was an effort to resume reading. It seemed that John Kent did his own research after he spotted what looked like Arabic correspondence on Alex's desk. He also discovered that a laboratory at Grishin Genetics GmbH, Alex's old company now merged with Capsella, still operated in some capacity in Berlin. Guy highlighted the address then picked up a Berlin map David had left out.

'Westfälische Strasse,' he said to himself and found it on the map. 'What goes on there?' On a previous visit to Capsella John Kent had met department heads and molecular geneticists, and he cross-referenced information with the public Human Genome Project. Apart from Britain's Sanger Institute, the other research organisations involved were all based in the USA. John learned that requests had been made to Capsella at its other centre in Newark, New Jersey, not to apply for patents on any sections of the human genome. Capsella's response had been evasive, and in September the matter would be raised at the annual convention of the Institute of Genetic Sequencing and Analysis, or IGSA for short.

Guy could not recall Raymond mentioning this and he wondered how Grishin Genetics played into it all. There was more. On one of his Berlin visits John Kent happened to be in a taxi when he thought he saw Alex Grishin enter an austere office building not far from the Brandenburg Gate. John learned that the address in Behren Strasse was the Russian Consulate in Berlin. Guy wondered why Alex had met with Russians. John Kent obviously realised that Capsella, and maybe Grishin Genetics, did more than Alex had disclosed.

Guy wanted to find out about IGSA. A computer search pointed him to *IGSAconvention*, a website with details of the Institute's annual convention at The Roosevelt Hotel, New York. Scheduled for early September, it would be attended by pharmaceutical companies, biologists, academics and computer experts involved with the Human Genome Project. The programme included keynote speeches on the latest developments in human genomic research, and plenary sessions on health issues and the potential impact of eugenics. Specialists would also present topics on the technology for sequencing DNA, and research into the genomes of plant species. And there would be the usual round of back-slapping, wining and dining.

On the website's home page Guy clicked on the *Keynote Speakers* tab and at first he did not recognise any of them, until he scrolled down to one name that pole-vaulted from the screen:

Dr Alexander M. Grishin
Chief Executive Officer, Capsella-Biotech GmbH
<u>Subject</u>: Gene Patents   <u>Time</u>: 14:00 Thurs 6 Sep
<u>Venue</u>: Terrace Ballroom

It occurred to Guy that he could sign up as a Convention delegate and accompany Jessica to New York, until he considered the career implications if anyone at Herron International found out. It might also prove awkward for Jessica.

He returned to the John Kent report. On the inside cover he noticed faint pencil marks that he had not seen previously: *Editing / IBEC*. It did not look like Raymond's handwriting, so perhaps John Kent had scribbled these words. Guy wondered what they meant.

He sighed, closed the folder and placed it back underneath his mattress.

When he met up with Jessica in Kensington Gore the next day, Guy glowed from a strenuous workout as they strolled under a clear blue sky towards the Royal Albert Hall. The music still rang in their ears as they arrived at Jessica's apartment, where they settled down to supper with a bottle of 1990 Sauvignon Blanc that Guy had brought.

After supper they snuggled up on the sofa. It may have been the mix of alcohol and affection that prompted Guy to say, 'I cannot get you out of my mind, Jessica. I don't want you out of my mind, ever.'

'I can't concentrate whenever I think of you, dearest.' She ran her index finger down the length of his nose and over his lips, and gave him an enraptured look.

'Darling, can we…?'

She smiled.

'Darling, please, I want you! Like now?'

Elated with the pleasure that awaited them, they soon found themselves in the familiar surroundings of Jessica's bedroom. Before long they both stood naked amongst the pile of discarded clothes, breathing heavily as they held each other tight. Jessica encouraged Guy to lie on his back on the low Hülsta bed where their noisy union was followed by a mutual flow of gentle kisses until their heartbeats gradually slowed and they enjoyed a few hours' sleep. When they awoke at dawn they made love again, but with more tenderness this time.

Over breakfast later that morning amid the aroma of fresh brewed coffee, Guy dropped the question.

'Jessica darling?'

'Yes?'

'There's a small favour I need to ask of you.'

'What is it, dearest?'

'The other day you said if I needed help, to let you know.'

'Of course.'

'Well, I wonder if you could do a small job for me while you're in New York.'

'If I can, sure,' said Jessica as she began to pour the coffee, 'what did you have in mind?'

'Research, kind of.'

'What sort of research? I'll be busy the moment I touch the ground in New York.'

'It's about an organisation called IGSA, the Institute of Genetic Sequencing and Analysis.'

'Is this to do with Herron International?' she said guardedly. 'I mustn't interfere with anything that affects Pop's business.'

'Well, yes, but I'm anxious about one of Herron's clients, you remember that firm I visited in Berlin.' Over the next few minutes Guy explained to Jessica the significance of genomics, its role in medical science and the potential benefits such as gene therapy, that could all be scuppered if certain material ended up in the wrong hands. He talked of fears of misuse such as designer babies, eugenic sterilisation and racial classification. She asked how any organisation could control access to genetic data and Guy replied that international patents, for example, would compel other users to pay for it.

'If most of the information is destined for the public domain and the common good, where's the problem?'

'That's the whole point,' said Guy, 'if just a small fraction of genetic data is kept in private hands, scientists and researchers will be denied access to the complete sequence of the genome.'

'Guy, you've just been suspended from Herron. Don't get involved in any of this, at least until you're re-instated.' She looked worried.

'It's the way I am, Jessica, if something's not right I get drawn to it.'

'If this German company is a client of Pop's firm, I'm not the one to intervene.' She placed her hand on his lap and gave him a sympathetic look, 'Too close to home. Sorry.'

Guy nodded. 'That's all right.'

The two lovers boarded the Docklands Light Railway and parted company near Jessica's Covent Garden office. Back at his flat Guy found he had turned off his cell phone when the Proms concert began and must have left it switched off all night. When he switched it on it bleeped with a fresh text message. Raymond's PA wanted him to call and make an appointment with the Chairman as soon as possible. Guy wondered if it meant that the company's disciplinary process was about to get underway, or had Jessica's step-father learned of their relationship?

CHAPTER 9

As a film set for several Hollywood blockbusters, Somerset House is unrivalled. Not that Raymond was aware of the fact as he walked from the Strand through a triple stone archway. He strolled through a vast quadrangle with floodlit fountains and through double doors into the main reception area. Originally built as a riverside palace overlooking the Thames, this magnificent London landmark is also used for art displays and cultural events. Its eighteenth century neoclassical architecture, galleries and spaces are ideal for exhibitions and shows such as the Fashion Preview being staged by Jessica's company that Friday evening.

'Perhaps Herron International should have sponsored this.' Raymond saw signboards, posters and promotional literature displaying the *MBS* logo informing everyone that the evening's Fashion Preview, and next week's main event in New York, were sponsored by Maynard Baker Securities. He was ushered to interconnecting rooms where drinks and canapés were being served. He soon spotted Jessica. She was talking with a woman dressed in an immaculate dark suit who must have been about ten years her senior. They turned their heads as Raymond approached.

'Hello Pop, welcome to Fashion Bound! I'm so glad you could make it.' After they kissed, Jessica introduced him to the other woman, Ali, a director of Maynard Baker Securities.

'Very nice to meet you, Sir,' she said. They shook hands. 'You must be so proud of your step-daughter.'

'Very. I'm delighted that Fashion Bound has a commercial sponsor this year.'

'We're planning to back her next year as well, provided it works out this time round.'

'I hope so too,' said Jessica. 'We must firm up the arrangements when we meet next week.'

The rooms became loud as they filled, and even louder as guests filled themselves with more champagne and canapés. Ali excused herself while Jessica introduced Raymond to some of her team as they waited for Ben. He turned up earlier than predicted and was already on his first drink when he was approached by Ali.

'Good God, you've changed your suit real quick Sir. How did you manage that?'

Ben was baffled and assumed he was being targeted by a guest who had drunk too much. 'Well, I'm an actor, so it's my job is to switch costumes as quick as lightening!'

'You don't say? But Jessica told me you ran a finance house in the City.'

'That's my brother! Look, we haven't met before, I'm…'

'Yes we have, a few minutes ago, over in that corner…'

'Er, I'm Ben Herron, twin brother of Sir Raymond Herron. Where did you see him?'

'I'm sorry!' Ali held one hand to her mouth and blushed. 'But you two look and sound so alike, how weird is that?'

'We're identical twins.'

'God, what a gaffe, please don't tell Jessica or your brother what's happened, I feel stupid.'

'No worries,' said Ben.

They introduced themselves, oblivious to the horrific fate that awaited one of them in less than two weeks. The woman looked around to see where Raymond was standing and pointed him out. Ben joined him. As the two brothers stood side by side Raymond became aware that some guests gave them inquisitive looks.

They took their seats on the River Terrace under a vast marquee where the programme got under way: new fashions worn by models in a glittering show of laser lights and funky music that quelled the traffic noise from nearby Embankment. At the end Raymond and Ben heard the congratulations being offered to Jessica and her team.

'I hope it goes as well for her in the States next week,' said Ben.

'Of course it will, she's a marvel.'

After the Preview as the three unwound over dinner in a restaurant, Raymond was certain of one thing about that evening: Jessica was missing Guy. She had informed Raymond and Ben that the next day she would have lunch with her boyfriend, making sure they knew she and Guy were in a relationship. Raymond gave a benign smile at the time, again asking himself at what stage the bedroom would feature on the couple's agenda if it had not done so already. The prospect of Guy Shepherd as a future stepson-in-law had not escaped his mind either.

It was past midnight when Raymond returned to his residence in Pelham Crescent, a semi-circular terrace of white nineteenth-century houses, fronted by cast-iron railings with evenly spaced porches facing a beautifully maintained garden. He was worried by the lack of response so far from Guy.

Earlier that week they had met, not at Raymond's office, but at Guy's insistence on a bench in Finsbury Circus, a public park between Moorgate and London Wall. Other lunchtime bystanders and sun worshippers took little notice of a City gentleman and a blonde athlete in running gear, seated on one of the benches that faced inwards towards Finsbury Circus' manicured bowling green and covered bandstand.

It was even hotter than the day of the polo tournament earlier that month, but on this occasion there were fewer initial pleasantries. 'Is this about the disciplinary procedure?' Guy sounded apprehensive as if he was about to endure a no-holds-barred slugfest.

'I'm not here to fuck around. Where is it?'

'Where's what?'

'You know damn well what,' said Raymond. 'John Kent's report. How did you get it past security?'

'You don't know that I did get it past security.'

'I do know it can't be found at our Adams Court office, so who the hell else took it from the building?'

Guy raised an eyebrow.

'Don't piss with me. Look, do you want to hold on to your job at Herron, or not?'

'Of course I do,' said Guy. 'I'll face being disciplined, you can dock my pay, place me on a formal warning, do what the hell you like. I'll conform.'

'So why don't you conform and own up that you nicked the bloody Kent report? Earlier you admitted seeing it.' He hesitated a few seconds then spoke in a softer tone, 'You know what's in it, don't you?'

Guy nodded.

'Do you believe any of it?'

'No smoke without fire.'

Raymond sighed. He looked beyond Guy and watched musicians unpack their instruments under the shade of the bandstand.

'It's not just about the race to sequence the human genome, you know.'

'What isn't?' asked Guy.

'My enthusiasm for Alex Grishin and Capsella-Biotech. My obsession, you might say. There's a lot of money to be made, but there are other drivers too.'

'Such as?'

'Alex and his team think they've discovered how to edit DNA. The implications for the future of medicine are huge, and so is the money. Genomic sequencing is only a first step. What's more, this is my one chance to finance the battle against genetically inherited illness, the nemesis that deprived me of the woman I loved.'

Guy nodded but said nothing.

'And there's one other thing I'm not so proud of.' He looked at Guy's passive face. 'The Herron family firm before the war. Our family wealth stems from investments in American eugenics. My grandfather met aristocrats who persuaded him to fund US firms that made materials for human sterilisation. You'd be staggered if I told you the names of establishment figures from both sides of the Atlantic who got involved…'

'I learned about that at school. Later copied by the Nazis.'

Raymond looked at his feet as he explained to Guy that in those days there were some who campaigned for euthanasia as well as sterilisation in order to create the perfect race. 'Wholesale murder of the undesirable, it was crazy. I wasn't around when all that sickening nonsense was going on. Even so, it's good that I'll soon profit from an incredible product that will genuinely benefit society.' Raymond looked again at the bandstand where spectators gathered as the conductor gave instructions and got ready. He changed the subject. 'I've picked up a vibe that you and Jessica have become an item.'

Guy lowered his head and his cheeks reddened. He was leaning forward, elbows on his knees with both hands clasped. He stared hard at the bowling green as if to steel himself to make an admission.

'I can't be harsh on anyone who makes my step-daughter happy. She took it badly when her mother passed away.'

Guy turned his head and gave Raymond a sympathetic look. 'That must have been an awful time for both of you.'

'It was.' He paused for several seconds and crossed his legs. 'Huntingdon's, bastard of a disease, it runs in her family. Rips into the nervous system. Until Elizabeth died I'd never realised how grief could be so intangible, and yet so heavy. Somehow we coped, Jessica better than me.' His eyes moistened. 'Once, a few weeks after the funeral when I was alone in the house, I lay on my bed and wept for almost two hours, until drained of all sorrow.'

'I guess that was only natural.' Guy sat up straight.

'The funny thing was, afterwards I felt better. I could even admit to Jessica that it was less painful to think of us both at Elizabeth's bedside in her last hours, holding her withered hands as she slipped away.' He gave Guy a paternal look. 'It was my concern for Jessica that gave me strength in those dark days.'

Guy took a deep breath and said, 'Your step-daughter's a wonderful person and yes, we're an item. It's for real.' There, he had said it. He and Jessica were lovers. Would Raymond explode?

'She's taken to you Guy, I can tell. Isn't it remarkable what can happen in only three weeks or so?' He gave a dry chuckle. 'You two haven't been idle, that's for sure.'

Guy gave a coy smile.

After watching the musicians for another few moments Raymond said, 'Sign a sworn statement, Guy.' It was a command. 'You will agree to have nothing more to do with Capsella-Biotech, never to divulge the contents of John Kent's speculative report, and you'll affirm that you hold no other copies of it.'

'And in return?'

'These are my terms: we'll meet at my lawyer's office where you will make a sworn affidavit and hand over the original report, with any copies, to me. In return, I'll make out somehow that this whole damned episode was purely my oversight.' He stared intensely at Guy. 'Do we have a deal?'

Guy hesitated. He was not quite ready to make a full admission. 'May I contact you shortly?'

'Please do,' said Raymond with a hint of satisfaction that this young toughie would grab the lifeline he had just been offered. 'But for heaven's sake let's both move on from this bloody nonsense.'

As they stood to depart Raymond said, 'By the way, I've informed Alex Grishin that my partners should approve the four hundred million dollars for Capsella-Biotech's new computers. He's pleased, and he asked me to thank you for the part you played.'

'My pleasure, not that I did that much if the truth be known.'

'You conducted a corporate review and drafted a convincing proposal. Important steps.'

'Of course they were, now that hundreds more millions are to be made.'

Raymond winced. 'Alex is in good form at the moment but be warned, he's not someone you should ever cross.'

'Why's that?'

'It's common knowledge he suffered mentally after Afghanistan, and it was not by chance that he moved to Berlin.'

'He earned an exemplary service record, didn't he?'

'There's more to him than that, he should never be underestimated.' Raymond paused, then said, 'Pick your enemies with care.'

'Is that a threat?'

'A warning,' said Raymond. 'Given everything that's happened, if you return to work - rather, when you return to work - I think you should have no more to do with Alex or that company of his.'

'Point taken.' Guy broke off, interrupted as the band struck up a jazz piece. 'I'll get back to you soon,' he raised his voice over the music. 'Enjoy Jessica's Fashion Preview.' They shook hands.

Guy jogged along a footpath bordered by flower beds, past the bandstand and out into Moorgate. As Raymond cupped one hand over his eyes to shield the sun's glare and watch him leave, he noticed how Guy's physique drew admiring glances from several young female passers-by; and from one male observer too. Raymond began to walk in the opposite direction with that serene air of entitlement that goes with financial success and the expectation of a luxurious retirement. As he did so he recognised the George Gershwin piece played by the band: *When You Want 'Em, You Can't Get 'Em*.

CHAPTER 10

Saturday September first was warm but wet. Jessica had joined Guy at a brasserie in Mount Street, Mayfair. They sat at the rear of the conservatory raising their voices over the slapping of rain against the windows. She wore a blue and white striped skirt matched by a velvet hairband that swept back her chestnut locks over a white blouse.

Wearing suede shoes, chinos and a Tattersall shirt with rolled up sleeves Guy, with some trepidation, revived the IGSA annual convention and his unease about Capsella's business aims.

'I've already said I'm cagey about getting involved,' said Jessica. 'Where is this genetics institute, anyway?'

'IGSA is based at Newark.'

'I suppose New Jersey isn't that far from where I'll be…'

'I meant another Newark, the one in Delaware.'

'I shan't have the time to trek that far.'

'You wouldn't have to. At the same time as your trip, IGSA is holding its annual convention at The Roosevelt Hotel in Manhattan.'

'That's Madison Avenue, minutes' walk from my hotel.'

'Exactly. Is there any chance I could persuade you to register as a day-delegate and attend a keynote speech next Thursday? I'm sure it won't infringe on your step-father's work. Capsella's finance will have been arranged by now.'

Jessica frowned and looked at her diary.

'<u>Please</u>, darling,' said Guy at his most seductive.

'Thursday sixth of September, I'm supposed to meet a director of Maynard Baker Securities at the World Trade Center that afternoon.'

'How important is your meeting?'

'It's about sponsorship for next year's Fashion Week, but I could postpone it. The weekend is taken up with my fashion event, so I'd have to meet her on Monday or Tuesday instead. Let me see.' She studied her diary again and looked upbeat. 'All right, I'll email the team at Maynard Baker and try to fix a later appointment. But… no promises!'

'Brilliant, thanks so much,' said Guy and leaned forward to kiss her.

A waiter brought them salade niçoise with chilled white wine – Sauvignon Blanc again – and topped up their tumblers with water.

'What exactly do you want me to do at the conference? What's the keynote speech about?'

'The speech is about gene patents,' said Guy, 'and this is what I want you to do.'

An hour later wearing macs, Jessica with her umbrella at the ready, they hugged and kissed in the foyer of the brasserie and stepped out into the persistent downpour to go their separate ways. Jessica needed to pack for her flight to New York the next morning. Guy, sheepish, had admitted that his and David's priority later in the day was to watch England play Germany live at Munich in a qualifier for the 2002 Football World Cup. 'It should be a fantastic game,' Guy had said, 'everyone's hopes are pinned on Owen and Beckham.'

It continued to rain as Guy walked under mushroom clouds through the puddles in Berkeley Square towards Green Park underground station. As he raised the collar of his mac to stop water dribbling down the back of his neck he felt an emptiness, as if a vital part of him had gone. He realised how much he adored Jessica and would have loved to accompany her to the States. Still, her business commitments were due to end after the first six days of Fashion Week, and they had agreed to meet again at Jessica's apartment on the fifteenth after her flight home, to watch Last Night of the Proms.

He quickened his pace and weaved his way along the pavement to avoid determined shoppers in their dripping raincoats. To his mind there was so much more to Jessica than just her looks and the sex - she was good humoured, cultured and professional: over lunch she had described how her Fashion Preview had gone at Somerset House the previous evening and from comments made by designers, models and buyers alike, the event had been a surefire hit.

'I hope she's as smitten with me as I am with her,' thought Guy as he left the wet pavement and sloshing gutters behind him and hurried down the steps into the muggy sanctuary of the tube station. 'I've never fallen in love so quickly before and I'm damned if anyone will get in my way.' He took the escalator down to the Victoria Line, hopped onto the next southbound train and grabbed hold of a support rail above his head. The carriage doors slid shut behind him with a thud.

On Sunday at around eleven o'clock Guy awoke to a different kind of thud, this time from a cup of strong tea being placed onto his bedside table.

'I thought you might need this, mate. I'm off out for some fresh air.' David turned and left the bedroom.

'Thanks!' croaked Guy, groggy and bleary eyed. The previous night had been astounding – the Munich Olympic Stadium had erupted when Germany scored in the first six minutes of the game, but the noise from Guy and David seemed just as loud when Michael Owen scored England's first goal seven minutes later. By full-time England had beaten Germany five goals to one with Owen's three goal hat-trick the undisputed highlight. Earlier Guy had placed a bottle of champagne in his fridge and a heavy night was enjoyed by the two exultant fans.

Now his head whirled and he needed the hot tea. He took several sips and heard yet another 'thud' as David shut the front door to set off for a morning stroll. He began to regret the previous evening even though the football had been electric. He also regretted hesitating over the terms Raymond put to him when they had met under a banner of truce in Finsbury Circus.

That afternoon Guy had entrusted David with a bit more about the Kent report.

David's advice was unequivocal. 'For God's sake do as Raymond asks, or you could go down for nicking company property. Prison life isn't a lot of fun, I can tell you.'

'Really? How would you know?'

David avoided Guy's eyes. 'Look, my point is that you don't have to admit any wrong doing.' His cheeks flushed. 'Raymond's about to let you off the hook!'

'I've got my relationship with Jessica to thank for that.'

'You owe it to her to make a clean breast of the situation. Who knows, you may become part of Raymond's family one day. I take it you'll ask me to move out of here soon...'

'Bloody hell David, don't jump the gun! Jessica and I have been dating for three weeks. Anyway she has a fabulous docklands pad that meets all our, well, you know, intimate needs.' He smiled. 'Of course you can remain here, that goes without saying. It's been great to rekindle our friendship.'

'You'll agree to Raymond's terms?'

'I have to.' Guy had not informed David about Jessica's role at the IGSA Convention that coming week. 'Before I contact Raymond again, I need to ask you another return favour, old mate.'

'How can I help this time?' asked David in a way that implied he had already guessed how.

'I need to engage your research skills again. Would that be okay?'

The beep from Guy's phone signalled a new text message:

02 SEP 2001 16:15
Arrived safely am at hotel.
Weather glorious.
J. xx

'Jessica's touched down,' said Guy.

'A pity you couldn't go too,' said David. 'You would've had the time now I'm your official researcher.'

'I've got to swear an affidavit, don't forget.' Guy still felt in a quandary, unable to quell his instinctive curiosity about Alex now that he had been warned to steer clear of the man who looked like his father. It was as if Guy was being drawn back to a time of hate and resentment. He hoped that Jessica would be all right if she were to bump into Alex at the IGSA Convention. She had promised not to mention her connection with Raymond or Guy to anybody, so she should be safe enough.

It was on a hunch that Guy had asked David to research Alex's post-military background, including any possible explanation for his move from the States to Berlin. David was flattered by his friend's request for further help, and with a business trip to the west country over the next few days he would have time in the evenings to give it a go. That suited Guy who at last sent a text to Raymond agreeing to meet next week.

What suited Guy less however, was the response from Raymond's PA a couple of days later. Guy had to return all the paperwork - that bit was fine - but the lawyer's appointment on Tuesday the eleventh was with a Ms Dolman of Messrs Chapman and Cook in Lincoln's Inn Fields.

'Christ, I don't fucking believe it,' Guy mumbled to himself, 'how bloody embarrassing.' But he accepted there was nothing he could do to change the arrangements.

In the meantime Guy remembered how his longstanding friend and flatmate had gone red in the face when tweaked about prison. Perhaps nothing would come of it but later, alone in the flat at his laptop computer, Guy could not resist typing 'david bond prison' into a search engine. He was about to be surprised how a simple action could be clad with significance. He clicked on a link that took him to an article in an old edition of the Manchester Evening News headlined *Policemen Jailed For Rampage Through Home*. A jury had returned guilty verdicts on two policemen, constables Nicholas Peter Williams, 26, and David Timothy Bond, 24, for affray and an attempt to pervert the course of justice. 'Bloody hell,' muttered Guy, 'this must be the same David Bond I've known for so long.'

In 1992 the two off-duty officers were in a pub in a Manchester suburb. They made a lot of noise as they left the premises at closing time, and caused a local resident to protest from a bedroom window opposite. The officers made obscene gestures and shouted at the man to appear at his front door, which he did, dressed in pyjamas with a cricket bat in his hand. It was alleged the two policemen forced entry into the home. Unaware that they were policemen, the man struck constable Williams on the head with the cricket bat, and a brawl followed. The officers later claimed that constable Williams was only struck outside the house, but they were charged with causing the punch-up and fabricating their story. They were found guilty and sent to prison for two years.

'Blimey! Is that what David did before he sold software? As a copper it explains his appetite to investigate and research things.' He clicked on another article from a 1993 edition of the same newspaper that described how the two policemen had lost subsequent appeals against conviction. The article concluded that both prisoners were stoical and passing the time behind bars studying software design on a correspondence course.

As the newspaper had referred to one of the police constables as David Timothy Bond, Guy opened up his Outlook email to remind himself of David's exact email address: it began with *david.t.bond*. A visit to the website of David's current employer settled the matter: David's career profile described him as a former policeman from Manchester who qualified as a software designer in 1996. At this point Guy recalled David's earlier remark about running the Berlin marathon in aid of… what was it called? *Macro*? He found the homepage of an organisation with that name, but it turned out to be a community resource centre in Ireland.

'That's not it,' thought Guy and clicked away until reaching *Nacro*, a charity that reduces reoffending and helps people with convictions to move on with their lives. 'That must be the one.' He clicked back to take another look at the first newspaper article. 'This is news to me. David has a secret.'

A 'ping' from Guy's laptop signalled the arrival of a new message in his in-box. Jessica had been able to postpone her appointment with Maynard Baker Securities to the subsequent week, which would free up time to attend the IGSA Convention on September sixth. It was to be two days later on the morning of the eighth when she would leave Guy a voicemail message about an important find she had made: by then she believed Alex could put the Human Genome Project at risk but she needed to probe a bit more and would have to call back later.

Just then David returned caked in sweat from a training run.

'It's the final of the US Open next Sunday Guy, will you watch it?'

'You bet. Who's your money on?' Guy stood up and turned away from the laptop.

David took a bottle of water from the fridge. 'Lleyton Hewitt is in with a chance.'

'True, he's played fantastic tennis this season.' Guy went to the sink to deposit a used coffee cup. 'What time's the match start?'

'Not sure. You know I'm off to Exeter for a few days, sales meetings and stuff, so I'll watch it in my guest house.' David shut the fridge door, took several gulps of water and grabbed a hand towel to wipe his forehead.

'Can I use your computer to find out what time it starts?' Before Guy could answer, David had his finger on the touchpad of the laptop and the dormant screen came back to life. The first words he saw on the screen were *Policemen Jailed for Rampage through Home*.

CHAPTER 11

Seated in the drawing room at Ashworth Manor, Raymond took a call from New York. It was Jessica to thank him for coming to her Somerset House Preview, and for dinner with Ben later that evening.

'An absolute pleasure my dear. Congratulations again on the superb Preview.' Raymond wished her all the luck in the world at New York Fashion Week. 'I can't wait to hear about it when you return,' he said. 'Why not nip over here the Saturday after…'

'Sorry, Pop, I've a date that evening to watch Last Night of the Proms, let's meet up the week after.'

'Good, I'll email a suitable date.' With affectionate farewells their call ended.

'A date to watch, but not <u>attend</u> the Proms,' he reflected. 'On TV I suppose, at her place or Guy's?' These immodest thoughts came to a halt when his cell phone pulsed:

02 SEP 2001 21:13
Re: our Finsbury Circus discussion. I agree to swear, sign, and hand over all docs. How about week of 10 Sept?
Pse confirm time & place. Guy.

'That's more like it,' murmured Raymond, confident that closure now lay within his reach. 'It'll be a load off my mind as well as Guy's.'

The next morning his PA arranged the lawyer's appointment for Tuesday the eleventh. Raymond leaned back in his chair to rest his feet on his desk. He was dazzled by the prospect of those one hundred million dollars although he never truly understood the science behind the product that would generate such fabulous wealth. However, he was quick to grasp its potential to defeat hereditary conditions such as Huntingdon's Disease, a destructive predator that seriously galvanised him. It was about a year since Dr Alexander Grishin's initial pitch about his mysterious claim of a cure for genetic mutations. Until then Raymond had never heard of Capsella-Biotech nor of Dr Grishin, but he was soon captivated by the Russian entrepreneur's style and his obvious grasp of a complex subject.

At a second meeting Raymond found himself in the drawing room of Alex's suite at The Savoy. Alex described how changes in a DNA sequence lead to mistakes or 'mutations' in the properties of living cells to cause inherited conditions such as Down's Syndrome or Cystic Fibrosis. However, convinced that he already led the race to sequence the entire human genome, Alex had another big money spinner in mind. Raymond was intrigued, and wanted to know more.

Alex said his company was working on a product developed from bacteria that would enable scientists to edit the genomes of living organisms, humans included. It had the potential to revolutionise the treatment of incurable diseases and genetic disorders.

'We call the system Identical Bacteria Enzyme Corrector,' he said. 'IBEC for short. We adapt a molecule of bacteria to match any DNA sequence. The adapted molecule is 'carried' by a special enzyme to the faulty section of DNA, then used as a cutting tool to delete or edit the mutations with remarkable accuracy. Think of it as a correction to one misspelt word in a large encyclopaedia with pinpoint accuracy and at great speed.'

Raymond was astounded by IBEC's apparent capacity to identify one faulty genetic 'letter' among billions, and repair the defect. 'How difficult is it to use this IBEC method?'

'It's so simple even a novice could follow the instructions. Why not visit one of our labs? We'll give you a demo.'

Raymond was hooked by that meeting with Alex, a Russian molecular geneticist with a charisma that drew people to him like coins to a magnet. At last Raymond had found an opportunity to fight inherited disorders including his mortal enemy, Huntingdon's Disease. If he could make a personal fortune by destroying the hereditary illness that so cruelly attacked Elizabeth's nervous system, and protect Jessica into the bargain, then his conscience was clear and he would give all he had to secure a deal.

He looked around his plush office, the firm's throne room and the legacy of his grandfather and father that symbolised his family's ascendency. Without further interference from the likes of Guy Shepherd he would soon create a new personal endowment. Nobody need ever know that Herron International's investment in Capsella would also cover the final stages in the development of the IBEC system, which would handsomely reward him and Alex.

Raymond promised himself to look after Ben's financial needs, discretely of course. Jessica and any future family of hers need never worry about money again, not that she had done too badly for herself so far, it had to be said.

'And what difference will it make if countries or institutions pay vast sums for IBEC or Capsella's other genomic material?' he reflected. 'Even politicians now accept free market competition as the surest way to drive up standards in the health sector.' He recalled with satisfaction a socialist politician who once remarked how intensely relaxed he was about people getting filthy rich. 'So there you are Mr Mandelson,' Raymond said to himself in mitigation, 'like you, I'm signing up to the ethos of New Labour.'

CHAPTER 12

From: David T Bond
Sent: Wednesday 05 September 2001 20:43
To: Guy Shepherd
Subject: Comrade Alex & stuff

Guy,

I'm so sorry for the way I blew my top the other day when I discovered you'd seen those news articles online. Since my journey down to Exeter, I've had time to reflect and I accept it was wrong to accuse you of snooping, as I know most of the news reports are in the public domain.

Thanks for the sympathetic way you calmed me down that evening. My police colleague and I behaved very foolishly in Manchester all those years ago, although we'll always dispute the way the charges were framed. But that's history, and when I did 'time' it gave me the opportunity to embark on software studies since when I now have a decent job – thanks to Nacro. So some good came from that unfortunate episode, although I stick to my earlier advice that life behind bars isn't fun!

Back to the present, while I get ready for my sales meetings here in the west country I'll have time (no pun intended) to start that research you asked me to do into Alex Grishin. I'll revert straight away if I make any discoveries.

Regards,

David

From: Guy Shepherd
Sent: Thursday 06 September 2001 19:12
To: David T Bond
Subject: RE: Comrade Alex & stuff

Hi David,

Of course I accept your apology re: our spat. It was tactless of me to leave that newspaper's web page open on my computer, and I'm sorry for any hurt.

Let's say no more about it, except that from our frank exchange the next day I admire how you must have picked yourself up from the whole prison experience, brushed down and got on with life.

Best,

Guy

From: David T Bond
Sent: Saturday 08 September 2001 21:52
To: Guy Shepherd
Subject: RE: Comrade Alex & stuff

Guy,

VMT for your kind remarks. Glad we're still friends!

I've now been able to investigate Alex G. Thankfully I've had a couple of evenings to myself in this lousy guest house (but it's better than a 2-man cell!)

*You remember I found a website for mentally disturbed combat veterans? It's called **MindCrusade**. Take a look, a lot's in English and the blog section includes historic contributions from sufferers of Post-Traumatic Stress Disorder (PTSD).*

And guess what - click the blog's Archive tab and scroll down, & you'll find one former blogger was Dr Alexander Grishin who shared his thoughts with fellow PTSD sufferers, & his entries seem based on his personal experiences.

Cheers,

David

Guy looked at the archived PTSD blog. 'Christ,' he muttered, 'it rambles on for months if not years.'

The blogger named Grishin was an airborne infantry officer during the Soviet occupation of Afghanistan, until his capture. Guy reckoned he must be the same Major Grishin awarded the Order of the Red Star. He also blogged about his move to Berlin which suggested he must now be Dr Alex Grishin of Capsella-Biotech.

Incarcerated in a rebel prison camp in Afghanistan for about ten months, he witnessed terrible suffering in fierce combat and later as a prisoner. Grishin was one of the lucky few to be spared but forced to work for the Mujahidin until set free as part of a prisoner exchange.

He described how he seemed unaffected by his traumatic experiences after his release, until it all flared up some years later. Other bloggers stated that PTSD does that to people: it lingers in the subconscious for years but one trigger can make it erupt.

While working at the University of Maryland Grishin had a heated quarrel with his wife. When she discovered he had been sending money to a former lover he admitted he was bisexual and had an affair with a Russian male officer while on active service. He blogged that the marital quarrel was the 'trigger'. He became ill, nightmares and flashbacks caused unpredictable behaviour, when he would fly off the handle. The outbursts of violence broke up his marriage. Reminds me of Dad, thought Guy. Unable to cope, Grishin had a serious nervous breakdown and became suicidal.

He later received in-patient treatment for his PTSD, when he learnt that if you repress traumatic memories you just make them intrude more. The trick, he wrote, is to speak openly about your trauma and learn to take it to a happier place in your mind – easier said than done, he pointed out. He claimed gradually to 'manage' his condition for most of the time, but described occasional lapses.

On clinical advice he made a fresh start in a new location. He found work at the Max Planck Institute for Molecular Genetics in Germany to pursue his special interest, and to be closer to family stamping ground

---

From: Guy Shepherd
Sent: Monday 10 September 2001 07:48
To: David T Bond
Subject: RE: Comrade Alex & stuff

David,

Thx for sharing such intriguing info.

Afghanistan must have been terrible during the occupation. I once read a book on how Soviet troops believed in the Kremlin's strategy to reform a backward country – true maybe – but that belief turned to distrust when soldiers were ordered into search and destroy missions that routinely massacred hundreds of civilians. Hideous atrocities were committed on both sides. Ironic, isn't it, that the USA & Saudis provided aid to Afghan rebels in those days...

Hope all's well, and you managed to watch Lleyton Hewitt beat Pete Sampras in the US Open on Saturday.

Wish me luck with my affidavit meeting tomorrow.

Guy

CHAPTER 13

Pedestrians took little notice of the chauffeured BMW that drew up alongside the kerb in Lincoln's Inn Fields, the largest garden square in London. Located in the legal quarter where the homeless once slept rough, it was now home to Sir John Soane's Museum, outdoor tennis courts and a modern café. The Chairman emerged from his air conditioned saloon into the soft September sunshine and the discordant traffic noise from nearby Chancery Lane. Seagulls screeched as they circled overhead, a reminder of the square's proximity to the Thames. They eyed up picnickers sprawled on the square's neatly cut lawn and swooped low in search of lunchtime scraps. Confident that he was about to close the lid on the Guy Shepherd affair, the Chairman's sense of anticipation added a certain keenness to the afternoon. Careful to avoid the seagull droppings, he marched towards the eighteenth century red brick building fronted by a fine white neo-gothic porch. He took two steps up at a time, entered the front door with its brass plaque engraved *Messrs Chapman and Cook, Solicitors and Commissioners for Oaths* and strode towards the oak reception counter.

'I'm Sir Raymond Herron, Chairman of Herron International,' he said, 'I have an appointment at two o'clock with Angela Dolman.'

'Thank you sir, I'll let her know you're here. Take a seat in the waiting room,' the receptionist smiled and pointed, 'with your colleague?'

He went into the waiting room furnished with chic upholstered armchairs grouped around occasional tables strewn with legal journals. 'Hello, Guy, I'm glad you're on time.' He sat opposite Guy who looked impeccable in a grey worsted two-piece suit. 'Not off for a run today, I see. Do you have the necessary?'

'Don't worry Raymond,' he replied with a self-conscious look. He made a nervous gesture at his leather briefcase on the floor, 'I've brought it all.'

Raymond was puzzled by Guy's uneasy manner and wondered if it was caused by a touch of guilt. After several minutes a young graduate type approached and introduced himself as Ms Dolman's assistant, and invited the two of them to follow him to a meeting room on the second-floor.

'I'm sorry you had to wait gentlemen, our previous session overran a touch.' After they emerged from the lift Raymond observed how Guy's cheeks flushed as he hovered, reticent, short of the doorway.

'Here we are,' said the assistant. 'Sir Raymond, you already know Angela Dolman of course.'

'Hello Angela. Good to see you again. All well?'

'Very well thank you, Sir Raymond. Welcome back to Chapman and Cook.'

Raymond turned in Guy's direction. 'Angela, I'd like to introduce you to Guy Shepherd from Herron International.'

Guy took a leap into the abyss, 'In fact, we already…'

'Good to see you, Guy,' the lawyer intercepted his fall, extended her right hand and gave a steady glare. 'I understand you're to swear and sign for us today?'

'Absolutely, er, Angela,' he maintained a flustered cordiality even though it must have felt strange to shake her hand. 'I've brought along the…' but he never finished the sentence. Raymond went the jaded colour of someone about to faint, staggered sideways and clasped the arm of a chair.

The lawyer rounded on her assistant, 'Quick, water. Hurry!'

Guy went to help Raymond. 'You're breathless Raymond, what's happening?'

'I must go outside for some air. I'll be all right, I just need air.'

Guy and the lawyer helped him to the door where a glass of chilled water was now held at the ready.

'Thank you.' Raymond took a few sips and forced a smile at the assistant. 'Whisky would have been even better.'

They returned to the entrance hall and escorted Raymond through French windows into a sunlit courtyard. He was already less pale and said, 'It's Ben. Something's happened, I must call him.'

Raymond sat down on a wooden bench shaded by a cherry tree and composed himself, while the other two looked on. As Raymond took out his cell phone he could just hear Guy and the lawyer talking in undertones.

'Christ, Angela, until the other day I honestly had no idea you dealt with Sir Raymond's affairs, for God's sake.'

'I don't always,' she hissed with a certain coldness, 'but the senior partner's abroad and I cover for him while he's away.' She frowned.

'How are you, anyway?'

'I'm all right, but it looks like you've got yourself into a spot of bother if today's agenda is anything to go by.'

Raymond was too wound up to take much notice of them, and he dialled a number on his phone. 'Ben? It's me. What's up?'

'I'll stay with him,' said Guy, 'we'll return to the meeting room once this is sorted out.' The lawyer looked doubtful but Guy insisted, 'Don't worry, he'll be fine with me.'

'All right.' She turned and left.

Guy hovered at one end of the courtyard as if to examine potted plants lined up against a wall, although Raymond figured that he was in eavesdrop mode.

'No I haven't seen the news, why should I… what?' Raymond seemed appalled by what he was hearing. 'Jesus Christ, you're kidding! When did you learn all this?' He looked up at Guy with a serious frown. 'But Jessica's over there now. God help us, Ben, no wonder I picked up your shock… one thing at a time, please! For heaven's sake let me call her and check if everything's okay. Yes of course I will, thanks.'

'What is it, Raymond?'

'I need to call Jessica because...'

'*MY GOD!*' The receptionist's high pitched cry came from indoors. Her shout was so anguished that the two of them rushed inside. 'Look at the news,' she called out, 'look at it, for goodness sake!'

'Is it the New York plane crash I've just heard about?' asked Raymond.

'Look at my computer screen, it shows repeat clips of an aircraft hitting a skyscraper...'

At that point the lawyer's assistant reappeared, flustered. Raymond, a bit garbled, said that his twin brother had relayed the terrible news just in from America, a personal shock because his step-daughter was on a visit to New York. Diverted by the receptionist's agitated outburst however, Raymond, Guy and the assistant leaned over the counter to peer at scenes of the North Tower of the World Trade Center engulfed in gigantic flames.

'Turn the sound up,' demanded Guy. She pressed the volume control and the noise and shouts of collective anguish could be heard from the streets of Lower Manhattan. Then the sound of an aircraft's jet engine drew near and the public cries rose to new levels of horror and disbelief, as the camera swung up and caught a shot of another plane that flew smack into the South Tower. Incredulous, the four of them watched the second massive explosion and the huge orange flames bursting from the plane's fuel tanks.

'What in God's name is going on?!' exclaimed Guy, but he was interrupted when a door flew open and a middle aged man appeared, looking stunned.

'Have you seen what's happened in New York?' He stared at the four glued to the images. 'It a multiple terrorist attack, being replayed on all the TV channels.'

'This is terrible!' choked the receptionist.

'I must call Jessica, right now,' Raymond's voice cracked with emotion.

'You can use the empty waiting room over there, sir,' said the assistant.

Raymond and Guy took refuge in the waiting room as more staff assembled to watch the hideous replays of the planes' impact. Raymond's call was diverted to Jessica's voicemail, so all he could do was leave her a message to call back.

'Call her office,' suggested Guy. 'Perhaps they've been in contact with her.'

'Good idea,' replied Raymond, aware of Guy's anxious expression. He spoke to one of Jessica's staff who explained that they had tried to contact her as well, by phone and email. Raymond asked when they had last communicated with her - it was by email a couple of days ago. She was due to phone her office in London late yesterday afternoon but had not done so, which puzzled them at the time.

Raymond led the way back into the reception hall where a larger gaggle of people continued to look at the computer screen.

'One of our clients has an office in New York, I'm sure it's in The World Trade Center,' one junior member of staff remarked.

The ring tone from his cell phone caused Raymond to rush back into the waiting room. Guy followed, he looked guarded but reassured as if to foretell it would be Jessica to say she was all right.

'Raymond Herron.' He nodded in encouragement at Guy and hissed optimistically that the call was from Jessica's office. He listened intensely, until his face drained of colour.

'Oh Christ… God, no… please find out what you can and keep me informed.' He looked at Guy, whose eyes began to moisten. 'Oh how terrible… yes, I'll let you know straight away if I hear anything. Of course.'

Raymond saw Guy's adam's apple move up and down as he swallowed hard and asked, 'What's happened to her?' in a dry, shaky voice.

'There's no easy way to say this,' Raymond's gaze met Guy's in mutual angst for several seconds - an eternity. 'Jessica had an eight-thirty appointment with Maynard Baker Securities today, at their office in the North Tower of The World Trade Center.'

Guy held his head in his hands. It took a moment to compose himself before he looked back at his girlfriend's step-father. 'Do they know if she turned up?'

'Not yet. But I do know she's always been a stickler for punctuality.' He paused. It was his turn to dab watery eyes with a handkerchief. 'And her PA just told me…'

his voice faltered as a wave of emotion swelled within him, '…the first plane struck at a quarter to nine.'

'Holy god,' murmured Guy, and hung his head. Nobody in reception heard them as staff gawped at the gruesome scenes unfolding before them.

'Look at the North Tower, bodies are falling from the top.'

'That person just fell while still alive!' cried another. 'Christ almighty!'

A stunned silence hung in the air until another exclaimed, 'God, the South Tower's collapsed in a massive cloud of dust, it's horrific!'

Raymond and Guy walked back to the reception hall. Raymond wiped tears from his eyes for a second time with a handkerchief that was already damp.

'It's no good, sir, US airspace is closed. All flights to and from the States are suspended till further notice.'

Raymond and Guy had hurriedly retrieved their briefcases and left Chapman and Cook's office. Their lawyer was pre-occupied in a desperate attempt to contact a Manhattan client, while all thoughts of the affidavit were vaporized in the ensuing disorder. In the quiet and more comfortable space of Raymond's house in Pelham Crescent he and Guy made phone calls that achieved nothing, including attempts by Raymond's PA to book him onto any flight that might be headed in the general direction of the US.

'Please keep trying,' said Raymond to his PA. 'Do whatever you can. Charter a private jet if necessary, I must get there.' He put the phone down, poured out two generous measures of whisky and offered one to Guy.

'God, I need that, thanks,' said Guy. Then, as if to reassure Raymond and counter his own numbness, 'We mustn't give up hope. Jessica may have missed her appointment.' He swallowed some whisky. 'Even if she hadn't, as soon as the first fireball exploded she would've cleared off immediately.' His words contrasted with noisy scenes from Raymond's television. It was now six thirty UK time, and replays were broadcast of the moment the North Tower collapsed and scenes of the rest of the day's carnage.

'I can't watch any more of this stuff.' Raymond switched off the television. 'Look, if Jessica's safe why hasn't she returned our calls? Why hasn't she phoned us or her office to say she's all right?'

'It's tough, but think about it, she may have been injured and on her way to hospital.' Raymond noticed Guy grimace at the thought. 'Perhaps she lost her phone in the general chaos.'

For a few moments they sipped their whisky in silence, then Raymond saw Guy flinch as his cell phone vibrated.

'Guy Shepherd. Hi David. I've heard, yeah it's terrible. A coordinated terrorist attack. What? No there's not much you can do right now, thanks. I'm with Raymond, we're worried sick about Jessica. We can't contact her, neither can her office. Okay, thanks for the call. Cheers.' Guy looked up. 'That was David Bond, my flatmate. The other day I told him that Jessica would be at New York Fashion Week and he now wants to know if we need any help.'

'That's kind,' said Raymond. 'We might need all the help we can get.'

'Actually, David's brilliant at gathering information and...'

Raymond broke in, 'Oh, I'd promised to call Ben back. He sounded devastated when we spoke earlier. I better update him if only to say there isn't any more news. Yet.'

Guy nodded and swallowed the rest of his whisky.

'I better get along,' said Guy after Raymond had finished his call to his twin brother, 'unless you'd like me to stick around a while.' He stood and picked up his briefcase.

'I'll be all right thanks, Ben will be here in an hour or so. He's a stalwart and we'll support each other.' For the second time that day his gaze met Guy's in mutual anxiety. 'I'll keep in touch with Jessica's office, and they know to call me if they hear anything. Don't worry, I'll call you straight away with any news.'

'That's fine Raymond, and I'll do likewise.' They shook hands. 'I'm so, so sorry...'

'Chin up. And you're right, of course, there's always hope.'

Raymond shut the front door behind Guy. Through the Georgian fanlight above the door the evening sun gleamed onto an oil portrait of Jessica as if singled out for a blessing. Her face stared back at her stepfather from its position on the wall. He returned to the sitting room and refilled his whisky glass. He sat down, and for a few seconds pondered how he and Guy would cope should the worst have happened to Jessica. He then asked himself how it was that Guy seemed to know the lawyer from Chapman and Cook, and why it caused embarrassment. Thoughts about the lawyer took his mind full circle to the sight of Guy as he strolled from Pelham Crescent moments earlier, carrying his Polo Ralph Lauren briefcase.

'Hell, I forgot to take John Kent's report from Guy,' he suddenly remembered, and took two big gulps of whisky. 'Oh, stuff it,' his shoulders slumped, 'I've got more urgent worries now.'

CHAPTER 14

Any tragedy is tough to handle, but without all the facts everything freezes making it difficult to move on. For Guy time stood still on Wednesday, twelve September. Emotional and torn by guilt, he had not heard from Jessica or her office where he phoned earlier as her desperately worried boyfriend. Raymond had not called either, and Guy wondered whether to call him but one thought weighed: at his own insistence Jessica rescheduled her World Trade Center appointment to the eleventh. 'What <u>have</u> I done to her? It's all my fault...'

It seemed Raymond was driven by false hope. Perhaps he would display Jessica's photograph on Manhattan billboards as others were doing. If by a miracle he found his step-daughter, dead if not alive, it would be a resolution of sorts. Guy dreaded having to admit to Raymond being the prime cause of Jessica's rescheduled eight-thirty appointment that day.

The next morning Guy's distress was converted to all out grief by a text from David:

13 SEP 2001 09:15

Sorry to send awful news

Just can't believe it

Click on the link below from M.B. Securities

David

Tears brimmed in his eyes. 'Oh, *GOD!*' He was too
drained to speak about it with Raymond. Instead he
texted the web link and his message of condolence.

However he did call Jessica's office who said they too had seen Maynard Baker's tragic web page, although they would not give up hope yet.

Guy on the other hand had already given up every prospect of hope. Tormented by anguish and the unbearable guilt, to him it was obvious what had happened to Jessica. He was overwhelmed by the vision of his girlfriend crushed beneath millions of tons of skyscraper, all because a certain tosser called Guy Shepherd persuaded her to change a meeting date. It made him sick to think that the searing heat in the North Tower may have forced her to 'choose' whether to burn to death or jump from one of the top floors. Whichever way she may have died would have involved several minutes of unimaginable horror and pain.

Over the next few days Guy's mind flooded with vivid impressions, memories of her gestures and many things that she had said during the times they spent together. He would stare at the front door as if Jessica would walk in and run a hand through his hair. Her presence hung in the still air of his flat, and one thought penetrated him like a dagger: 'I don't deserve to live,' he groaned in remorse. He wept until empty, and felt the grief depicted by Raymond that day in Finsbury Circus: intangible yet heavy.

He received a text from Raymond to thank him for his sympathy. Nonetheless, US civil air traffic would resume by the end of the week and he was booked onto a Saturday flight.

'I must do my own search,' his text was pitiful, 'all is not yet lost.'

Guy was more troubled by Raymond's forbearance than by everything else the poor man must be suffering. Nevertheless he acknowledged Raymond's message, wished him luck and invited him to call if he needed any help. He even signed off his text: *Love, Guy.*

A natural follow-up to bereavement is anger. For Guy, perhaps influenced by Alex Grishin's blog at *MindCrusade*, to repress his anger would make his feelings more intrusive. But unable to take his thoughts to 'a happier place in his mind' he asked himself who was to blame. To punish himself would be a futile attempt to right an irreversible wrong. To hunt down dead hijackers was not an option. To target the political class would be a waste of time. There was only one other thing to bear the brunt of his rage.

'Capsella Biotech, and Dr bloody Grishin.' Guy not only grieved, he also began to plot. Influenced by his suspicions about Capsella-Biotech he shouldered the responsibility for Jessica's terrible predicament on September eleven. Alarmed by Capsella's agenda to profit from genetic science and his distrust of Alex Grishin, the least he could do if only for Jessica, was to prove his suspicions.

In fact Guy was surprised how easy it was to concentrate while upset. He stood at the kitchen counter, grabbed a sheet of paper and a pencil and wrote down several bullet-points. He knew one possibility was to do nothing, but he was meant to be the go-getter Guy Shepherd, business professional and sportsman – people like that never sit around. He drew a line through the first bullet-point, 'do nothing'. He asked himself whether he should alert the Human Genome Project about Capsella-Biotech, but a quick internet search confirmed the Project was not a regulatory body. Such a move would drag Raymond into the public arena, which he had to avoid out of respect for Jessica. So Guy drew another pencil line, this time through 'contact HGP'.

He soon realised the need for raw evidence that pointed to Capsella and Alex Grishin. He knew a few people with the IT skills to hack into Capsella's computer system or Alex's private email and computer files. The idea was risky and might leave an audit trail implicating anyone brave enough to take the risk. Thus a line was drawn through 'hack into Alex's computer'.

And so it continued, pencil lines sliced through more options systematically discounted on practical grounds or to protect Jessica's step-father. Eventually his hand hovered for a few seconds over the final bullet-point; he frowned and began to chew the top of the pencil. A few moments later he grinned and wondered why he had not thought of it sooner. It was a blunt approach, illegal even, but if it worked Guy would get hold of information seen by John Kent, perhaps other evidence as well. And the likes of Raymond need never know...

It might just work.

On Saturday fifteen September Guy heard David walk through the front door and wheel his suitcase into the living area. The two friends studied each other in total silence for a moment, then embraced and patted each other's backs.

'Christ, mate, I just don't know what to say.'

'You don't have to say anything, David.' They released their hold.

'You poor bloke, I know how much she meant to you… how have Raymond and his brother taken it?'

'Raymond's in pieces but clings to hope,' said Guy with moist eyes. 'He flew to New York today, he won't admit defeat. As for Ben, he kept his brother company at Pelham Crescent but I haven't spoken to him.'

'If there's anything I can do.'

'Thanks, you're a real sport.' Guy swallowed hard. 'Think of it. Jessica would've been back in London now,' he said with raw bitterness, 'we'd planned to watch the Proms.'

'Give that one a miss, for Chrissake,' replied David, 'the programme includes Beethoven's Ninth as a mark of respect but you don't want to wallow in that.'

'No, I couldn't face it.' He sighed. 'It was bloody tough listening to that National Prayer Service yesterday.'

After a short pause David asked, 'Fancy a stiff drink?'

'God yes,' said Guy.

Half way through his third brandy and ginger Guy opened up. 'David, are you religious?'

'Not especially. Why?'

'When Raymond and I visited his lawyer the other day, it turned out that the person in charge of our case was Angela – you know, my previous girlfriend, who's become a devout Christian.'

'How very peculiar.'

'How bloody embarrassing, more like! Anyway…'

'The affidavit got signed, I take it?'

'Did it hell, we were just about to do the necessary,' Guy's speech was slurred, 'when our session was torpedoed by the bombshell from Manhattan. It's left us with unfinished business, not that I give a shit.' He drained his glass and flicked his fingers at David to pour him another drink. He was getting pissed. What the hell.

'Anyway, I can't help the urge to be spiteful,' he spat the words out, 'like, to quiz Angela where was her precious God while all those poor fucking sods were burnt alive or dropped to their deaths. Or crushed.' His voice choked with resentment. 'Jessica among them I expect.'

'Stop it!' David was unusually sharp, and hesitated before he handed Guy his refilled glass. 'That question applies to all tragedies – Titanic, Aberfan, IRA bombs, you name it.' He then spoke more gently, 'Ripping into other people's beliefs is just what those stupid terrorists want, to stir up hatred.'

'I suppose you're right.'

'Those bastards don't believe in things like equal rights, individual liberty and the rule of law, all the hard-won freedoms we take for granted.'

'Okay, but I'm still bloody angry with the likes of Al Qaeda, that US President, the Bible punchers who'll peddle the deeper significance of suffering, and I'm angry with Capsella fucking Biotech.'

'Don't get worked up, it doesn't help.'

'Do you know who I'm <u>most</u> angry with?' Guy pronounced every syllable as if to hide his drinking. 'ME!' He stood up and flung his tumbler at the kitchen tiles where it shattered and spilled broken glass, brandy and ginger onto the floor.

David gaped for a moment, speechless but steadfast when he walked over to the kitchen and cleared up the mess. In the silence he found it difficult to understand why Capsella was on Guy's hate list, nor could he quite fathom his friend's self-loathing. Meanwhile for the second time that week Guy stood stock-still with his head in his hands.

'Christ, I'm sorry about last night, I behaved like a complete idiot.' This time he was sober and drank tea, not brandy.

'That's all right,' David replied. 'I plumbed the depths once, different situation, banged up in jug. And to watch your own cellmate weep buckets, well, enough said.'

Guy gave a weak smile.

'Despair leads to anger, I sort of get that,' said David, 'but can I ask you one thing? Why be so angry with yourself and Capsella?'

'Keep this to yourself?'

'Of course,' David nodded, 'after all, since my time in choky became common knowledge we don't have any more secrets.'

'Quite,' Guy took a gulp of his tea. He explained how his suspicions about Capsella had prompted him to enrol Jessica's help in New York, which resulted in her rescheduled appointment at the World Trade Center.

'God, I had no idea,' said David after listening to his friend's outpouring. 'But you mustn't blame yourself, how could you have known what Al Qaeda would do?'

'But don't you see?' Guy said, 'I can't sit around here and do sweet fanny adams. I'll go mad.'

'Have you thought of joining Raymond in New York?'

'Yes I have, but his is a lost cause…' his voice faded. 'I don't know. I've offered to help but I should wait to hear back from him first.' He looked straight at David, 'Besides, I've got a plan I want to share with you, action we should take out of respect for Jessica.'

For a few seconds David's face said it all: *We? What the hell's he cooked up now?* 'What is it?'

Guy outlined his audacious plan. When he hinted that David's help might be needed yet again, it was no surprise, David's reaction was predictable. 'Careful where you tread for heaven's sake,' he said, 'if Raymond and Dr Alexander whatsisname ever find out, the shit will hit the fan. Are you sure you know what you're doing?'

'It's a roll of the dice,' said Guy in an upbeat voice, 'I could win or lose.'

Describing his bold scheme to David that day gave Guy a sense of renewal and redemption, like a crusader roused.

PART TWO

Notes for Guy
IGSA convention 6th Sept
Gene Patents

1)   Intro: Alex states his research activities began
       when he founded Grishin Genetics, now part of
       Capsella-Biotech GmbH, Berlin & New Jersey.

2)   PowerPoint pics: directors' bios, company
       structure, operations.

3)   Sequencing the human genome (confusing...) he
       uses GenBank data provided by Human Genome
       Project (HGP).

4)   Noisy protests. Alex responds, 'GenBank in
       public domain, free access' etc.

5)   Capsella likely to complete sequencing ahead of
       HGP, investment opportunity, (Pitch for funds?
       Guy would cringe!)

6)   Capsella to file preliminary patent applications
       for 20,000 gene fragments. (What's this mean?
       Must ask Guy.)

7)   Alex states his patents would be legal, & help
       prevent rogue organisations from holding global
       health community to ransom.

8)   <u>*Audience cries of betrayal.*</u> *Alex defensive: 'HGP is free to file its own patent applications anytime.'*

9)   *Audience member says HGP puts its data into public domain via GenBank, so why won't Capsella do the same? Alex indignant: HGP is publicly funded, Capsella is a commercial company.*

10)   *Press reporter asks: HGP has sequenced over 2 billion base pairs, how many has Capsella sequenced? Alex evasive, says 'much more than that'. Then says Capsella already has 6 big pharma clients - that number will increase.*

11)   *Reporter asks if Alex knew Capsella's stock price had risen 10% today. Alex smirks - says no, he wasn't aware*

CHAPTER 15

Raymond made his way through queues of passengers delayed by tight security controls, towards the first class lounge for his flight to New York. While waiting to board he discreetly observed other passengers, quiet and patient but perhaps a little nervous. Once seated in the jumbo he felt no anxiety about taking to the air, no sense of pending disaster. At JFK Airport he and fellow travellers faced further disruption caused by the backlog of stranded aircraft waiting to take off. At least the seven-hour flight and the hold-ups had given Raymond plenty of time to read and re-read several newspaper articles about the week's catastrophic events.

In JFK arrivals hall he briefly imagined his step-daughter there to greet him, a notion that evaporated as he made his way outside, unaccompanied, to hail a cab. With help from Jessica's office he had reserved a suite in the Carlyle Hotel on Madison Avenue, where she had stayed and where he now asked the cabby to take him. But moments later he changed his mind and asked to be driven to the site of the collapsed Twin Towers.

'It's sealed off but I guess you can get as far as the security cordon,' said the cabby.

'Could you take me there now?'

'Ground Zero looks like it's been nuked, you sure you wonna go there?'

'Please.'

On Broadway the cab reached the cordon sealing off the salvage operation, and halted near satellite trucks and television news hacks doing their stand-ups. Raymond got out of the cab and walked among huddles of onlookers who stared at the news cameras, while others gaped in disbelief at the vista of desecrated ruins. The acrid smell of smouldering rubble still permeated Lower Manhattan. He approached a National Guardsman at a barrier who described the task that lay ahead. Raymond frowned and gazed at what could have been a film set for Dante's inferno: a wasteland of empty streets, dust and paper, shells of trashed buses and cars. He saw one news reporter point at water flowing from a solitary pipe protruding from the rubble like a warrior's spear, a defiant survivor. Raymond felt strangely exposed and vulnerable. The recovery work was hindered by structural problems with buildings like One Liberty Plaza, used earlier as a temporary morgue. Engineers also had to deal with unstable office blocks while teams of sniffer dogs searched for any more survivors. Even though some dead had been recovered, the National Guardsman said, most were unidentified body parts of rescue workers and pulped remains of victims who had plummeted to their deaths. Body fragments with personal effects such as wallets or purses made some identification possible, and a system was in place for victims' details to be collated centrally. Raymond was given the number of a call-centre that handled all enquiries and victim identification. Later, when he booked into his hotel he asked about Jessica Parry.

'We haven't seen her since the start of the week,' replied the receptionist.

'Did she settle her account?' asked Raymond.

'Her room and breakfast were paid in advance, but she was supposed to check out the day before yesterday and there are charges to be settled.'

'I'll pay it now.'

'Thank you sir… is there a problem? She hasn't used her room since Monday…'

'There's a problem all right,' said Raymond, 'Miss Parry's my step-daughter and nobody knows where she is. She had an appointment at the World Trade Center last Tuesday and I'm desperate to find out what's happened to her.'

'Oh God… I'm so sorry. Let us know if we can help in any way, sir.'

After Raymond paid Jessica's account he took the elevator to his suite and tipped the bellhop who wheeled in his suitcase. He closed the door behind him and walked over to a window. The landscape of concrete structures and glazed office blocks looked like random Lego pieces that could topple over with one flick. He drummed his fingers on the window sill and noticed thick dust on the outside, a stark reminder of why he was there. He took some mineral water from the mini-bar, flopped into an armchair and absorbed the insulated silence. After a few swigs he wondered how the hell to start his search.

'May I see the room Jessica Parry occupied earlier this week? Number two-six-one.'

'Why, sir?' A different receptionist was on duty.

'I explained to your colleague that I'm her step-father and she's gone missing.'

'The room's occupied by other guests, sir. If you want Miss Parry's belongings, they're stored in our House Manager's office.'

'May I pick them up?'

'We'll need identification, sir.'

Raymond rolled his eyes. 'Will my passport do?'

'We've already seen your passport. We need proof you're Miss Parry's step-father.'

'Look, the only ID I've got is my passport. Can I speak to your House Manager?'

'She's off duty until Monday. Our week-end manager is here, but they'll both insist on additional ID before you take Miss Parry's belongings.'

'Give me strength.' Raymond sighed. 'I'll speak with your House Manager on Monday.' He returned to his suite and the respite of the mini-bar.

He ordered a meal from room service then texted his PA for additional items of ID to be couriered to his hotel by Monday morning latest, whatever the cost. He signed off with an apology for messing up her week-end. He dialled the number given by the National Guardsman but got diverted to a call queue and placed on hold for twenty-minutes, not surprising in the circumstances. When he got through he was told that lists were being compiled of casualties taken to hospitals, and of remains stored in morgues, and the data would then be matched with information from frantic relatives or friends. Raymond was assured that nobody called Jessica Parry had been reported by any hospital so far, although some unconscious casualties needed to be identified. Likewise there were no morgue reports of a body, or a body part, linked to her name. The operator then took Raymond's phone number and email address, and said they would notify him of any developments.

It was dark by the time he ate supper, fettuccine and a green salad. Exhausted, he prepared to take a bath and retire. Before he went to sleep he turned on NBC News and watched updates on nine-eleven. In one clip the camera closed in on water coming out of a standpipe jutting from the debris, and Raymond recognised the reporter's face from earlier that day. As he switched off the bulletin he remembered to text Ben that he had safely arrived across the pond but had nothing to report, yet. Raymond reached for two Seroxat tablets and a glass of water on his bedside table, swallowed the pills and turned off the overhead light.

Next morning he heard on the radio that hundreds of crushed bodies would never be found, an inauspicious start to the day. With twenty-four hours until he could collect Jessica's belongings, he decided to conduct searches of his own. Hotel staff provided contact details of New York hospitals with emergency response teams equipped to handle major disasters and mass casualties. He worked through the telephone numbers repeating the same enquiry. He gave up if they put him on extended hold, but some were quicker to respond. One hospital operator referred him back to the same call-centre number he had dialled the previous evening whereas others connected him to internal departments, but the answer was nearly always the same: no record of an injured or deceased Jessica Parry.

However, one response differed from the rest. At New York University Downtown Hospital in Gold Street, between Brooklyn Bridge and Ground Zero, an unidentified woman in a coma seemed to fit Jessica's description. Plus, other victims' remains in the hospital morgue had yet to be identified. Raymond took a deep breath and asked if he could visit. He reserved a chauffeured limousine for later that afternoon, and emailed his New York office with details of the hospitals and instructed his staff to continue the same process on his behalf the next day.

The black Lincoln wound its way through the Manhattan grid until it arrived at the hospital. Raymond had to wait a few minutes while an epileptic Hispanic woman was lifted down from an ambulance and wheeled in by the crew. Once inside he was introduced to one of many emergency physicians specially drafted in.

'I hope I shan't take up too much of your time,' Raymond said in a nervous, apologetic tone.

'Far from it,' said the doctor. 'We need all the information we can get, and appreciate your visit.'

'What's your role here?' asked Raymond, trying to sound calm as he was led down corridors past staff, patients and visitors.

'I work at Columbia University Medical Center but for now I'm attached to the Victim Identification Teams.'

'That can't be easy.'

'Easier than some. A buddy who's a trauma surgeon had to amputate limbs from survivors trapped in Ground Zero rubble, it was the only way to get them out alive.'

'This woman we're about to see, er… is she an amputee?'

'I'm afraid so,' said the doctor with a compassionate look, 'she lost both legs and her left arm, and she's still in a coma.'

'Oh my God!' Raymond went deathly pale. As they approached the door marked I.C.U. he was on the verge of panic.

They entered the intensive care unit where Raymond was led to a dimly lit bay. His view of the bed was partially obstructed by apparatus, spouting wires and tubes. The doctor touched his shoulder with one hand and gestured with the other that he should step towards the patient. From where he stood he could see that the patient's body was covered by sheets from the neck down. A frame held up the bedclothes over the space of the missing arm and legs, and breathing was controlled by machinery that Raymond assumed was life-support. The only sound from the patient was her breathing as if on auto-pilot. Raymond raised his head and observed the mute saline drips.

The doctor gently touched his shoulder a second time. Raymond moved closer. Unconscious, she lay on her back, the familiar length of blood-stained chestnut hair outlined her battered face with its scars and cuts. He stared at the patient for a while, then shook his head. 'This person's not my step-daughter. I'm sorry doctor.' He could see the likeness, in particular the colour and length of the hair, but she was not Jessica. The tide of relief lasted for only an instant because the doctor then invited Raymond to accompany him to the morgue in the basement. For a second time he began to panic.

The next twenty minutes were the most harrowing of Raymond's life. The morgue attendant explained that most of the human remains were body fragments, and the only way to make an identification was from attachments such as shoes, pieces of clothing and jewellery.

'What about DNA or blood testing?' asked Raymond, his voice unsteady, desperately buying time to compose himself. His face had gone pale and he realised this hands were shaking.

'I'm not sure to what extent these human remains can be matched with DNA samples, it's not really my territory.'

'It is possible you know. The Duke of Edinburgh once provided DNA to help identify the remains of the Russian imperial family.'

'Fair point, but I think they only found eight skeletons at Ekaterinburg. Or was it nine? Whatever, with thousands dead in New York it's a massive operation, so any visual identification will facilitate the process. Otherwise our pathologists will use whatever method they can whether it's DNA, blood groups or dental records.'

He recognised none of the items shown to him, most of which were attached to blooded arms, torsos and feet, and as his stomach churned he asked to be shown only the remains of females. The attendant said it was not always possible to tell the gender from a morsel of someone's body. Raymond almost fainted a few minutes later, when a refrigerated drawer was pulled open to reveal one half of a lady's decapitated head with an earring still attached to the ear lobe. But the most gruesome of all were those who had dropped to their deaths at a minimum velocity of one hundred and twenty miles an hour. Their bodies had pulverised on impact and now looked as if they had been ripped open by rabid dogs. Barely recognisable as human, their slivers of clothes were again the sole means of identification. Raymond was pretty certain that none of the clothes were Jessica's except, perhaps, for one item. It was a torn piece from a pink and green floral dress that at first he thought he recognised, until he realised it was attached to a mashed arm and shoulder of black ethnic origin.

'I'm sorry to have wasted your time, doctor,' said Raymond at the end of this nightmare, relieved to be away from the morgue and back at reception on the ground floor. He felt he was about to be sick.

'These things have to be faced, sir, and you weren't to know.' The doctor held out his hand. 'Thank you for visiting. I know it's difficult, but good luck with your search.'

They shook hands and Raymond gave the doctor a weak smile. He walked out of the glass doors and firmly gripped a metal handrail as he descended the steps down to the sidewalk. The sun made him blink just as his phone rang. It was Ben.

'God, am I relieved to hear you, Raymond. Something's not right, what've you been up to?'

'I'm about to puke up.'

'Why?'

'I'd like to see you confronted by refrigerated body parts, and not know whether the next limb you look at will be your own step-daughter's…'

'Christ, so that's why I've had such a traumatic dream.' It was past midnight in Britain and Ben explained he had been woken by a hideous nightmare about Jessica. He sounded reluctant to give graphic details, in any case Raymond proceeded to do the job for him:

'I've been to a mortuary, Ben. It was awful, I'm sorry if you picked up my thoughts. Headless bodies, bodiless heads, hideous lumps of half clothed dog meat…'

'You've been through the mill, Raymond, I'm so sorry. Any news? Can I do anything?'

'Not now, there's still no clue as to Jessica's whereabouts. But I haven't gone through her belongings yet.'

'Call me if you need help.'

'Thanks Ben. You take care.' He climbed into the back seat of the waiting Lincoln and wept all the way back to the Carlyle Hotel.

Raymond had a disturbed night, his mind visited dark places, so it was a relief to get up early and take a pre-breakfast stroll round a lake in Central Park. Afterwards in the restaurant a muted flat-screen television trailed news that New York Stock Exchange was about to open for the first time since the eleventh.

'Two fingers up to Al-Qaeda,' thought Raymond as he smeared marmalade onto a piece of croissant. He felt a bit less downcast. He wondered about the stock price of Capsella-Biotech in the present climate and recalled his last visit to Capsella's labs in Newark, New Jersey, when he was so astounded by the remarkable new process he was shown that he omitted to discuss the company's market value. Capsella's premises in Broad Street included a laboratory where Alex Grishin had used a high powered electron microscope to demonstrate the IBEC system. Enlarged images appeared on a monitor screen and Raymond watched, spellbound, while Alex talked him through the process using a mutated version of the plant *Capsella Rubella*. A molecule of bacteria, pre-programmed to match a DNA sequence in the plant's genome, was carried by a special enzyme straight to the target sequence of DNA. The enzyme cut in to both strands of the DNA double helix, to delete the defective DNA and allow corrected versions to be inserted.

'Unbelievable!' To Raymond it was magic.

'It's believable all right,' Alex had said, 'and we've already used IBEC on mice with genetically induced blood cancer. They were cured in a matter of months. Before long medics will apply this system to humans.'

Brought back to the present by a waiter pouring him more coffee, Raymond looked at his watch. He was about to ask at the lobby for Jessica's possessions when a text arrived. He feared the worst news from the call-centre, but it was Alex.

17 SEP 2001 15:23
First tranche of Herron International's funds have landed, excellent. Will set plans in motion. Samir still on side. Please call re: second tranche of money. Alex.

Raymond saved the message, left the dining room and made his way to the lobby. When asked by the House Manager to prove his relationship to Jessica he was better prepared. His PA had couriered Jessica's and her mother's birth certificates, together with his certificate of marriage to Dame Elizabeth Parry. When Jessica's luggage was eventually wheeled into Raymond's suite and placed on his bed, he gave the bellhop a heftier tip.

It was sobering to look at the personal belongings of a loved one yet not know whether she was safe, injured or dead. His phone rang and he cursed. If it was Alex he could wait till later. In fact it was his firm's New York office about contacting the remaining hospitals: one of the partners had volunteered to work the telephones on Raymond's behalf.

He started with Jessica's suitcase, but did not get far. It was locked.

'Shit! Where's the key?' He paused, and noticed that her handbag was not there. Next he tried to open her briefcase. It was locked on a combination so he tried using various dates of birth, house numbers from Jessica's previous addresses, and so on. He thought he might ask room service to send up a screwdriver and spanner to force the luggage open, but it occurred that one of the cases might be alarmed in some way. Besides, he realised the keys may not even be in her briefcase as she may have taken them with her. This prompted another line of thought: why did she not take the briefcase to her appointment at Maynard Baker Securities? And if the hotel receptionist last saw Jessica on Monday evening, did anyone see her on Tuesday morning when she left for her World Trade Center appointment?

The House Manager was an amiable and attractive woman. In different circumstances Raymond might have fancied her.

'I'm sorry to take up your time but I must work out my step-daughter's movements last week.'

'Sure, I understand,' she replied with a caring smile, 'how can we help?'

Raymond explained he was unable to open Jessica's luggage, but the House Manager regretted she could not do anything about that.

'Did she leave any possessions in a safe deposit?'

'Oh, I hadn't thought of that. Give me a moment.' She phoned the registration desk, but the answer was negative.

'Fair enough,' said Raymond, 'but one thing troubles me.' He understood that Jessica was last seen on the evening of Monday the tenth of September, and he asked to play back CCTV footage of the hotel entrance.

'That's possible, of course.'

'How long would it take?' asked Raymond, as he recalled the recent footage of Guy Shepherd's oscar-winning performance on Herron International's CCTV.

'Well, twelve hours of tapes could take just as long to re-play I'm afraid.' She paused. Her eyes brightened. 'Here's an idea. We have electronic records of when guests use magnetic keys to enter their rooms. When they step out of the hotel their keys are clocked at the registration desk. We could work out Miss Parry's movements.'

'So we would look at shorter CCTV clips?'

'I hope so. Leave this with me sir, I'll see what can be arranged. How may I contact you?'

'Try the suite first, but here's my card with cell phone number.'

Back in his suite Raymond tried more combinations on the briefcase lock. It was a six-digit device with three numbers on each lock. He tried obvious codes such as 111-222, 222-333 and so on, but these attempts failed. Not normally one to swear or get violent, he picked up the briefcase in frustration and slammed it down on the floor.

'FUCK!!' He gave the briefcase a piece of his mind: 'Capsella-Biotech can sequence up to three billion DNA letters, even faster with my firm's money, yet I can't get six bloody numbers in the right order!' He kicked the briefcase across the floor. 'Bugger it!'

With hands on hips he stared at the briefcase for a few moments until his more rational, analytical brain came on-stream. What were the chances of selecting six numbers in the right order from a choice of only ten numbers? One in a million? One in five hundred thousand? Who knows. He had to accept that the odds were formidable. He sat on the bed with his head in his hands, 'Jessica, where are you, for God's sake?'

It was around noon and a glass of whisky had calmed Raymond. Then... why had he not thought of it before? He grabbed his phone and called Jessica's office in London just as staff were winding up for the day. It was answered by a young intern, and Raymond asked if she knew any numeric codes or office pin numbers that Jessica might have used.

'Yes, Sir Raymond, our main entrance has a six digit keypad code. It's brilliant, you set the alarm's timer and get out of the office quick before the police...'

'Never mind that, what's the code?'

'Oh, I can't tell you. It's confidential.'

'Don't be ridiculous! The chances are my step-daughter who's your boss might be dead. Just give me the goddam code!'

There was a muffled pause.

'Sir Raymond, this is the communications manager here, the intern you just spoke to is in tears. What can I do for you?'

'Look, I'm sorry I've upset one of your people, but I'm in New York and unable to examine Jessica's possessions because her briefcase is combination locked. It would be a great help if I could try your office entrance code.'

'I understand. It's 15-06-92. The date we moved into this place.'

'Thank you.'

'We've still heard no news from poor Jessica and we fear the worst, how have you got on over there?'

'There's no trace of her. Like you I'm about to lose hope, but I promise to let you know of any progress.'

'Thank you, and we'll do the same of course.'

He balanced the briefcase on top of a dressing table so that the two combination locks faced uppermost, adjusted the numbers to 150-692 and pressed the release catches. They did not budge. He also tried the same sequence in reverse. Nothing. A pointless phone call had left a kid in tears, but it was worth a try.

'Shit,' he muttered, and he started to think that a spanner and screwdriver might be the one option left. But hang on... he had another thought... what about Guy? Would he have any ideas? The keypad to Jessica's apartment block has a combination code, and Guy might know it.

Guy did not answer his phone, maybe the network was unavailable, so Raymond left a voicemail message.

Then he remembered Alex's text. He dialled Capsella-Biotech's Berlin office.

'Hello Raymond, how are things with you?' Alex sounded even more alert than usual.

Raymond chose not to mention his personal crisis - the less emotional, the more focussed he would be. 'I'm safe in one piece, but I have to deal with urgent stuff in New York. I got your text message, you wanted me to call you.'

'That's right. But, look, had I known you were in the States we could have met.'

'Oh? What've you been up to?'

'I was in New York to address a genetics institute. After hold-ups and delays I got back to Berlin last night. God, did I get a shock when those hijacked planes …'

'Yes Alex, the world was shocked. What did you want to talk about?'

Alex wanted to thank Raymond and his team for the first injection of financial capital. He explained that the new Spectra computers had already been ordered on the assumption that Herron International would provide the rest of the money, and they would be installed by the end of October. His firm would then accelerate its work to sequence the remaining elements of the human genome code, which should make the IBEC system more attractive than ever to Samir and his political masters.

'Oh, and Raymond, something else has happened in respect of the international patents which I must run past you…'

'Alex, there's a lot going on here,' said Raymond, 'must we talk about this now?'

'It can wait I suppose. Let's catch up when you're back in Britain.'

Raymond tried Guy's number once again, and this time got through.

'Hello Guy. Have you got a moment?'

'Of course. Any news?'

'A few unanswered questions after a grim hospital visit, that's all. Look, I need your advice, sorry if it sounds daft.'

'No problem.'

'I've got Jessica's luggage but I need the code to unlock her briefcase. I've tried every combination I can think of but no luck. Would you by any chance know the keypad code where she lives?'

'Yes, it's Beethoven's Moonlight.'

'What do you mean?'

'Easy. The first time we slept… erm, I mean, when she first invited me over to her place I teased her it was weak security to have the first three digits the same as the last three.'

'So?'

'She told me they're the opening six notes of the Moonlight Piano Sonata, 513-513. Will it help?'

'Hold on a moment…' Raymond put his phone down by the briefcase and carefully aligned the numbers on the two locks: 513-513. For a few seconds he delayed the next move, then positioned his thumbs on the two release catches. He held his breath for a short time and pressed the catches.

'Bugger!' he muttered as nothing happened. In desperation he reversed the same numbers: 315-315. He swore a second time, convinced he was getting nowhere until with a defeatist grump he pressed the catches again.

'Bingo!' he shouted as the locks sprang open with a healthy metallic click. He picked up his phone, 'Guy, you're an absolute star!'

CHAPTER 16

It was two days since Raymond's call from New York, and Guy was relieved his boss had sounded in quite good spirits despite the lack of progress. The missing suitcase keys were inside Jessica's briefcase together with her passport. The locked suitcase also contained handwritten notes that Raymond intended to go through. For now Guy was anxious because Raymond had not called again with an update. Guy doubted anything in Jessica's luggage could possibly be of any help, meanwhile it never occurred to ask himself why Jessica had not taken her briefcase to the World Trade Center meeting.

His anxiety was matched by fear, not just of Jessica being a casualty, but fear of his own reaction once her anticipated fate was confirmed. He was also preoccupied with his own scheme which at least diluted his grief. He had made preparations over the previous forty-eight hours, which included reassuring David who worried about risking another spell behind bars.

'You just have to create a diversion, David, that's all,' he had said to his wary helper, 'I'll be the one who takes all the risks. Your job is to operate the remote control.'

'Okay, a return favour for old time's sake. I'll do as you ask but absolutely nothing more.'

'Brilliant! You won't even need much time off work, we'll do it at the end of the week.'

'If anyone asks, I'm off to Germany to train on the marathon route.'

'Agreed. Once our work's done, on the Saturday we could both have a go at part of the route if you want.'

On Thursday afternoon Guy flew from London City Airport to Berlin Tempelhof, so named because the airport's original site belonged to Knights Templar in medieval times. From the arrivals hall he walked over to a row of desks, dumped his Bergen backpack and a separate suit hanger on the floor beside the *Hertz* counter and hired a car. An hour later he checked in to a modest but comfortable Gasthaus in the Zehlendorf district, a short drive from Capsella's headquarters in Wannsee.

Guy had a lot to do before picking up David the following day. His first job was the reconnaissance phase of his plan, best done after dark. Meanwhile, bratwurst beckoned. He left the Gasthaus and strolled towards the seductive aroma of 'bratty' sausage and chips that wafted from a nearby stall, and stood in the short queue. A teenage lad and a woman were serving customers while meat sizzled on the grill.

'Mit Mayonnaise oder ohne Mayonnaise?' said the lad when it was Guy's turn.

'Mit Mayonnaise bitte,' said Guy in a lousy accent.

'Are you English, mate?'

'Yes. What brings you to this part of sunny Deutschland?'

'My gap year. That'll be six deutschmarks fifty pfennigs, or three euros and thirty cents, please.'

As Guy paid he noticed two separate cash tills, one contained deutschmarks and the other was stuffed with euros. He reckoned the word 'stuffed' just about summed up the single currency idea. 'One day,' he thought, 'millions of people will regret that their political masters ever adopted a one-size-fits-all interest rate.'

He carried his bratwurst and pommes frites in an airline-style tray with its plastic fork to the forecourt of the Gasthaus. He sat at a table shaded by a large umbrella emblazoned with the words *Schultheiss Pilsener* which at first he misread as *Scheithaus Pilsener* – less tempting – but soon realised that this particular brew was part of the hotel's brand and he decided to try some. He nipped inside to the bar signed *Herzlich Willkommen* in large letters and placed his order.

Outside again he sucked the heady white froth from the top of his beer glass and enjoyed its bitter-smooth taste. Fortified by beer and bratwurst he returned to his room for a short rest. An hour later, woken by his cell phone alarm, he got up and opened the window shutters and let in the final vestiges of daylight, and for a few minutes he watched the orange sun grow dim on the roof topped horizon. His sour, tacky mouth made him think that *Scheithaus* was not such an unsuitable brand name for the beer after all.

Despite his enthusiasm for a challenge Guy was surprised how nervous he felt. Perhaps he was worried that the next day he would depend on David who had a simple but important job. When David finally agreed to help he seemed quite calm about it. Even so, he appeared tetchy during a conversation the previous night, worn out after a long training run, slumped on a beanbag and absorbed in a paperback.

'Can you speak German?' Guy had asked him.

'Why?' David looked up. 'Can't you see I'm reading?'

'I know, but something I saw at Capsella's office in Germany has puzzled me. Look at these notes.'

David rolled his eyes, but relented and looked at Guy's scribble from his visit to Capsella-Biotech:

Capsella Rubella oder 'Rot Schäfer'
Es begann sich selbst zu befruchten vor
circa 200,000 Jahren
Und ist ein ausgezeichnetes Modell für die Untersuchung
der Wirkung auf sein Genom

'What the hell's it about?' David looked perplexed.

'That's what I'd like to know. The only words I understand are Schäfer which means Shepherd, my family's old surname, and the bit about two hundred thousand Jahren, or years.' He looked thoughtful. 'Oh, and Capsella Rubella is a plant used by Alex's people for DNA research.'

'Easily solved,' said David, 'A chum at work speaks fluent German, I'll call him.'

A few minutes later Guy looked at the piece of paper with the translation provided by David's colleague:

Capsella Rubella or 'Red Shepherd'

Started to self-fertilize around 200,000 years ago
An excellent model for studies of the effect on its genome

'I wonder why they use the Capsella plant for genetic research?'

'It tells you in the last line, Guy. I'm knackered, can I get back to my bloody book now?'

Guy drove from the Gasthaus and joined Potsdamer Chausee that took him south west and under a railway bridge towards Königstrasse. Passing Wannsee lake he spotted the right fork from his last visit, turned, and drove towards the familiar driveway through the wooded area that would lead to the main gate of Capsella-Biotech. He switched off the car's lights. The driveway was less recognisable in the dark. On his last visit he had noticed a number of rides that ran through the woods at ninety degrees from the driveway, and as his eyes started to adjust he kept a look-out for the first ride. He soon made it out, just visible alongside a row of silver birches that glinted in the delicate light of the new moon. It was wide enough to back up his car with room to spare on either side. He took care not to over rev and keep the noise down, and when he got out of the car he noted with satisfaction that the ground was firm – he preferred not to get bogged in. He grabbed a plastic bottle of mineral water from the glove box, took a swig and replaced it inside. As a final precaution before closing the car door he made sure his cell phone was switched off.

His shirt, trousers and trainers were black, as was the running hat that concealed his blonde hair. He looked upwards and his eyes reflected the starlight from sections of the clear night sky exposed by the gap between the lines of trees. With his night vision he had little difficulty in making tracks along the main driveway in the direction of the glazed buildings of Capsella-Biotech. He kept to one side of the drive as he crept forward, ready to take refuge in the trees that bordered his path, moving slowly to avoid any noise from his footsteps. To keep his balance while he crept forward he held out his palms parallel to the ground like a tightrope walker. The night silence was only broken by the sound of bugs, the hoot of an owl and the occasional distant car on the main road. He breathed in the scent of pine, and as he got nearer to his target he felt drops of cold sweat trickle from his armpits down the inside of his clothes.

He could soon see the floodlit perimeter fence that lay siege to the buildings. He hopped over a ditch and crept into the trees and was startled by the noise from the layers of dead leaves that brushed as he trod. He hunkered down behind some shrubs and remained completely still for a few minutes.

'That answers my first question,' he thought, 'the bloody place is floodlit.' At another hoot of an owl he looked up with a start, but all he could see was the mosaic of tree branches silhouetted against the night sky. He parted some shrub leaves and peered through the gap to observe the activity near the gate. He would need to get closer, but he could make out a security guard who stood beside the entrance barrier and then he watched a dog handler approach the guard from inside the boundary fence. 'That answers my second question. Dogs.'

While Guy was in a good position to monitor the guards' routine he took time to crawl as quietly as possible further into the wood where, from careful scrutiny while propped on his knees, he reckoned he could sneak over to another observation point if he wanted. He carefully manoeuvred back to his original stop-off, produced a small notebook and pen from his hip pocket and settled down to a period of surveillance. His first thought was that whereas the perimeter was floodlit, the buildings were not, perhaps on the assumption that nobody would ever break out of Capsella even though intruders might attempt to break in.

It took Guy half an hour to work out that the guard at the entrance and the dog handler were the only two people on active patrol. At some stage they must stand down or swap with others on a roster, and he wondered where the replacement guards were. Did they have accommodation, or would a vehicle turn up with new guards and relieve those ending their shift?

'Who supports them when there's an alert or if an alarm goes off?' Guy asked himself. 'There has to be a standby team within the perimeter.'

He was right. A new shift eventually appeared from behind one of the buildings to relieve the guards Guy had been watching. He continued to take notes, just able to read his own handwriting thanks to the slivers of starlight that filtered through the branches overhead.

At around two in the morning Guy moved from his observation point deeper into the wood, a painstaking process to avoid making any noise. He stole through the undergrowth and crouched to avoid the low branches as he took each meticulous step from one tree to the next, to find a new position where he hoped to view the side and rear of the complex. It took almost an hour to cover a distance of around two hundred meters, like a slow motion movie. He winced at one point when a twig snapped underfoot, to his sensitive ears the 'snap' sounded as loud as the crack of a breaking branch. Nothing happened, nobody stirred.

He found what he was looking for. Deeper into the wood he now had a good view through the trees across open space between the wood's edge and the perimeter fence. Beyond the fence, adjacent to the nearest smoked glass building, were two stand-alone portakabin huts. Beside them he saw four kennels with attached cages. In one cage a dog lay asleep.

'I won't go closer,' he thought, 'don't German Shepherds have sixth sense?' The 'twin telepathy' between Raymond and Ben came to mind. 'If humans can do it maybe dogs can,' he surmised, 'I hope my thoughts don't trigger anything now.'

He guessed that both portakabins probably had enough space for four bunk beds in each, with basic washing and cooking facilities. Nothing more. It was clear that the antenna on one of the roofs was not a television mast, so Guy assumed that landline communications were backed up by radio should reinforcements be needed. He stayed motionless as the dog and its handler toured the inside of the perimeter, both unaware of the single pair of eyes that observed their every move. A small pouch attached to the handler's belt caught Guy's attention, it looked like a pistol holster until he heard it crackle - a radio handset. When they disappeared round a corner he looked about and realised that earlier he had failed to notice a telegraph pole on the edge of the tree line. Some wires, a power cable and perhaps a telephone line, ran from the top of the pole over the perimeter fence to a junction box fixed to the wall of the main building. From there more cable was linked to the top of one of the portakabins.

'A job for David.' As he jotted this down he also logged that no security patrols appeared to operate inside the buildings, only on the outside.

Three hours later he decided that he had seen enough and now needed to extract himself. It would take a while to manoeuvre back to the car by which time it would almost be dawn. With his notebook secure in his hip pocket he looked once more towards the complex to ensure that the coast was clear and began to inch away. Again his actions were slow and cautious but he crept to the area of his first stop-off without incident. Once out of sight of the guard at the entrance barrier all he had to do was head back down the main driveway towards the ride and the hidden car.

The unmistakeable rustle of leaves made him freeze. Motionless, his heartbeat raced, the adrenalin surged. Something or someone was about twenty meters behind him. He shivered and his legs trembled. The moment's silence was broken by a second rustle, this time a little nearer.

Shit! One of the dogs! His mind raced, there was nothing for it but to dash bloody fast to avoid being bitten to shreds. He took off like a sprinter exploding out of the blocks, tore past trees and shrubs and raced out onto the driveway.

'Hey! Was machst du da?' shouted one of the guards from behind him. Guy heard a dog bark. His legs no longer felt weak, and they worked at a pace he had never previously experienced as they carried him of their own accord. He could hear the creature behind him as it ran through the woodland in an attempt to get parallel and close in. He thought he heard it growl which caused his legs to propel him even faster along the driveway. Now the animal overtook and for a split second he heard it crashing towards him, when suddenly it hurtled out of some shrubs straight into his path.

He did not have time to stop. He tripped over the wild boar as it careered across the track, grunting, and scurried into the woods on the opposite side. Guy smacked into the surface, winded by the impact and with grazed hands and limbs, but with self-pity not an option he leapt to his feet and continued to sprint along the driveway. He ignored the distant shouts and the excited bark of a guard dog as he struggled to breath, and turned right at high speed into the ride where his hire car stood.

'Fuck me, that hurt!' he panted as he got behind the wheel and slammed the car door. 'Enough running for one bloody night!' In no time he had the car northbound on Königstrasse with his foot hard on the gas, and sped to the safety of the Gasthaus in Zehlendorf.

In the shower jets of water stung his cuts and grazes but he was too tired to care. He wrapped himself in a towel and sat on the edge of his bed. He set his cell phone alarm for later that morning then went to close the window shutters. Exhausted, he lay on the bed and fell into a deep sleep.

The shrill cell phone interrupted Guy's graphic dream. He woke up with a start and reached for the phone, then with his head stuck to the pillow he fumbled with it to switch off the repetitive jingle.

'Sod it, I was enjoying that.' He and Jessica had been in Berlin's picturesque Tiergarten to watch a magnificent show of music with fireworks set off from boats on the River Spree, until his cell alarm destroyed the illusion. But he guessed why his subconscious had conjured up such an extravaganza, a thought that prompted him to swing his legs off the bed and start to shift. He took another shower, shaved and went down to the ground floor.

It was another warm day and he enjoyed a late breakfast of coffee with fresh baked Brötchen. His next task was to drive to a down-at-heel address in the

Wedding district north of the city centre where he had arranged to pick up essential supplies. When he got there he parked in Pankstrasse opposite a dingy apartment block, its walls smeared with graffiti, a short walk from his destination. He grabbed his backpack from the rear seat. As he walked three things struck him: not many people, litter and the stink of drains. This was no leafy garden suburb. He passed a Lebanese shisha café where a liquorice aroma came from two plump men who lounged under a canopy smoking a hookah pipe; their hooded eyes followed him. Guy tensed, quickened his pace and crossed the cobbled street towards a shabby store with tired fruit and vegetables displayed outside, beyond which was a Halal butcher. He then realised why the area seemed strange – he had not seen any women. Pedestrians, customers in the shops and bars, players in a sordid amusement arcade: all were men and even they were few in number.

He was relieved to reach the address where he had arranged to pick up the merchandise. The price was extortionate but at least the elderly Turkish trader had prepared the right quantities of everything Guy had ordered. After the short walk back to the car he swung the full backpack onto the rear seat, aware that he could be an object of local curiosity, and was glad when he drove off towards Zehlendorf. On the way he was tempted to park up and take a stroll in the Tiergarten – it might make him feel closer to Jessica whose hand he had held in his exotic dream. The place was certainly less eerie than Wedding but he decided it would be just his rotten luck if his new box of tricks got nicked while leaving the car unattended. He went straight back to the Gasthaus.

The Gasthaus proprietor gave Guy a curious glance as he breezed through the front entrance with the Bergen strapped to his torso, strolled past the reception desk and entered the lift. In his room he laid all the materials out on the bed to be sure they were complete, including the batteries, then placed them back to await David's arrival. He looked at his watch and decided it was time to pick up his loyal accomplice from Tempelhof. David, owed a day's leave from work, had booked a late morning flight.

'This is a quaint place.' David's room in the Gasthaus was next door to Guy's.

'It's discreet.' Guy leaned against a dressing table and looked on while David unpacked, but flinched when he placed his hands on the table's edge. 'Come on, it's stuffy in here. Leave all that. I'll explain over a glass of *Scheithaus*. It's beer, you'll like it.'

They sat outside in the shade and sipped their ice cold pilsner. David remarked that one thing he liked about the continent was the relaxed licensing hours. 'Beer any time is a good motto,' he said.

'Dutch courage any time,' Guy replied, who went on to describe his near miss with the wild boar. David rocked with laughter and nearly choked on his beer.

'Laugh as much as you want, David. I almost shat myself, visions of animal teeth embedded in my buttocks…'

'I'm sorry to laugh,' David's shoulders heaved as if to shake off any sign of nerves, a release of tension perhaps, 'but it's fucking hilarious!'

They were alone in the forecourt, nobody else was listening.

'If you screw up tonight, it'll be your arse on the guard dogs' menu,' said Guy with a stern expression. 'Look, when we've had our beers I'll talk you through the sequence. Apart from my close shave with the wild boar I did a thorough recce of the place last night, so you shouldn't have any problems with your slice of the action.'

They returned to Guy's room where David was shown the goods and how to operate the remote control device. Guy spread a map out on the bed, drew some diagrams and briefed him on the other details. David had few questions, the job seemed pretty straight forward to him.

'I must get there by five o'clock,' said Guy, 'we'll set off at half-past four. After you drop me off, park the car here,' his index finger pointed at the map, 'until I give you the call.'

'No probs, though rather you than me. I'll go to my room and get the contents of your Bergen sorted out.'

A few minutes later as Guy readied himself, his cell phone vibrated with a new text from Raymond.

'At last, I wondered when he'd be in touch again.' He opened the message, the main body of which comprised just two words:

21 SEP 2001 14:03   YOU'RE FIRED.

CHAPTER 17

Raymond sat at a corner table opposite the piano in the Carlyle Hotel bar and raised a glass of malt whisky to his lips. His elation at unlocking Jessica's briefcase had soon turned to alarm after he read her notes written for Guy.

It seemed obvious what Alex was up to. Patents cannot be kept secret, so the IGSA Convention gave him a platform to disclose Capsella's plan with limited impact. Articles and correspondence would no doubt appear in *Science* and *Nature*, there may be more debate, even protests, but with any luck it would all die down rather than become explosive. Alex must have judged that this disclosure made business sense, a fair calculation given the company's stock price had gone up literally while he addressed his audience.

But it was Jessica's follow-up notes that most disturbed Raymond: she later recorded that during a short break after Alex's presentation she had gone to the main lobby of the Roosevelt Hotel for tea, and tucked herself away at a small table between two pillars in the mezzanine area above the bar. A few minutes later and to her surprise, on the other side of the pillar she heard Alex with someone who must have been a trusted colleague. Piano music interfered but Alex had said something like 'I've just about seen off the enemy' and, unable to make out everything he was saying, there was talk about triggering a debate over Capsella's commercial strategy. His colleague sounded less convinced and asked whether *not mentioning the firm's unique editing tool (something-something-inaudible) the exclusivity promised in the anthrax negotiations.* Jessica jotted this down together with Alex's loud reply, *Shut your fat mouth you prat, you never know who might be listening. Drop by my room around seven, and I'll fill you in on Samir.*

Raymond could only guess at how accurate his step-daughter's notes were. Had the two men really talked about anthrax? Or had Jessica misheard? ANTHRAX? What in God's name was Alex playing at? And why refer to Mr Samir, how was he involved? <u>*Contact Guy*</u> was underlined in Jessica's feverish scrawl. She had also heard a waiter ask for Alex's room number, and noted his response: *Bill these drinks to 1227.*

It had been the right decision. Whichever way you looked at it, Guy had to go. Already suspended from his job, there was no excuse for entangling Jessica in the affairs of Capsella-Biotech and by association Herron International. Raymond had never discussed business matters with his step-daughter - work and family were kept separate.

The whisky deepened his gloom, amplified by the trauma of visiting two other morgues. Earlier he had also visited Herron's office in midtown Manhattan to thank the partner who had phoned hospitals, medical centres and helplines in the quest for Jessica. The partner was sorry that his efforts had not succeeded yet, and offered to carry on.

'Actually there's something else you can do,' said Raymond. 'Tell Human Resources in London to sack Guy Shepherd. Immediately.' He pointed with his right index finger for emphasis. Everyone else in the office looked up and stared. 'Chairman's orders. Any queries, call me direct. It shouldn't be complicated as the bloody man hasn't even worked his probationary period yet.'

The partner gulped. 'Sure. I'll call London now, sir.'

'You have my full authority. Meanwhile I'll text Guy to tell him he's fired.'

Guy must have coerced Jessica to delve into Alex's work, why else attend his presentation at the Institute of Genomic Sequencing and Analysis? She would never have done so of her own accord. Raymond had already heard of IGSA and presumed that it endorsed the international Human Genome Project. He now knew about the audience's downbeat reaction to Alex's presentation on gene patents. As he put his empty glass down on the table with a disparaging clunk, he was approached by the Assistant House Manager. Their staff had reviewed magnetic key data, narrowed the times of Jessica's movements and matched them with the CCTV recordings. Would he please come to the House Manager's office?

Raymond soon grasped that there was nothing unusual about Jessica's whereabouts during her first week at the hotel. The corroborated magnetic key data and CCTV clips confirmed she left the Carlyle each morning and returned late in the evening, as expected of a busy executive staging a fashion show. It took place on Saturday the eighth, to critical acclaim according to one press report that the House Manager now produced. Jessica's team flew to London the following Monday, while she stayed to negotiate sponsorship for 2002 New York Fashion Week.

Jessica's activity on Monday puzzled Raymond. She could not have known that in one day's time the world would change forever as she handed in her key card to the registration desk at nine o'clock, but it was not clear what she did immediately afterwards. One CCTV camera filmed her walking from the registration desk, but the next shot was of her leaving the main entrance behind a man in an open-necked shirt and linen jacket at nine-thirty. So, what had she done in the intervening half-hour?

'She may have gone to a quiet corner of the bar to read a paper,' said the House Manager, 'or to the ladies washroom where there's no CCTV.'

Raymond raised his eyebrows. 'Half an hour to visit the ladies?'

The House Manager shrugged. 'The real puzzle is that she never came back to the hotel.'

'Are you sure? Could she have returned without picking up her key card?'

'That's possible, but there's no record of that, or of her entering her room again. We would have to play back the entire CCTV tape for the whole day in the hope of spotting her...'

'Don't,' said Raymond. 'Do any images show whether she met anyone, or left the building with another person?'

'No, I think she was alone in all the clips.'

'So, what did she do from the morning of Monday the tenth until her fateful meeting at the World Trade Center the next day?'

The House Manager gave him a compassionate look. 'There's one possible clue,' she said. 'In most clips your step-daughter carried her briefcase as she left and entered the hotel. Except on the Monday morning when she walked out empty handed.'

'When she also left all her other belongings behind,' he said. 'Perhaps we'll never know why.'

A call to Jessica's London office only deepened the mystery about the twenty-four hours leading up to the Twin Towers attacks. Fashion Bound Ltd had received no further contact from her since Saturday, the day of her fashion show, when she emailed her UK colleagues to say it had gone like clockwork, a huge success with the prospect of future sponsorship. That message was first seen by her London staff a couple of days later when the office had opened at the start of another week. In Jessica's Outlook diary her stay in the USA after the Preview event was blocked out with *In New York*, and no other details except the time of her return flight. Meanwhile the company's finance officer had looked at Jessica's corporate credit card account, and informed

Raymond that the last entry was dated Sunday the ninth – several rounds of drinks for her dedicated team.

'What about her personal bank card?' Raymond had asked.

'I wouldn't know, but she rarely if ever uses her own funds on business trips. She makes most purchases on the business credit card to get the corporate travel insurance. Any personal spending is settled up here after she gets back.'

Raymond had wondered if Jessica might have copied or faxed her hand written notes to Guy but reckoned, if she had, Guy would have mentioned it when they spoke the other day about the combination code to the briefcase. It was doubtful Guy could cast further light, in any case it would be awkward to contact him now he had been fired. It seemed that no lines of enquiry would bring his step-daughter any closer, despite tantalising unanswered questions.

For a start, in his presentation to the IGSA Convention Alex had not talked about IBEC, his unique system that could edit genes – that was no surprise as the intention always was to get IBEC patented <u>before</u> its inventor talked about it. But Raymond had no idea that Alex had begun to file a raft of gene patent applications. How does anyone patent a gene, for heaven's sake? It was one thing to patent a scientific invention such as IBEC but surely genes are the product of nature just like ants or tulips… and Raymond felt sure that nobody had ever patented animals or plants. Any person or organisation that patented only a few thousand genes

(Alex's words) could in effect become the global key holder that controls access to the complete Human Genome.

As for anthrax, maybe Jessica had misheard. Raymond began to think of other words that sounded similar: *Backpacks – Tampax - Baghdad's*. Ah, Baghdad… that could explain Alex's reference to Mr Samir. If Jessica's notes were accurate, Raymond would have to raise the matter of gene patents when he next talked with Alex. Perhaps he could say he had read a report in a scientific journal. But it vexed him how best to quiz Alex about an overheard word that sounded like 'anthrax'. As he thought about this he reminded himself that Jessica had not misheard the name *Mr Samir* – she had even spelt it right. He felt goose bumps on his neck.

'There's a poem by Henrietta Huxley that I want printed on the front cover.'

'I'll get the printers to put it in the order of service. We can proof read it after you get back.'

Raymond had called Ben to say that the search was over. He wept on the phone as he explained to his twin brother that the end point had been his visit to Saint Thomas Church on Fifth Avenue, described as the finest parish church in North America. When he entered the place for some quiet time to reflect and compose himself, the organist happened to be playing, practising for a recital probably. Raymond had entered the building via the back of the nave, careful to avoid stepping on the words *Peace on Earth to Men of Good Will* inscribed on the stone floor. Leaving behind the noise of traffic and pneumatic drills, he sat in a wooden pew under one of the chandeliers suspended from the high ceiling and looked towards the altar, with its large sculpture of a cross surrounded by kneeling angels. The church was almost empty apart from a steward and a couple of elderly sightseers. Raymond watched them saunter past the altar steps as if to venerate the sculptured cherubs. The couple drifted off to the back of the nave to admire the high stained glass windows. During the next half-hour Raymond twisted his hands while his imagination unreeled. Every move in the hunt for his step-daughter seemed to make her disappear, like a fisherman casting a fly upstream but unable to land his catch. Before long Raymond succumbed to the sacred music and comforting atmosphere of the neo gothic church.

Before his visit to the church he had already been in touch with a longstanding Cambridge friend, now a board director at *One2One*, and asked for a fast-track review of Jessica's cell phone account only to reveal there were no outgoing calls since the night of Sunday September nine. Raymond also listened to other people in his hotel and on streets, he read newspapers and watched TV bulletins, and they all said the same thing: no more bodies, just rubble and dust.

'Ashes to ashes, dust to dust,' said Raymond on that desolate phone call to his brother.

'For God's sake come home.' Ben was pleading. 'Please. You need the support of someone close to you.'

'I'm on my way Ben. I'll let you know when I'm due to land at Heathrow.'

CHAPTER 18

The hire car turned off Königstrasse towards the perimeter fence of Capsella-Biotech and slowed to a halt fifty meters short of the security barrier. Guy, immaculate in a navy two-piece suit, got out of the car while David remained at the wheel. It was five o'clock in the afternoon. Once Guy had passed security without hindrance, David turned the car round and drove away.

As instructed, David pulled up at a Wannsee 'Parkplatz' beside a café at the water's edge. He found it easily enough, near a zinc statue of a lion, a replica of a nineteenth century war monument and not far from a villa used by the Nazis for their 1942 Wannsee Conference – the final solution. There, with Guy's Bergen filled with the goodies, and armed with a paperback book and a chocolate bar he awaited his friend's next instruction.

Guy's ploy was simple, and he had gambled on three assumptions. The first was that his now defunct Herron International business card plus his passport would get him through security, even though he had no appointment. Second, he planned to sneak behind the indoor trees in the atrium and nip into a male washroom without being noticed. He succeeded at both. The security guard simply pointed him towards the main entrance and told him in broken English to go straight to reception. Before he passed under the porch with its large display of the four base letters of DNA he noticed for the first time an intruder alarm, something he had not seen the previous night. Inside people milled around, and within five minutes of being dropped off he hid behind a closet door in the men's WC where he waited; and waited.

Guy's third bet was that Capsella's internal security would be minimal after the premises closed for the day, given the external protection he had already witnessed: the perimeter fence, the arc lights, the patrols with guard dogs, the landline and radio communications, together with the intruder alarm he had just observed. While the accuracy of this assumption would be put to the test, he was not too concerned about any internal CCTV footage unless his movements were monitored live. He did not want to be caught in the act, but if he got found out after the event Capsella could hardly sack him. He thought he had learned his lesson from his exploits on camera at Herron International, and suspected Alex Grishin and his lackeys had so much to hide that it would deter them from reporting him to the authorities.

For now he was in self-imposed solitary on a lavatory seat which seemed to parody his abrupt sacking from Herron. On that last score all he had to go by was Raymond's brusque text, but no doubt a formal letter would follow. Without news of Jessica's whereabouts and after such a hasty dismissal from the Chairman, of all people, Guy soon figured Raymond must have discovered that his step-daughter had gone to the IGSA Convention. Paperwork or some other evidence in her briefcase or luggage would have made it obvious. Given

Raymond's grief you could hardly blame the poor man in whose shoes Guy would probably have reacted the same way. In one sense it was almost a relief to untie the contractual knot with Herron, to operate as a free agent and investigate what Alex and his crew were scheming. Now more than ever he owed it to Jessica to get at the truth, even so, the irony of launching his mission from a cubicle in the men's WC at Capsella-Biotech was not lost on him.

He looked at his watch and could still hear people and movement from beyond the washroom door. He thought of David relaxing beside the scenic south bank of Wannsee Lake munching a snack, admiring the yachts moored nearby or reading his book, and Guy crossed his fingers in the hope that his lifelong companion would not do anything stupid like fall sleep. Tempted for an instant to text David with *STAY AWAKE!* he suddenly remembered he had not switched his cell phone to silent mode. He took it from his jacket pocket.

Suddenly the washroom door opened and he heard footsteps on the tiled floor. He stiffened and almost dropped his phone as someone brushed past his cubicle door and went to a urinal. Guy sat motionless thankful he had silenced his phone seconds earlier. He listened to the discharge from the man's bladder accompanied by groans of relief and wondered if it could be Alex, but surely the CEO would use his own closet on the directors' floor? Besides, this fellow did not seem to groan in a Russian accent. To Guy he sounded more Teutonic especially when, fully relieved, he whistled the tune to *Edelweiss* as he did up his flies. At least, Guy hoped, that was all he was doing with his flies, nothing more, and he smiled briefly at his lewd thought until the man went to a basin to wash his hands and farted like a protracted crackle of thunder. Seconds later the vile stink erased Guy's smile as he held his nose in silent disgust.

'Too much garlic mayonnaise with his bratwurst,' he thought as the man walked out.

He waited for around an hour after the last sounds of human activity, such as receptionists' chatter when they switched their phones to auto-message, the valedictory remarks of other staff, 'gute Nacht' and 'bis Morgen' and various doors being closed. It was a long silence, no cleaners or janitors as far as Guy could tell. How he might have coped had someone locked the washroom door from the reception side remains unanswered - thank goodness, he thought, as the washroom windows were barred on the outside. He was just about to unlock the cubicle door when someone else entered the room. He heard the footsteps make their way to the window, which was followed by sniffing and a pause – maybe to admire their reflection in the mirror. The person moved towards the furthest cubicle and pushed the door so that it swung open against the inside partition.

'Oh God, he's opening the cubicle doors!' Guy knew his visitor would see the red *Besetzt* or 'Engaged' sign on the cubicle door handle.

The person came to Guy's cubicle and thumped on the door. 'Wer is da?' *Who's that?*

'Schäfer!' said Guy in what he hoped was a guttural accent.

'Beeilen sie!' *Hurry up!*

'Ja,' said Guy although he had not understood. The man shuffled out through the main door.

Guy waited another hour. Nobody else entered the gents' that evening but he wondered where the janitor person might be lurking. He could not afford to wait any longer so he crept out from the cubicle past the urinals and opened the door that led back into the empty, dimmed reception area. In the half dark he hardly noticed the glass roof and steel beams that had seemed so impressive in daytime.

Guy knew he could not be seen through the building's one-way tinted glazing, but he could make out the perimeter guard changing shift at the main gate. He looked at his watch. The changeover time matched the pattern he had logged the previous night. Less than a minute later he was upstairs on the directors' floor. From a balustrade he peered down at the fig trees and the three water pools, but the floral double helix of DNA was less obvious. He turned and walked towards the familiar sign on the CEO's office door: *Dr Alexander M. Grishin, Chief Executive* and felt a twinge in the pit of his stomach. He breathed more rapidly and glanced behind him as if to check for Alex's heavy minders. Instead he found himself looking at the door to the Director's toilets, and he stole inside thankful for temporary refuge. With its white tiles and marble and chrome plumbing, the place was at odds with the faint pong of a blocked drain. He leaned back against the door and took out his cell phone. Anxious that he might find Alex's office locked and still nervous about getting caught, he closed his eyes and resolved to pull himself together. Stay calm. Keep focussed.

'Move now,' he texted David.

His friend responded, 'Will do.'

'Good man,' thought Guy, encouraged that his accomplice was alert, 'he better get the rest of it right, or I'm stuffed.' He ventured back into the passageway and placed his right hand on the handle of Alex's office door.

As he predicted, the door was unlocked. A belief that nobody could break in undetected must have given Alex and his staff a false sense of security - they had not thought that an intruder might simply walk into one of their offices out of hours. Nonetheless, as a precaution Guy turned the knob below the inside door handle to lock himself in. There were no filing cabinets in the room and Guy reasoned that if his PA kept stuff filed somewhere, it would either be easy to get at and thus of no real interest, or locked away and therefore inaccessible. He walked across the room towards Alex's teak desk. Outside the sun was going down behind the trees and less light came through the one-way window. Confident that he could see but not be seen he sat at the desk and began his search, knowing exactly how much time he had. The desk's surface was empty except for a few personal items lined up along one edge which Guy ignored, and he started with the drawers. One of them was locked, but he pulled open the other ones which contained the usual junk of spare pens, old journals, blank notepads, a tube of peppermints, a half-eaten chocolate Berlin Bear and a cell phone charger, until he came to the bottom right hand drawer where he found a loose pile of papers.

He placed these documents onto the desk and sifted through them. At first there was little to attract Guy's serious attention. A meeting agenda, correspondence from Capsella's brokers about stock price movements, a science professor's invitation to lunch in Berlin's famous KaDeWe department store and an itinerary for Alex's recent trip to the IGSA Convention in New York. But then Guy found something. It was a print-out of the PowerPoint slides used for the presentation on gene patents, the speech that Jessica had agreed to attend, and he folded up the sheets and put them into his jacket pocket. So his initial calculation was wrong – these documents were easy to access <u>and</u> of interest. The remainder of the pile now grabbed Guy's full attention so that he took no notice of anything else in the room – for the moment.

In the complete silence of the CEO's empty office he flicked through the remaining papers until he came across a secure fax message. Addressed to Raymond and signed by Alex, it began with condolences at the death of John Kent, then referred to an arrangement with someone called Karim Samir. Guy frowned. The message mentioned a DNA editing product and payments into bank accounts in Zurich. The final bit referred to patent applications, something Guy would read more about later from the PowerPoint dossier in his jacket pocket. He asked himself if Alex and Raymond were planning to patent some new DNA product as well as file for gene patents. He flicked through the rest of the documents and began to think he would find nothing more. Until he got to the very bottom of the pile.

Guy held up the single sheet. His hands trembled. It was another secure fax, this time from Karim Samir to Alex, from which two lethal words leapt out. Biological words that reminded Guy of the 1979 Sverdlovsk Incident in the Soviet Union he had learned about at school. Still holding the sheet he lowered his hands onto the surface of the desk. He looked up, too stunned to notice a certain black and white photograph amongst the other pieces of memorabilia arranged in a neat row along the edge of the desk.

'What the hell… this is dynamite.' He knew he was onto something. With no need to hang around or mull over what might be at stake, he stood up and shoved the chair backwards. He thrust the two fax copies into his other jacket pocket just as a text arrived from David, 'In position,' to which Guy replied, 'Stand by.'

And that was when he saw it.

As he looked up from his cell phone his eyes settled on the framed black and white photo. He turned pale, made a dive for the swivel chair and sat down again. Perched on the edge of the chair and breathing heavily, he drew himself up close to the desk and stared at the picture for a whole minute in sheer disbelief. He needed absolutely no prompt to understand where or what the picture was: Podbielski Allee. Unquestionably Podbielski Allee, Berlin. And without doubt the pre-war German home that belonged to his great-grandfather, Carl Schäfer. The shape and design, gables and stonework, garden and front door, all matched the tattered photo Guy kept in the kitchen of his flat. He was baffled as to what possible connection Alex could have with his ancestor's house. He even wondered whether Alex might have researched the Schäfer family, although it was unlikely. He picked up the frame, slid the photo out and held it for a moment. He turned it over. *Berlin 1931* was hand-written in faded ink on the back. This picture was no new acquisition.

'Jesus Christ,' was all he had time to mumble before he heard a jolt. He flinched and looked at the office door. The handle moved up and down twice. He went rigid and tried not to move a muscle, but his hands had not stopped trembling since he had picked up the first fax message moments ago, and they trembled even more now. He had not expected the security people to enter the building. He kept as still as possible for around five minutes, his eyes transfixed by the house in the photo, his ears tuned to any sound that might indicate trouble, until he felt sure that whoever it was had moved on. It may have been a cleaner or caretaker. Or Alex? 'God, I hope not,' he thought.

Guy checked his watch. His time was up and he had seen enough. He returned the rest of the papers to the bottom drawer, and inserted the photo back into the frame which he replaced on its spot marked by a gap in the dust on the desk's surface. He did not need to take the photo with him - for his whole life he had known exactly what the image looked like. Outside, from the lights on the perimeter fence Guy could tell it was getting dark and decided to spur David into action. He texted the pre-arranged instruction, 'Cut it.' He waited for David to text 'okay' but no reply came which made him anxious.

'Come on David for God's sake, tell me you've got my bloody message!' It was like waiting for the curtain to rise and the show to begin. But a few minutes later Guy knew his accomplice had received the order when there was a loud crack, a flash and all the perimeter lights went out.

'Good work!' he thought. David had cut all the wires at the base of the telegraph pole that Guy had seen on his recce. It should mean that telephone lines were neutralised as well, an added bonus.

Guy made for the office door. If he bumped into domestic staff, too bad, he would shove past them. But the way was clear and he raced down to the main reception area in the atrium. He heard shouting.

'Was ist das Problem?'

'Scheisse! Warum sind die Lichter ausgeschaltet?' *Why are the lights turned out?* Dogs barked. People were running.

'Schalten sie den Backup-Generator!' *Switch on the backup generator!* The scene outside looked and sounded chaotic. Time for the next move. He squatted beside a fire exit door and texted David, 'Ignite.'

Both men knew what would happen next.

David had spent part of that evening laden with the Bergen full of fireworks, furtively crawling on all fours to a clearing near the edge of the woods hidden from the perimeter fence. Earlier he had studied the instructions that came with the Power-Con firing system, a remote control device that ignites fireworks from a distance. Controlled by a radio signal, at the touch of a button Power-Con could set off up to ten fireworks at a time.

In the dog compound a distressed guard dog yelped in terror and cowed as the first barrage of fireworks screeched upwards, exploded and crackled in the evening sky. A cascade of bright flares shot out from each rocket until a vast area glowed pink. Guy watched from his position near the reception desk and grimaced as the multitude of radiant flares gently descended – he had not expected Blackpool Illuminations, he paid good money for an ear-splitting noise, not fairy lights. But he broke into a grin when the flares did their stuff and exploded like random hand grenades. In an instant the incendiaries were extinguished but the dogs were now demented with fright. Two shat themselves. A third pulled so hard on the leash that its handler was dragged through the fresh crap.

It was the moment for Guy to make his escape. He pressed down on the metal handlebar of the fire exit, pushed the door open and sprinted out into the dusk.

The security alarm immediately set off, its shrill clang accompanying him as he headed straight for the main gate. No security guards blocked his way, no dogs, no wild boar. He hurtled past the security barrier and ran at full throttle down the driveway that he now knew quite well. As he did so, he heard the 'whoosh' of the second salvo of rockets that he hoped would cause as much havoc as the first bombardment. He could not resist the temptation to slow down, turn and admire the display. Once again the evening sky dimmed after the pink flares detonated, their ear-splitting explosions smothering the incessant jangle of the alarm bell while guards and dogs continued their hysterics.

He was now at a safe distance from all the clamour and did not need to run any more. He wiped the sweat from his brow and walked in the twilight along the last leg of the driveway towards the ride in the woods where he expected David to be ready with the car. When he reached the ride his heart stopped. He could not see the car, or David.

'Where the bloody hell is he?' He stood motionless. The sun was almost down and he inhaled the still, balmy air that carried the security guards' distant shouts and the squeals of frenzied dogs. For a few moments Guy dithered whether to search for the car or stay where he was, but the guards and dogs began to sound less remote. His stomach fluttered. If he did not get a move on it would be his turn to shit himself. He could not keep still and do nothing so he started to walk along the ride. He kept close to the edge so he could nip into the trees if needed.

'Shit!' he hissed under his breath. 'Where's David?' Just as he reached for his cell phone a vehicle engine sparked into life. He scrambled behind some trees and squatted. Two headlight beams projected from a concealed track on the other side of the ride. Guy held up his hands to shield his eyes from the lights, unable to identify the car or its driver.

The car emerged from a small space between the trees, out onto the ride. Guy emerged furtively from his hiding place and trotted towards the car until he could just make out David's face behind the wheel. David gave him thumbs up and reached across to open the passenger door.

'Phew!' said Guy as he jumped into the front seat. 'You had me worried for a moment.'

They returned to the Gasthaus where they confronted each other in David's room, horns locked, voices raised.

'You stupid prat!' Guy yelled and pointed at David.

'It not all my fault!' David shouted. 'You're the one who told me to move the car as fast as I could. "Go like shit off a shovel" those were your exact words!'

'That didn't mean you could leave behind a trail of evidence, you ass!'

'I didn't leave a trail, it was only two items…'

'One of them has my name written in indelible ink on the inside flap, how could you be such an idiot?'

'Jesus Christ Guy, if I hadn't trekked all the way to Berlin so that you and Capsella could celebrate fucking bonfire night, you might never have…'

'All right, all right.' Guy held up the palms of his hands in submission, his voice still grouchy. 'Listen, I'll back off, okay? Let's just think this through. Somehow I've got to get that damned Bergen back.'

After he positioned the fireworks David had made his way back through the woods to a firing point nearer the parked car. As soon as he had triggered the second rocket blast he placed the Power-Con transmitter into the Bergen and carried it back to the car. In the excitement he leaned the Bergen up against the car while he tapped his pockets and fumbled for the car keys, at which point he made his big mistake. He got into the driver's seat to start the engine, switched on the headlights and drove onto the ride to meet up with Guy but accidentally left the Bergen behind. He did not realise what he had done until they were at the Gasthaus and Guy asked, 'Where's the backpack, is it in the boot?'

They were a little calmer now. 'I'll drive back and pick it up,' said David.

'Don't be stupid, the place will be crawling with the very people we need to avoid.'

'Why not? It's only the first bit of the driveway…'

'No David, it's too risky.' There was a moment of silence. 'Fuck it. Let's go downstairs for a drink.'

They sat in silence at the Gasthaus bar. In one corner of the room an elderly German couple were drinking their way through a bottle of vodka. For several minutes Guy gazed at the surface of the couple's table until he looked the other way towards David, took a gulp of beer and said, 'I'm sorry for the way I spoke just now.' He looked straight into his friend's eyes. 'It was bang out of order and I've a lot to thank you for.'

David nodded. 'That's okay. Looking back over the years since junior school, I suppose we've got a lot to thank each other for.'

'It's just that I'm still cut up about losing Jessica.' Guy's voice cracked. 'At first I was numb, but now it's sunk in that I'll never, never see her again.'

David sipped his drink deep in thought for a while. 'Tell you what, Guy. You suggested a run tomorrow, remember? Part of the marathon course? Well, let's do it, but change our route to include Königstrasse.' He gave Guy a sly smile. 'Get my drift? We might even find ourselves near the forest perimeter,' there was a hint of mischief in his voice, 'and who would suspect two joggers out early on a Saturday morning?' And so it was they both rose just before daybreak and quickly dressed in trainers, shorts and sweatshirts. In token disguise David wore a baseball cap while Guy sported a pair of wrap-around dark glasses. At first light they set off at a gentle pace until they got into their stride. Their breath steamed in the cool air. Guy was surprised how many other runners were out at that time of day, until he remembered that hundreds would be in their final stages of training for the Berlin Marathon next weekend.

In less than an hour they arrived at their original rendezvous, and soon found the same spot where David had parked the car. Sweaty and puffed, they paused for a few moments to catch their breath as thin shards of early daylight broke through the trees. Guy stood, legs wide apart with his black running shorts tight around his thighs, pushed up his sunglasses onto his tussled mop of hair and squinted. He heaved a sigh, coughed up some phlegm and spat. The only other noise was the rhythmic cooing of resident wood pigeons and a song thrush's distinctive chirrup from a tree top. Accompanied by this repertoire both men began to comb the area and they soon added to the dawn chorus by using small branches to brush aside the dead leaves, remnants of a forgone autumn now moist with fresh dew. The only man-made objects they found were two nub-ends of smoked joints and an old Smirnoff bottle. The latter contained no vodka, but a used condom had been meticulously stuffed into it by someone no doubt as keen on hygiene as they were on getting stoned and enjoying safe sex in the great outdoors. Guy gingerly picked up this receptacle of spent passion which curiously made him think of the elderly vodka drinkers he had seen in the bar the night before, held it up to his eyes for a few seconds and peered through the glass at the shrivelled genie inside. His observations were suddenly interrupted by a clatter of wings as two wood pigeons took off from their perch and flew away. He tossed the bottle with its tell-tale contents behind a cluster of shrubs, and fleetingly speculated whether Smirnoff could be Alex Grishin's favourite tipple.

'Sod it,' said Guy. He lowered his sunglasses back to his eyes. 'Those bastards must have already searched the area and picked up my Bergen with the Power-Con transmitter inside.' He placed both hands on his hips. 'They'll work out I was the cause of last night's mayhem.'

'Maybe some kids have nicked it,' said David hopefully, but the thin line of Guy's mouth indicated how doubtful that was. With nothing more they could do, they continued their run and arrived back at the Gasthaus about an hour later. After they had showered and changed Guy nipped out to buy himself a new suitcase for the flight home.

At Tempelhof Airport Guy and David went to a news stand while they waited for their flight, when they saw a late edition of the *Berliner Morgenpost* on one of the racks. Guy picked it up and saw an article headed: *Feuerwerk im Wald*. It was a short piece and another passenger helped them translate. Suspected pranksters had cut the electricity supply and let off fireworks near a genetic research facility based at Wannsee. It did not say what the police or anybody else intended to do about the incident. As it was a short article Guy reckoned that little damage had been done. There was no report of a forest fire because David had aimed the fireworks so that smouldering fragments dropped onto Wannsee lake, not dry land.

Besides, the spectacular events of that Friday had paled into distant memory after Guy told David what he found in Alex's office - the IGSA presentation on gene patents, the two faxes and the picture of his family home. At first David was speechless when Guy showed him the papers.

'This material is dangerous,' said Guy.

'It's also evidence,' said David, his face shell-shocked. 'How much do you think Raymond knows?'

'I'm not sure but I ought to find out. Even if he only knows some of it, he may have found more among Jessica's belongings, though I suspect that wouldn't amount to very much.'

David thought that it might be possible to research the house in Podbielski Allee and its connection with Alex Grishin. Guy said he was still in a state of disbelief about the photo so it would help to find any link. Then he had watched David hold one of the faxes in his hand. He had been astonished by the same two words that troubled Guy and said, 'I just don't know what to make of this,' he looked up at Guy, 'what's Bacillus anthracis?'

CHAPTER 19

And if there be no meeting past the grave,
If all is darkness, silence, yet 'tis rest;
Be not afraid ye waiting hearts that weep,
For God still giveth his beloved sleep
And if an endless sleep He wills, so best.

Henrietta Huxley

If anyone had told Raymond that one day he would attend his own step-daughter's memorial service, it would have left him astounded. If he was then told that death had to be assumed without finding her body, he would have been speechless. Hardly surprising then that *Dark Cloud* had descended.

Raymond had the poem printed on the front page of the order of service. Composed by a follower of Charles Darwin, it would placate any agnostics among those at the sombre memorial service in St John's, the eleventh century church in Ashworth, and he was confident that Jessica would have approved of the piece. The vicar was less enamoured with its mild insinuation of nature versus faith but, undeterred, when the church bell ceased its toll and the solemn organ music ended the reverend lady opened with the bidding:

'I am the way and the truth and the life says the Lord, no one comes to the Father except through me.'

She then reached up to light a large white candle on top of a wrought-iron stand positioned in front of the chancel where the catafalque would normally be. She greeted the congregation that packed the church to give thanks for the life of Jessica Elizabeth Parry. Raymond had no idea his step-daughter had so many friends and admirers, but here they were from the worlds of fashion, media, university, school.

With several discreet wipes of their eyes, Raymond and Ben choked their way through the first hymn. To begin with, the singing almost faltered but the organ soon fortified the congregation who belted out the last verse, a resounding congruence of voices and wind pipes that swirled up and reverberated back down from the church rafters. Many spirits were lifted until later when a former university friend stood before the congregation, guitar in hand, and sang a folk song Jessica had loved as a student. In front of the flicker of the candle the woman performed Pete Seeger's popular ballad that parodies the futility of war and conflict, *Where have all the flowers gone*. Raymond maintained his poise throughout most of this ordeal until the last verse when he broke down. Ben, no better, placed a fraternal arm around his twin brother and squeezed.

During the vicar's poignant eulogy Raymond glanced sideways at the pews occupied by Jessica's work colleagues, dressed in black, some sobbed and dabbed their moist cheeks with handkerchiefs. He also recognised the editors of *Vogue* and *Look*, and Jessica's senior tutor from Durham accompanied by a man who turned out to be the university's Vice Chancellor. In front of them Guy and his flatmate sat still, rigid statues that glared straight ahead, tight lipped, their pale faces void of expression. The vicar mentioned the relationship between Jessica and Guy. She acknowledged the huge sense of loss that affected everyone, and cited an earlier comment by Raymond that Jessica was an indomitable and feisty child who had blossomed into the most loving and precious step-daughter. The service ended with a prayer about the spiritual journey of the soul, when it occurred to Raymond that the vicar made no reference to the absence of a coffin. The organist played as Raymond, Ben and the vicar went to the church door to receive the congregation as they filed out. After the last person had left, the vicar went back inside to extinguish the candle. A thin trail of smoke arose that carried with it the familiar scent of burnt wax.

Afterwards the mourners gathered in the magnificent galleried hall and reception rooms of Ashworth Manor. They were greeted by Raymond's housekeeper, and by Penny and Tuppence whose expectant tails wagged at the sight of so many visitors. Neither dog barked but panted noisily for a while until they fell silent, instinctively attuned to the repressed grief. Over the subdued chatter of afternoon tea the folk-singer, no longer in possession of her guitar, walked over to Raymond and Ben and introduced herself. She spoke of happier days when she and Jessica had been carefree students at Durham.

'How kind of you to sing for us at the service,' Raymond said, his voice unsteady, sadness engraved on his face. Penny loped up and flopped down at his feet.

'The least I could do.'

'Thank you,' said Ben. 'Not too great an ordeal?'

'No, a privilege,' she said with a forlorn smile, and turned away to refill her teacup and talk to others. Penny's tail thumped a couple of times on the floor.

After tea when most of the mourners had left, David said he would leave before Guy and make his own way home. He had been offered a lift to Hatfield railway station by the finance officer from Jessica's company. The housekeeper and caterers began to clear everything away, and Raymond suggested Ben and Guy stay on for a stiff drink. As Raymond poured out whisky his dogs scratched on the other side of the study door, so he let them in and the pair headed for the fireplace and the large hearth rug. Guy stared out of the window at the grey and the drizzle. Raymond handed him a glass and watched him gulp the whisky.

They sat down. The dialogue was awkward but polite with no mention of Herron or Capsella, and definitely no mention of Guy's recent downfall. Ben said they were lucky the weather had been brighter earlier that day, and he thought the church service and all the arrangements had gone well. He looked up at a row of 'at home' invitations on the mantelpiece. Among them he pointed at the pink admission card to the Buckingham Palace Investiture.

'At least that's something to look forward to in the next few days,' he said in an encouraging tone.

'I had invited Jessica,' said Raymond, his face expressionless. The other two exchanged uneasy glances.

'Well, I'll be there to support you on the big day,' said Ben. ' It's the Queen isn't it? A huge honour. Jessica was so proud, I hope that's some comfort to you.'

Raymond swallowed his drink and went to refill his glass. 'Still, I've got other important things to do.'

'If it's sorting out her affairs, probate and all that, I'm happy to help in any way.'

'Me too,' said Guy in a pathetic voice. He cleared his throat.

'That's not what I mean. First of all she has to be legally declared dead, a lengthy formality that can't be put off, but there's a perfectly good lawyer who'll take care of that side of things.' He remained standing. 'No, Ben, I must travel and meet some people. Ask pertinent questions,' he turned and looked hard at Guy who shifted uneasily in his chair, an empty glass in his hand, 'to find out what others might know, and how much they understand.'

Ben raised his eyebrows but said nothing.

Guy looked at his watch and shifted to the edge of his chair. 'It's time I made a move.' He cleared his throat once more.

'Let me run you to the station. I'm sure Raymond needs a bit of space,' said Ben.

Guy got up. Raymond forced a thin smile as they shook hands.

'Call me if there's anything I can do,' said Guy.

Ben stood. There was an edgy silence until Raymond said to Guy, 'I know how much you meant to Jessica. I never used to believe in love at first sight, to me it was just romantic fluff. But then she met you…' his voice cracked and tears rolled down his cheeks. 'You were everything to her,' he rasped in a tone that could have been either raw emotion or plain bitterness. Or both.

Guy did not look Raymond in the face. He nodded at the floor, bit his lower lip and walked out of the study followed by Ben.

When they had gone Raymond sank exhausted into an armchair beside the hearth. He puffed out his cheeks and sighed. There were some business issues that he needed to straighten out, issues that he thought he understood… even though he was about to become phenomenally rich he was desperate to grieve. He fixed his gaze towards the hearth rug where the two dogs had fallen asleep.

CHAPTER 20

'This is the final call to passengers intending to travel on Lufthansa flight LH 921 to Berlin Tegel Airport, please proceed immediately to gate nine.' Early on the morning after Jessica's memorial service two men were on the move again, one to run in the 28th Berlin Marathon and the other to right some wrongs.

The days leading up to Jessica's memorial had been busy. After a moment of pique when Guy chucked his dismissal letter into the nearest waste bin, he was asked by Ben to help with preparations for the service in St John's church. David, meanwhile, returned to work and spent his evenings at the Vista Gym to limber up for Sunday's marathon. He also researched Alex Grishin's possible links with the Schäfer family house in Podbielski Allee, and made progress of sorts. He came across *MyPedigree* an interactive website where he looked for a Grishin family tree. It was a start at any rate.

Guy started to review the facts: first, Capsella-Biotech was buying new computers to speed up sequencing of the human genome. Second, judging from the IGSA speech notes Alex planned to patent a few thousand genes, assuming it was legal. Third, there was a DNA editing product for which large sums of money would be paid. And fourth, somewhere in the mix was an 'anthrax formula' mentioned in a secure fax from Karim Samir. Raymond was in no state to divulge more information to Guy, by now a former employee. Even if

Raymond knew about Alex's IGSA presentation, it would be no more than the PowerPoint script Guy had pocketed during his recent incursion in Berlin.

The only person with answers was Alex Grishin, and two days before the memorial service Guy had made the decision to take a huge risk and square up to the man. He assumed Alex was unaware he had been fired from Herron International, and he would just blag his way and feign ignorance if he got quizzed about the fireworks incident. Meanwhile David did not even bother to dissuade him – there was no point, he knew exactly what his impulsive flatmate's response would be. So he was just as surprised as Guy when something unexpected occurred that proved Guy's reasoning.

As he was revving up the courage to call Capsella-Biotech, Guy's cell phone rang and he found himself talking with Alex's PA.

'Yes, I'd be glad to…. when did he have in mind? I'm at a funeral on Thursday but I can fly out on Friday I guess… no it'll be fine, honestly… what did he want to discuss? Okay… Friday afternoon… that's at Capsella-Biotech presumably? …oh, I didn't know he still had an office there, all right. If I get an early enough flight, four o'clock German time would be great, thanks.'

So Alex did not know Guy had been sacked. Or else that was what he wanted Guy to assume … even so it was unlikely that Raymond in his current frame of mind would have told Alex anything, yet.

Guy and David had booked rooms in the same Gasthaus in Zehlendorf. Discreet and low key, it suited their needs. They had separate agendas of course.

'You make me nervous,' said David over coffee in the Gasthaus bar, 'I wish you'd go to the Polizei.'

'What would that achieve?' said Guy irritably. 'The only hard evidence I've got is the paperwork I nicked from the Chief Executive's office at Capsella.' He shrugged. 'If I exposed Alex I expect he would sham ignorance and say I must have forged the documents. Even if the Polizei pursued the matter, they'd probably be more interested to know how I got hold of those documents and whether I knew who set off the fireworks.'

'What time's your meeting with Alex this evening?'

'At four, in Westfälische Strasse.'

'Where's that?'

'Wilmersdorf, north of here, where Grishin Genetics was based before it merged with Capsella.'

'Why's he want to meet you there?'

'Apparently Capsella's having new satellite telephone facilities installed at the Wannsee site!' Guy winked. 'Westfälische Strasse was mentioned in John Kent's report, it's not far from your marathon route on Sunday, about three-quarters of the way round.'

'I hope you're not being set-up,' said David.

'If I am it's of my own making.'

'That's what worries me.' David downed the last of his coffee.

'Look. This is about fighting corporate greed, preventing misuse of genetic science that could benefit millions of people,' said Guy with a tremor in his voice. 'I owe it to Jessica. I owe it to myself. It's the only opportunity I'll ever get.'

Guy's taxi pulled up by the kerb in Westfälische Strasse, an avenue not far from the Kurfürstendamm, or *Ku'damm*, a fashionable Berlin shopping boulevard.

'Ist es hier?' asked the driver.

'Jar, dankah.' Guy's dreadful accent again. He paid and climbed out of the taxi. On the avenue he stood and looked down the lines of trees, their leaves edged with traces of golden brown, a hint of autumn. He turned towards the building. Unlike the other blocks in Westfälische Strasse it was several metres back and separated from the pavement by a wide strip of lawn. He looked up at a sign on one wall, *Grishin Informatik GmbH* which he realised had to be computers. The former site of Grishin Genetics, it included a large office complex and what looked like a warehouse at the rear. He made his way through the car park, empty except for a black Mercedes at one end, and walked up to the front door. The place looked closed for the week-end but no matter, this was his one chance to extract grains of truth from Alex. He pressed the entry button and the speaker crackled.

'Da?' A deep throated Russian accent.

'Er, Mr Shepherd. I've a meeting with Dr Grishin.'

'I come down and letting you in,' the voice said.

'Ziss vay please.' He was greeted by one of the minders he remembered from his first visit to Capsella-Biotech, the uglier of the two men. Another Soviet veteran perhaps. Guy was frisked and had his cell phone removed.

'You get ziss back later,' he was told.

Guy replied with a nervous quip that he was not carrying a wire, a wisecrack that was ignored. He was then led along a corridor into a small grubby office where Alex sat with his feet up on a tatty desk. The rest of the spartan office furniture consisted of not much more than functional bookcases, a small cupboard and two chairs, décor that made Guy think of second-hand Ikea. His host did not rise to welcome him, but merely gestured towards a chair while he thumbed through documents in a ring-binder file, until he seemed more conscious of Guy's presence.

'Take a seat.'

'Hello Alex.'

'Journey okay?' Icily polite. He looked up from the folder with a forced smile.

'Fine thanks.' Guy sat. It was clear from the ensuing silence that there would be no small talk. 'Er, I believe you wanted to discuss the timing of the second tranche of finance, to bring it forward...'

'Oh, did I?' In one move Alex swung his feet down onto the floor, slammed the folder onto the desk and shouted, 'Why did you do it?!'

'Do what?'

'Christ man, you must think I came in on last night's banana boat. What do you mean *do what*? – you know exactly what!'

Guy froze. As he looked straight at Alex he could sense rather than hear the door open gently behind him. He did not turn his head but knew others were now in the room. His mind raced to fathom how to survive this grilling. He could almost feel the door close as it shut without a sound.

'We have you on CCTV.'

Guy remained expressionless.

'We also have a backpack with your name written inside, and a transmitter that ignites fireworks.' Alex glowered. 'And I've discovered certain documents are missing from my office. Oh, on the night of the power cut my security team found a fire escape door had been opened from the inside.' He leaned forward. 'What do you have to say, Guy?'

Steady breathing from the doorway sent a tingle down Guy's spine, he was aware of their eyes on the back of his neck, their presence like ominous ghosts. By now he had guessed who they were but fixed his gaze on Alex and said sharply, 'More to the point, what do you have to say?'

'Eh?' Alex looked puzzled, evidently unused to anyone else having the nerve to stand up to him. He stared back at Guy as if to command respect, but it made Guy think more of a boar's head served up on a platter.

Besides, Guy was getting pissed off with this conceited, self-righteous bully whose Russian accent jarred his nerves. He also sensed that if this man ever felt exposed or cornered he would lash out, rant or go into a frenzy; Guy had despised his father's rages and now loathed this bigoted look-alike in front of him. It was that look in his eyes, and all it needed was one single trigger according to the blog at *MindCrusade*. Guy maintained an outward appearance of calm.

'I take it you've reported everything to the police?'

'We don't need that kind of hassle…'

'Oh? Don't you? I thought you might say that.' It was Guy's turn to cross-examine. 'What about your thriving computer business here, how's Grishin Informatik GmbH doing these days?'

'People don't need to know what goes on here,' said Alex with a dismissive wave of one hand. 'We've some storage space, a warehouse round the back rented by an IT distributor, and we let them get on with it. We don't get in each other's way and it justifies the signboard out front.'

'So Grishin Informatik is a front. For what? To patent a few genes if such a thing is possible?' Guy shook his head, 'I don't think so.' He held his stare. 'To edit DNA? That's one way to make a lot of money. But perhaps there's more money to be made from…' he paused, 'the anthrax formula. I presume Mr Samir has the answer to…'

'For Christ's sake! You've got us wrong, Guy.' Another forced smile, 'I'll tell you what we do here. From the papers you pilfered I expect you've worked out part of the story, so I'll explain the rest, okay?'

Several thoughts rushed through Guy's mind: he had been summoned here on a pretext, and had taken the bait in order to pull together strands of information from material stolen from this quick-tempered zealot. Yet the same man was now about to reveal industrial secrets while two pit-bulls blocked the door. It did not augur well. Guy shivered.

Alex stood with his hands in his pockets and paced to and fro behind the desk like a high school teacher deep in thought. Then he stopped and smiled.

'We don't understand each other, do we, Guy? I'm in business to revolutionise medicine, to create a scientific earthquake, and you are a corporate financier incapable of playing by the rules.'

Guy said nothing.

'You have to learn the rules of the game. And then you have to play better than anyone else. Who said that? Einstein. I take it your superiors at Herron International know nothing of your little sortie last week-end... no, I didn't think so.'

Alex sat down again, and pointed.

'You, sir, have got the wrong end of the stick. You've acted illegally, picked up butt-ends of information, put two and two together and somehow made thirty. I don't know what drives you, but let me help you see the light.'

Guy raised his eyebrows.

'You're right, I do intend to patent a few thousand genes. There may be legal challenges but it presents a fabulous business opportunity.'

Guy could not contain himself any longer. 'That's where I've grasped the <u>right</u> end of the stick. If you lot have the intellectual property rights to just a tiny fraction of the human genome, nobody can access the complete sequence without paying royalties to Capsella-Biotech.'

Alex grinned and said, 'Spaseeba.' *Thank you.* 'You're quick off the mark.'

'You make me sick.' Guy was about to lose it. 'To think that billions of dollars of public money has been spent to sequence the human genome and make the data freely available at GenBank...'

'Get real! This is business for God's sake!'

'And what about DNA editing?'

'Ah, the IBEC system. I was coming to that.'

'What's IBEC?' Guy was genuinely puzzled.

'It's a process to edit DNA with absolute precision. It'll have a sensational effect on the future of medicine. Mankind will be able to reverse the effects of genetic disorders, and neutralise most hereditary conditions.'

It prompted Guy to think of Huntingdon's Disease, the illness with a strong hereditary trait that took Jessica's mother and probably would have afflicted Jessica in her turn. With so much at stake it was clear why Raymond supported this enterprise.

Guy folded his arms. 'IBEC or whatever it's called sounds a fantastic contribution to science. Why don't you patent that, instead?'

'It's already patented, no worries. What's more we've got serious buyers and that's where our agent Mr Samir, comes into the picture. He represents a client that's signed up for our product, for a specific reason,' Alex then used a word that Guy had never heard before, 'a phage.'

Guy looked blank.

'You don't understand, do you? It's why you've grasped the <u>wrong</u> end of the stick. I'm talking about a man-made virus that destroys bacteria, known as a phage. The client will use our IBEC system to produce a more sophisticated phage as an antidote to anthrax. An antidote to bio-weapons.'

'Who the hell's threatened by biological weapons these days?'

'Here's a bit of history for you. In the nineteen seventies an international Biological Weapons Convention banned the production and stockpiling of weapons of mass destruction. But the old Soviet Union maintained a bio-weapons programme and kept it hidden from western intelligence.'

Guy looked astonished. 'If it was hidden how did anyone find out about it?'

'Vladimir Pasechnik, head of a Biomedical Institute in what was called Leningrad. He defected to Britain and convinced his interrogators that his country had stockpiled tons of strategic bio-weapons. Thousands of people were employed by the setup under the guise of a bogus civil research programme.'

'Surely all those weapons were destroyed?'

'Even if they were, Russian research went a stage further. Pasechnik was interviewed by one of your people, Dr David Kelly, a microbiologist at Porton

Down. Comrade Pasechnik claimed his people had raised biotechnology to a new level and produced genetically engineered viruses that cause unknown symptoms in victims.'

'What has all this got to do with your phage product?'

'Listen. A while back the Russians came to realise that the human population would soon enter the post-antibiotic age. Although they developed the phage as the ultimate protection against biological attack, they later saw it as an alternative to antibiotics. In the post-Soviet era they possessed a marketable product that destroys lethal bacteria, but the technology was cyclical. Every time a new virus was developed it required a new phage to defeat it, which prompted the creation of another new virus, and so on.'

'Hence the need to edit the DNA,' said Guy, as the coin began to drop.

'That's what we're selling. We have one Middle Eastern client that's desperate for the rights to our IBEC system, so they can update their anti-anthrax phage. And with IBEC they won't need any more support from their Russian friends.'

From that last remark Guy guessed it. Mr Samir must be Arabic, his client would be a country in the Middle East and an ally of Russia. 'You're selling to Iraq, aren't you.' It was a statement, not a question.

Alex said, 'We know that Iraq operated a biological warfare programme long before the nineteen ninety-one Gulf War. Another defector who once supervised Iraq's weapon development has said as much. But since the Iraqi's were chucked out of Kuwait they've changed their tune. Their research programme now aims to develop phages to protect the population.'

'Do you seriously believe that? How much are they paying you?' Another question struck Guy – how much were they paying Raymond?

'The Iraqis were humiliated when the allies liberated Kuwait,' said Alex, 'and they still feel threatened by neighbours like Iran. There's never going be another Gulf war, the western Allies don't have the stomach for it, but the Iraqis still want to protect themselves. What's that fancy slogan you financial people use? Hedge your bets?' He paused. 'As for the deal, well, let's just say that they're paying us a fair market rate.'

'That's fucking marvellous isn't it! You're now telling me Capsella-Biotech is above all suspicion. Except when your patent applications get approved no person on this planet will access the complete human genome without royalties going into your coffers. Meanwhile you're making millions on the side selling a phenomenal DNA editing tool to arseholes like Saddam Hussein...'

'What's it to you, you interfering little runt?' Alex nodded at the two heavies who had remained silent throughout the entire exchange. In Russian he said to them, 'I've done with him. You know where to take him.' They opened the door then stepped forward to grab Guy by his arms.

'Hey? Leave me alone!' They pulled him up and pinned his arms behind his back which made him stand ramrod straight, and started to drag him towards the doorway. He resisted fiercely and used his heels to propel all three of them backwards until they crashed into the far wall of the corridor, then he tried to thrust forward but they had him secured by his arms and shoulders. 'Bastards!' His face contorted in pain. 'What the hell are you doing?' He looked at Alex and shouted, 'If you're so bloody innocent why treat me like this? Are you scared who I'll tell?'

'Me? Scared?' Yet another forced smile. 'I'm not giving you the chance to tell anyone.' Alex leered at him with cold eyes, leaned forward with both fists on the surface of his desk and said in a hushed, seething voice, 'Never, never, fuck with me.'

Those words resounded in Guy's ears as he was frog-marched along the corridor where they halted opposite a door. With his forearms pinned behind his back it hurt too much to put up a fight. One of the minders then stepped out in front of Guy, turned to face him and kicked him in the genitals. Guy screamed at the paralysing pain. Unable to flinch with his arms locked, he tried to raise his knees up to his chest and clenched his watery eyes shut while the other minder somehow managed to hold on to him. Both men bundled Guy into the room. There was no window but the light was on. Apart from a small table the place was empty like a disused store room. He was released with a firm shove that made him fall and curl up on the floor.

The door closed and the lock clicked. He felt he would puke up any minute. He did not know how long he lay in that foetal position clasping his testicles. He felt permanently deprived of his manhood, an eternity before the agony subsided to a pulsating ache when he made the effort to sit up. Eventually he stood.

Guy limped to and fro until one of the men brought him a roll mat and a bowl of cereals. He hardly touched the cereals which he left to go soggy. He sat on the roll mat and sighed. The room was airless which made him hot and sweaty. The question that recurred most in his mind was whether Capsella-Biotech's activities were legal. If not, perhaps he could go to the police, but that would implicate the Chairman of Herron International who may not understand the extent of Alex's negotiations with a rogue state. Perhaps Raymond simply believed that a fabulous profit was to be made from clients queuing up to buy the IBEC wonder product. Even if it was acceptable to supply Iraq with a defence against bio-weapons and if Capsella was operating within the law, the question remained as to what was going on here at Grishin Informatik. And how did those Swiss bank accounts square away with the corporate finance provided by Herron International?

Alex's chances of success with the patent applications were something that Guy could not weigh up. He knew nothing of the procedural intricacies but his hunch was that Capsella-Biotech would have a struggle on its hands. As for the photograph of the house in Podbielski Allee, he was mighty glad not to have raised that yet... the look in Alex's eyes, one single trigger... for now there were more important things to consider. Nothing would be achieved locked up in this dump and he needed to get out. He would then have to work out how to stop Alex in his tracks without compromising Raymond – Jessica would never have wanted her step-father to face the rigour and humiliation of exposure.

Suddenly a key turned in the door and the two cohorts walked in. They were on to Guy before he could even stand, giving him no chance to run off. They gripped him under the armpits and lifted him up.

'Get off me, you jerks!'

One of the men stood in front of him while the other moved behind, out of sight. For a couple of seconds Guy's right arm was free and he did not hesitate. He swung it back to strike a blow when for a split second he became aware of a swish of air, caused by the downward trajectory of an object aimed at his skull.

Then everything went blank.

CHAPTER 21

From: Raymond Herron
Sent: Friday 28 September 2001 11:28
To: Dr A. M. Grishin
Subject: Catch-Up

Dear Alex,

Sorry it's a while since we last spoke, but at last I can just about face putting it in writing that I lost a close relative in the World Trade Center outrage. We held a memorial service for her a couple of days ago and everyone's been hugely supportive.

It's a tough time but I must try to move on. My work is a great solace hence this message about a couple of things:

1. You should know that I've had to let Guy Shepherd go. It turned out he wasn't right for the company and I thought it best all round to nip the situation in the bud.

2. When you called me in NY you mentioned something about patents – what was it you wanted to say? When would be a good time for the two of us to talk?

Best regards,

Raymond

Sir Raymond Herron
Chairman, Herron International LLP
Adams Court, London EC2N 1DX

From: Dr A. M. Grishin
Sent: Friday 28 September 2001 14:12
To: Raymond Herron
Subject: RE: Catch-Up

Hello Raymond,

So very sorry to hear your tragic news - deepest sympathy. I honestly had no idea about your personal loss, but now understand why you were in New York so soon after 9/11.

Let me know if I can help in any way. I've loads of contacts in the States should you need assistance over there.

Rather than email each other would it be okay to talk this week-end? It's more secure. Contact me Saturday any time after 9am your time, I'll be in my office. When we last spoke I wanted you to know that the international patents for my IBEC system have come through successfully. We've done it! Hope this news brightens your mood a bit.

Surprised to hear Guy Shepherd has been put out to grass. He's meeting me here in an hour's time, did you know that?

What's going on?

All best,

Alex

From: Raymond Herron
Sent: Friday 28 September 2001 16:18
To: Dr A. M. Grishin
Subject: RE: Catch-Up

Dear Alex,

Thank you for your kind condolences and offer of help, it's appreciated.

Astounded to learn about your meeting with Guy, I should be asking <u>you</u> what's going on! Did he request to see you or was it the other way round? By now I presume you've had your meeting with him, so how did it go? What did you talk about? Anyway, please note that Guy no longer represents Herron International.

Delighted to learn that IBEC now has the necessary patents. I presume Samir and his contacts are in the picture?

By the way, the latest edition of Nature has an article about your recent New York speech – what's all this about filing for gene patents? I didn't known about that.

Best regards,

Raymond

Sir Raymond Herron
Chairman, Herron International LLP
Adams Court, London EC2N 1DX

From: Dr A. M. Grishin
Sent: Friday 28 September 2001 17:32
To: Raymond Herron
Subject: RE: Catch-Up

Raymond,

Before I knew you'd fired Guy I asked him over to Berlin to firm up Herron's second tranche of finance. From our discussion I reckon he's been snooping so v. glad you've sacked him. In a sense I've 'sacked' him too. He won't pester us again.

Re: the questions in your last message, let's talk them through tomorrow (Sat) if that's still okay.

Alex

'Guten Tag,' said Alex.

'It's Raymond.'

'Morning!' Alex moved both feet from his desk to the floor and rotated his chair to face his office window. It was a clear, dry day. He twiddled a biro in one hand while the other held the phone. 'Thanks for calling Raymond… listen, once again, sorry about your bereavement and I appreciate your call. Sure it's all right to talk now? Okay… excellent, let's try to keep things brief.'

'That's fine,' said Raymond. 'Er, I was staggered you met Guy yesterday. I still don't get why…'

'All under the bridge. We talked for a while then I got rid of him. He won't trouble us anymore.'

'I hope you're right,' said Raymond. 'You don't know him as I do. A loose cannon. Impetuous.'

'Which brings us to today's discussion,' said Alex, abruptly changing the subject. 'I hope you won't accuse <u>me</u> of being impetuous.' He turned towards his desk and dropped the biro into a plastic pen holder. 'I'll be blunt. Several months ago I made a working assumption that Herron International would deliver the required finance, so at the time I authorised delivery of the Spectra 6500 computers.'

'Bloody hell. That could have backfired,' said Raymond. 'What would you've done if we hadn't coughed up?'

'But Herron did agree to cough up, and you'll be a personal beneficiary…'

'Even so.' Raymond laughed wearily. 'Now you're the one who's the loose cannon…'

'Come on Raymond, I hoped my news would put you in a better mood. It means the Spectra machines will be installed very soon but in the meantime Capsella-Biotech has to honour outstanding credit, so we must have the second tranche of finance a.s.a.p.'

'Happy to oblige.' Raymond sighed. 'I'll get our operations team onto it first thing Monday.' He hesitated. This was surely the moment to question Alex about that overheard 'anthrax' conversation, but the very thought conjured up images of Jessica that almost got the better of Raymond. He closed his eyes for a few seconds and tried to recover his poise.

'Still there Raymond? You okay?'

'Alex…' he croaked.

'If this is too much, we can talk another time.'

'Alex, I must ask you something, um,' he faltered like a stammerer, 'we also agreed to talk about your…' a further pause, until all that came out was, '…about your bizarre plans to patent some genes. You've played that one close to your chest, what's it about?'

For someone who claimed that the phone call should be brief, Alex took his time to say he hoped to get patents for at least a few thousand genes. In theory it would give Capsella-Biotech part ownership – if only an infinitesimal part – of intellectual property rights to the human genomic code. He described how this scheme would prevent the medical community from being held to ransom by undesirable elements. Raymond's response that some might regard Capsella-Biotech as undesirable rankled Alex, as did the comment that attempts to patent a living organism would surely fall at the first fence.

'You're taking on too much, Alex,' said Raymond, 'why not keep to our original strategy to patent IBEC?'

'I've already said, IBEC is now patented.'

'Can't we just stick to that?'

'You can, Raymond. Karim Samir is fully prepared, he'll work with us to coordinate the delivery of IBEC to Baghdad and the payments to you and me. For my part I must press ahead with those applications for gene patents. It's a separate operation that needn't concern you.'

Raymond shook his head and spoke with calculated emphasis, 'Apply if you must. But do <u>not</u> let it disrupt sales of IBEC. I hope I've made that very clear.'

'Of course. Trust me, my friend.'

CHAPTER 22

He awoke on the concrete floor of a cold cellar that measured around fifteen metres square, with dirty tiled walls and a heavy wooden door. On one side daylight came through an oblong barred window out of reach just below the ceiling. As lodgings go, the place did not have a lot to commend it.

'This can't be right,' he thought, 'what the fuck am I doing here?'

Guy's jacket, tie and shoes had been removed leaving him in socks, trousers and a creased, blood stained shirt. His head throbbed. With an effort he sat up, looked around and breathed in the musty air before he touched his sore skull and examined the congealed blood on his fingers. His last recollection was the heated argument with Alex. The man must be demented if he thinks he can get away with the Iraq deal, and he wondered who else knew of Alex's intentions and whether Raymond understood the full extent of the plans.

Guy looked around his empty 'prison'. At one end about five feet above the floor, a horizontal wooden beam was fixed to the wall. On the opposite wall two metal ring bolts were screwed to the tiles about six feet off the ground. He tried not to look at these items in case they hinted at something sinister; goose-bumps came to his arms and legs. Still a touch unsteady, he managed to stand up and pad towards the cellar door which he was not surprised to find locked.

A couple of hours later he heard a door opening followed by the tap dance of footsteps, and hollow voices like a subdued monastery chant. A bolt clanked and the cellar door swung open. Guy looked up as Alex entered accompanied by his two ugly henchman who carried a trestle table that they opened out and placed in the middle of the room. Guy wondered why the legs at one end were shorter, causing the table to slant. They walked back out and returned a few moments later, one with a small suitcase that he placed on the floor while the other carried a watering can without its sprinkler. Alex held a dark metal object in his hand.

'You meddlesome little shit,' said Alex in a guttural tone.

'And a very good evening to you too.' Guy instantly regretted his derisive reply. Alex raised one hand and clouted Guy on the head with a Ruger semi-automatic handgun, loosening a tooth.

'Bastard,' hissed Guy as he clutched the welt on his face and tasted stingy salt in his mouth.

Alex bent down towards Guy. 'Before I get rid of you I'll make you suffer, Guy.'

Guy thought his captor smelled faintly of drink, reminding him of parental abuse years ago. 'What the bloody hell are you on about?' A trickle of blood ran down his fingers.

Alex turned to his lackeys and said in a cold voice, 'You know what to do.'

Guy still held his bleeding mouth when the two men unbuttoned his dirty shirt and ripped it from his torso. They tried to pick him up, but had not reckoned on manhandling the former captain of Warwick University's first rowing eight. His resistance was ferocious and it took all their strength, plus Alex's, to lift him onto the slanted table and slam his head down at the lower end. One of the brutes sat on his chest and the other on his legs while Alex produced a roll of extra strong duct tape from the case and twice wrapped it over Guy's ankles and under the table, then he did the same to his knees, arms and chest. Bound to the table, he made a token effort to fight back, but it was too late, he was pinned down by the double-wraps of tape round his body. He tried to lift his head, 'For Christ's sake!' he yelled but Alex smacked him back and taped his forehead to the table.

'You're about to go scuba diving!' sneered Alex. His men laughed, then one of them produced a cloth from the case.

'You SHITS!' Guy trembled. He knew what was in store but could say no more: the cloth was pressed over his mouth, nose and eyes, held in place by both thugs. Alex began to pour from the spout of the watering can onto the area of cloth that covered Guy's mouth and nose. As he held his breath not much happened at first, but when he inhaled by reflex, water shot through his nose and mouth into his lungs and stomach. It felt as if ice cubes had filled his chest. He tried to use his tongue to block the flow through his mouth, but he had no control over the cold stream through his nose. He was like a non-swimmer in chains, pitched into a deep river with no respite except to breath in water and await death. After what seemed an eternity, in truth about thirty seconds of agony, Alex paused for a moment but the cloth was still held tight over his face.

Then the second pouring commenced. This time it began with a slow trickle along Guy's legs, over his bare chest and neck that caused him to quiver in terrified anticipation. When the water reached the cloth over his face he was aware of his torturers' manic laughs. Unable to move, his tongue could not prevent the nasal dribble into his lungs. Previous victims of water boarding have described how the mind goes blank as total panic kicks in: Guy found out that this hideous torture does not just simulate drowning - he actually was drowning. Unable to cry out as his lungs filled, Guy's body shook and vibrated on the table. The veins on his tensed arm muscles enlarged as he tried, unsuccessfully, to escape this ordeal.

Alex nodded at his two accomplices and they lifted the cloth from Guy's face, for just a short spell. Guy choked and made death rattle noises as his lungs heaved and rasped. Alex took the now empty watering can out of the room, and came back a few moments later having refilled it.

'No more!' Guy could only just splutter, 'for God's sake, please, I can't take any m…' but the cloth went back into position and the third session began. Again he suffered the initial torment of a slow drip that started at his feet and progressed along the whole length of his quivering body. The two cohorts had to sit on Guy's shoulders as well as hold the cloth, as he juddered and quaked. At one point it seemed he might even break the duct tape but no such luck for this smothered victim who endured a further eternity (thirty seconds again) of drowning agony.

And so to the fourth pouring, administered with the same pitiless cruelty. Lost in pitch darkness under the infernal cloth, his life seemed to ebb away as he drowned. Guy was beyond desperation. His body vibrated so that it was fifty-fifty which would snap first: the tape or his bones.

Then it abruptly stopped.

'That's enough boys. Undo him.' Guy flinched as lengths of the sticky tape tore at his body hair. He was shoved onto the floor where he landed with a thump and spewed up fluid. With difficulty he got onto all fours and coughed, gagged and frantically gulped in air as if tasting it for the first time in his life. He made a horrendous noise but dared not utter a word.

'You know what to do next boys!' Alex ordered in Russian.

They grabbed hold of an arm each and dragged him backwards towards a wall, and forced Guy's right arm up to one of the ring bolts above his head, then used a nylon grip to tie his hand to the ring.

'Please,' he rasped, '*PLEASE! STOP!*'

The two of them managed to do the same to his left arm before they proceeded to tie more nylon cord around his ankles. His toes could just touch the cellar floor.

'After six hours with your arms up you'll beg me to cut you down,' said Alex, 'and after twelve hours you'll be screaming or unconscious.'

Immobile, Guy's legs were weak and shaky, and he felt hollow in the pit of his stomach as he glared back with a glint of real fear in his eyes.

The taller henchman had removed the trestle table and brought in a wooden stool from outside and placed it in the middle of the cellar where Alex sat and said to his men, 'Continue.'

From the small suitcase wire cutters, two pairs of thick protective gloves and strands of barbed wire were produced.

'Oh God! Not that. Anything but that!' gasped Guy, then he bawled as he was punched hard in the stomach. He threw up more water. Unable to double up, the pain was unbearable. The first barbed strand was wrapped around his ankles before the nylon cord was cut off, and the two other strands of wire replaced the nylon cords that had held up his wrists.

Guy's face creased and his eyes filled with tears as he tried to focus on his captors. He realised the wheels had fallen off all three of them, and thought he had nothing to lose any more.

'You utter cunts!' he gibbered.

'Give him another,' commanded Alex who grinned when Guy screeched at the merciless blow, writhed, and shrieked again in agony from the cuts inflicted by the barbed wire. Blood dripped onto the cellar floor.

'Oh God,' he whimpered, 'sweet J-e-s-u-s.' Such holy words and perhaps the nearest he would ever get to saying a genuine prayer, yet it must have been obvious that neither God, Jesus nor anyone else of sacred hue would redeem the atheist Guy Shepherd from his moment of peril.

'You've never experienced pain like this before, have you?' Alex gloated.

Guy could barely listen.

'Do you know what it's like to see a young soldier's stomach ripped open by mortar shrapnel, when he staggers towards you carrying his intestines in a helmet? Huh? No, you don't. It took him two weeks to die from gangrene, while under morphine the poor lad babbled how he would drink vodka with his comrades when he got home.'

Guy's delirious thoughts turned to Jessica whose company he now craved. If only, if only.

Alex narrowed his eyes and squinted at him. 'You've never seen a teenager scream for momma in his death throes, impaled on a cross like Jesus fucking Christ while they skinned him alive, have you?' He turned on his stool and pointed at his henchmen, 'These fellas and I saw it, right boys?' The men exchanged glances and nodded. 'You wouldn't know what it's like to have your own men tread on land mines, the shit of seeing those same boys' limbs hang from trees days later, would you? In one case it wasn't just a limb but the body, stoned to death then decapitated by the Mujahidin. The boy was eighteen.'

'What's all that got to do with anything, bugger it!' sobbed Guy.

'You just don't get it, do you Guy? Raw combat and brutal torture taught me to treasure the magic of creation and to relish life's fragile beauty…'

'What about the beauty of my fucking life? Let me down, for Chrissake, you bloody lunatic!'

'Give him another.'

Both henchmen gloated as they walked towards Guy who begged out loud, 'NO, *PLEASE!!*'

Their fists hit his stomach but his scream was muffled as he choked on his own vomit.

He squirmed, coughed up sick and water, and more blood dripped onto the floor. Barely conscious, he wondered if this torment was payback for his role in Jessica's tragic demise. With scarcely any breath left in him he managed to wheeze, 'You unhinged motherfucker. Raymond's daughter knew you'd shaft the Human Genome Proj…'

Alex leapt up and knocked over the stool. 'Raymond Herron? A daughter? Nyet! You're out of your damned mind… what do you mean?'

Guy winced, his mumble just inaudible. 'I meant step-daughter, Jessica Parry, she knew what…'

At the sound of her name Alex snapped, 'Damn it, nobody told me jackshit… take him down!' The men hesitated. 'Do it NOW!' The two obeyed, and caused

Guy to yelp and grimace as the barbed wire restraints were unfastened. He collapsed onto the floor.

Alex cursed. His victim was in no state to talk, and he turned to his men, 'We can't kill him yet, I need to mull things over. Leave him water and we'll shove off for a while.' At the door to the cellar he turned and said to the breathless body on the floor, 'When I return you better tell me what you know, or you'll suffer so much pain that you'll beg me to kill you there and then.' His men smirked and the three turned to leave. The door closed and the bolt slid shut. Confused and exhausted, Guy hardly registered that last threat.

Alone, bleeding and in terrible pain, he looked with nervous dread at the cold water that had been left for him in a thoughtfully placed metal piss pot. His ribs ached which made it difficult to breathe, his cheek was swollen, a molar wobbled on his lower left jaw and his sore wrists and ankles were caked in blood that had started to clot. When had he ever felt like this? He recalled overcoming the pain barrier when his rowing team was at its peak, but that was different - he had volunteered to row whereas he never asked to be treated like shit in a squalid cellar somewhere in the middle of Berlin. He sat on the floor with both forearms positioned painfully on his raised knees, his head lowered while the mop of tangled blonde hair flopped over his forehead. He shivered.

'God, what a mess,' he said to himself. He tried to weigh up what prompted Alex to release him from the barbed wire at the very mention of Jessica's name. If he ever got away from this shit hole he assumed he would never put that question to Jessica. Perhaps Raymond knew the answer. If not, Guy would love to kick the pants off this crazy Russian scientist to get his side of the story. He huddled against the wall, drew up his legs, sighed and after a while he fell unconscious.

He was woken by a loud metallic click and a fluorescent flicker. He opened his eyes and looked up at the ceiling where an auto-timer had turned on the light, its transparent cover freckled with insects that must have crawled inside and since expired. Guy resolved that whatever happened next he would never crawl, never expire.

Suddenly he was desperate for a crap. 'What the fuck do I do,' he wondered, until his eyes fell upon the metal pot. He shuffled himself up and winced at the perpetual ache in his genitals. As he attempted to sip the water he began to panic as if about to submerge, he felt queasy and breathless. His natural impulse was to hyper-ventilate but despite the hideous water boarding and with shaking hands and legs, he forced himself to drink a few drops while he shut his mind from the nauseous impression of drowning. Determined to crush his fear, he splashed his face and cleaned some of the clotting blood off his wounds before he poured the rest of the water onto the floor. 'God, now I need to pee as well. Oh what the hell.' He managed to squat over the pot and relieve himself and he used the remnants of his crumpled shirt to wipe clean. He placed the pot in the far corner of the cellar with all its foul contents, where he also dumped his filthy shirt.

The wooden stool that Alex sat on had been left in the middle of the room, so he decided to carry it to the opposite corner where he could sit and lean against the wall. As he moved he trod on a needle-sharp object which made him yelp and leap sideways. It was the strand of barbed wire used earlier to tie his ankles. Alex and his two muggers must have left it behind by mistake. He picked it up and took the stool to the corner, sat, and twiddled the barbed wire in his fingers. He started to think: those three would soon be back. He needed a strategy, and he also needed weapons.

His eyes roamed the room and he began to think of the cellar as a mini weapons store that contained one wooden stool, a repulsive chamber pot and a piece of barbed wire. He then started to think how to use them against his assailants. It would also help if he knew where the hell he was… of course, the stool! He placed it underneath the window, stepped up and raised his arms to their full extent so that his hands gripped the metal bars. With a herculean effort only made possible by years of hard graft on weights and pull-ups, he somehow overcame the fierce pain and hauled himself up to peer out.

'So this is where I am.' He craned his head to look outside to his right from where he could hear the distant sound of traffic. He carefully lowered himself back onto the stool.

An hour later he had devised a possible exit strategy.

CHAPTER 23

Raymond hung up, annoyed that Alex was taking delivery of the Spectra sequencing machines before the finance package had been confirmed, and depressed by his own reticence to ask Alex what Jessica overheard about anthrax. In need of fresh air he took Penny and Tuppence for a stroll through the orchard to the trout lake where he watched his dogs lark around at the water's edge. He sat on a tree stump for about half an hour and enjoyed the warm breeze. Moorhens took off and landed in a non-stop aquatic display on the bright ripples while a pair of swans paddled along the surface. As he observed these creatures unaffected by the presence of two dogs, he told himself that grief does not mix easily with business. Alone with the dogs and water fowl by the sunlit lake, Raymond's mind was a merry-go-round of thoughts and emotions that he desperately wanted to control.

He thought about Alex's bid to patent the IBEC system. A money spinner, yet it was hard for Raymond to get excited in his grief. Among the personal attractions of investing in IBEC was financial security for Jessica and her descendants, an ambition that now seemed futile. Even so IBEC, an ingenious way to wipe out genetically inherited conditions, signalled a fightback that his late wife would have supported.

In his last conversation with Alex, Raymond could not bring himself to raise Jessica's name or the anthrax question; thanks to depression his mind had blocked. Perhaps he was in awe of Alex, a brilliant scientist but not a man to cross. Raymond thought of previous battles while at the helm of Herron International, moments when he radiated courage in the face of opposition. Every time, win or lose, his self-esteem grew. Even after Elizabeth died, he found inner strength to be as tough as any company chairman. But today he was emotionally flattened, made worse by *Dark Cloud*. He leaned back. Distracted by a movement in the sky he looked up and watched a hawk circle in search of prey.

Given he may never know what Jessica overheard in New York, Raymond decided his only realistic option was to let Alex continue selling the rights to the IBEC system. It had begun with an agent called Samir, the intermediary between Alex and the government of Iraq. Other lucrative sales should follow. Despite his anxiety and grief Raymond was about to become exceedingly rich, as was Alex. Now was not the time to stand still even if Alex was up to something, so Raymond resolved to limit his own gains to profits from the IBEC sales – still an abundant sum. Herron International's only contribution was to bankroll the Spectra 6500 computers, nothing else. He also reminded himself that to sequence the complete human genome was a noble scientific goal of profound importance, and Herron International's funding would be hailed as integral to it.

Raymond fixed his gaze on the far side of the lake. Terry his gardener was planting yellow flag irises beside tall bull rushes that swayed in the light wind at the water's edge. As a young manager Raymond's favourite catchphrase had been: *When it gets tough, take action.* He did so now while he watched the dogs shake down and stretch out on rough grass. He decided to cobble together a simple plan, nothing fancy, just a few action points – the question was where to start. He took out a pocket notebook and jotted down ideas about next steps. In his study after the memorial service he had talked to Guy and Ben about finding out what others might know. While he watched the dogs panting side by side on the ground he recalled having to sign investment authorisations at Jacob & Cie in Zurich where Rudi Galler still expected lunch at the exclusive Pavillon restaurant. After a while a plan of sorts began to take shape, helped by the thought that a day or two in Switzerland might provide the distraction he needed. He decided to book a seat on the next available flight. Afterwards he would return via Berlin to ensure that Alex remained focussed on the final stages of genetic sequencing as well as on the IBEC sales.

He closed the notebook, put it back into his pocket and walked the dogs back to the house. The hawk continued to circle in the air.

It was no surprise to Raymond's PA that her boss would not return to the London office for a while. Nobody expected to see him at Adams Court so soon after his bereavement, and the senior Managing Partner had agreed to deal with most matters normally handled by

Raymond. William Vinson was a capable man and respected by fellow partners - future chairman material.

Raymond had yet to make an appointment with Alex, it was on his list. He wanted to impress upon the CEO of Capsella-Biotech the need to maintain focus, but had not yet worked out how best to put it. It depended on Alex's mood. A face-to-face encounter would help Raymond to 'read' the man, test his response and observe his body language once the courage had been summoned to put words like 'Jessica' and 'anthrax' to him.

CHAPTER 24

The distant ring of Sunday church bells could be heard as the three hard-bitten Afghantsi veterans entered the cellar to find Guy perched wretchedly on the stool in the middle of the floor. He had hardly slept and ached all over. The taller henchman carried the small suitcase and dumped it on the floor.

Alex grimaced at the sight of all the dried vomit, and gave a repugnant glance towards the reek from the metal pot's repulsive contents. He turned and looked straight at Guy.

'After your under-water swimming lesson we strung your body from that wall, remember? But this time we'll use the opposite side.' He pointed at the horizontal wooden beam fixed to the wall facing Guy. 'Before long you'll beg to be water boarded once more, and shackled to that first wall again.'

Guy gave the horizontal beam only the briefest sideways glance, careful not to give anything away. He looked back at his host with an impassive expression.

Alex lowered his eyes to inspect his hands, palms upwards and fingers bent to examine each nail in turn. After a few moments without another glance at Guy he asked in a steady, unhurried voice, 'Tell me Guy, what did Jessica Parry say to you?'

'She's not around to back me up. Nothing I say can be proved, so why don't you piss off you pathetic psychopath.'

Alex looked up and glowered. 'I'm seriously going to lose it. WHAT... DID... SHE... SAY?'

'PISS OFF!'

'Lift him!' The men came forward, took an arm each and looked back towards Alex.

'Guy, do you know where the term 'excruciating' comes from?'

'For God's sake, Alex, you need serious mental help.'

'SHUT THE FUCK UP!' He punched Guy on the side of his face. 'It originates from the ancient word 'crucifixion' - the most horrific, slow, painful death ever invented.'

Guy shivered.

'As the victim's legs get fatigued, the body weight transfers to the chest and arms. Minutes after being nailed up, the shoulder, elbow and wrist joints dislocate. We know, we saw it happen in that Mujahidin camp, didn't we boys?'

The other two leered at Guy who glared back.

'The victim becomes more active as he's forced to move up and down just to breathe, there's none of this fake motionless-fall-unconscious rubbish you see in the movies.' Alex spoke with manic relish. 'The unbearable pain is made worse by asphyxiation, death can take between six and forty-eight hours. And you know what, Guy?' Alex smirked lustily. 'The very thought pumps adrenalin straight to my crotch.'

'Fuck you.' Guy was determined not to reveal what he had in store for these demonic killers.

Alex looked at his assistants and shouted at them in Russian. To Guy it sounded something like, 'Don't just stand there, bloody get on with it!'

They struggled to drag Guy forward until his face was up against the wall below the wooden beam. Despite what he intended to do, he was almost ready to surrender. Alex opened the suitcase on the floor and lifted out a mallet and two large rusty nails, while the thugs each held up Guy's shaky arms until his palms were forced flat against the beam. His bruised, empty stomach and wrist injuries had drained a lot of his strength, yet his assailants still struggled to hold him up. When the unwary Alex approached from behind with mallet and nail poised at the ready, Guy knew if his strategy was to work it was now or never. It happened fast.

Sensing that Alex was close behind and about to hammer the first nail into his left hand, Guy struck with a backwards kick that crashed into Alex's groin. He squealed, collapsed and doubled up on the cellar floor. The mallet and nails clattered to the floor and distracted the smaller thug on the right for a second. Guy summoned all his reserves to wrench his own arm free, snatched the strand of barbed wire from where, luckily, he had laid it out on top of the wooden beam and lashed the lout in the face. The man shrieked and stumbled back towards the corner where he collapsed and only just missed the unsavoury piss pot. He thrashed about and screamed in Russian that the barbed wire was stuck in his eyeball, when the taller thug let go of Guy, sprinted to the case on the floor and reached for a handgun. But Guy's reaction was swifter: he leapt in the direction of the smaller man whose hands clasped his lacerated eye, grabbed the piss pot and hurled it like a jet-propelled Frisbee at the other henchman as he raised the firearm. The metal rim of the pot slammed into his mouth and smashed several teeth - the foetid contents ricocheted onto the man's forehead and slid down his face onto his shirt. He staggered and knocked over the wooden stool as he fell.

Guy sprang forward to pick up the gun. He gripped it with both hands and pointed the muzzle at Alex who was about to get up. With every intent to fill the son-of-a-bitch with lead, Guy pulled the trigger. Nothing happened. It was not cocked, or the safety catch was on, or both… As Guy fumbled, the toothless turd-spattered lout stood up, dazed. With his free hand Guy grasped the stool by one of its legs and swung it underarm with such strength onto the toothless man's shin that the crack of bone was audible. So was the man's reaction.

'AAGHH!! BASTARD!!' He screamed in a strong Russian accent, and twisted and squirmed on the floor.

Guy turned to find Alex tottering unsteadily, about to hit him with the crucifixion mallet. In a split second with one hand he snatched the mallet and seized hold of one of Alex's wrists, his other hand swooped down to the floor, dropped the gun and picked up one of the nails. He dragged Alex kicking and screaming to the wooden beam, and swore as Alex used his other hand to punch him in the legs. With all the power he could muster, Guy held the struggling Alex's palm and the nail in position against the beam, and hammered the nail into the back of the Russian's hand until it was pinned and bled profusely. Alex was pierced to the beam as he gaped at Guy in wide-eyed shock, then his face contorted and he let out an incessant wail.

'Better call a Soviet medic,' mocked Guy, shouting to be heard above the screeches and bellows. 'You sadistic maniac, I bet your dick isn't full of adrenalin now!' He picked up the gun and frisked the three convulsing bodies for their cell phones. The henchman with the cracked shin made an insufferable noise so Guy pistol whipped him, to shut him up and put him out of his misery, and to stop him writhing while Guy removed the man's trainers. 'I'll have those, thanks mate. Spaseeba.'

'Fucking monsters!' he yelled above the clamour, 'you make me sick.' He halted for a moment to review the carnage: one of his former captors had barbed wire skewered onto an eyeball that protruded from its socket, whilst another was nailed to a beam and had started to puke up. By now the third had come round and started to jerk in agony once again from the cracked shin bone.

'Sod it,' said Guy, 'I didn't hit you hard enough.'

All this was set amongst the debris of blood and vomit, a broken stool, an upturned piss pot, pieces of used duct tape and a sizeable expanse of stinking human excrement.

Guy put the handgun, cell phones and trainers into the case and closed the lid, picked it up and walked out.

Drained after the fight of his life, and drowned out by screams, it did not cross his exhausted mind how Alex had known Jessica. He slammed the cellar door behind him which stifled the anguished cries and stemmed the horrendous stench. The clank of metal echoed in the passage as he slid the bolt, then he paused to lean back against the door to catch his breath. With his eyes closed he slowly inhaled and exhaled the less repellent air. He looked up and shook his head. Despite his cuts and bruises he felt a strange grim pleasure. 'Hell, it must be the adrenalin.'

He carried the case along the passage and up some steps to a door that opened into a small lobby with a staircase. He faced a glass exit door and to the right of it an internal door. Guy put the case down and tried the interior door handle and was surprised to find it unlocked. It was a store cupboard filled with cleaning kit, a mop, a bucket, a floor brush and a vacuum cleaner with an upright handle. Hanging on the handle was his suit jacket. He grabbed it and rummaged through the pockets. His luck was in. After he was mugged on a London street he had got his tailor to stitch hidden pockets into the linings of all his jackets, a precaution against future attacks. He pulled out his wallet from the concealed section, slung the jacket back into the cupboard and peered into the recesses to see if his cell phone and shoes might be hidden there. Nothing doing. He grabbed the suitcase and made for the exit door, tugged at the bolts top and bottom and stepped out into sunlight and a cool breeze.

Guy was not surprised to find himself in the rear parking lot of Grishin Informatik in Westfälische Strasse. He flicked through his wallet to find his cards and cash intact. He shoved the wallet into his trouser pocket and turned his attention to the suitcase. He opened it and removed the batteries and sim cards from two of the cell phones. He kept Alex's phone in one piece but chucked the others into a nearby bin. After checking the gun's safety catch he put it in his trouser pocket. The shape of the bulge was obvious but there was nowhere else to hide the weapon; crossed fingers it would not go off by accident. Next he took out the pair of trainers and placed them on the ground. He concealed the suitcase behind a privet hedge, at which point he began to feel a touch of guilt for the ruthless treatment he had just meted out.

'What else could I have done to escape from those bastards?' he reasoned to himself. He used Alex's phone to dial 112 to call the emergency services and reported three hapless casualties in need of paramedic assistance in the cellars of Grishin Informatik GmbH – it was fortunate the operator spoke good English.

Guy gingerly put a finger into his mouth. His left molar was in place and felt less wobbly, although it still hurt. He then became aware of flies buzzing around the foul odour of his feet, and realised for the first time that his socks were soaked with much more than mere water.

'Ugh! What a whiff,' he pulled a face, 'I never thought my feet could be so smelly.'

This was not the time to fret about such niceties. He sat on the ground and waved the flies away. He peeled off his scummy socks and put the Russian thug's trainers on his bare feet, glad that they fitted quite well.

As he hobbled out of the parking lot he could scarcely hear the muted howls of his assailants. On a Sunday and with few other occupied buildings in the vicinity, Guy thought it unlikely anyone had heard the earlier commotion. He limped along Westfälische Strasse towards the faint sound of applause, whistles and horns that came from nearby Konstanzer Strasse.

The sound grew louder as he approached Konstanzer Strasse and he immediately knew what the noise was. While Alex and the two hoods had tried to humiliate and kill him the 28th Berlin Marathon had got under way. Somewhere along the forty-two kilometre route among many thousands of competitors would be David, who must have wondered what had happened after Guy failed to return to the Gasthaus from his meeting with Dr Grishin.

Guy stopped and rubbed the light stubble that embroidered his haggard face. He realised how bloody his sore wrists were. He wondered whether to steer clear of the general razzmatazz, but if he turned back now he might run into an ambulance crew and that was bound to include the Polizei as well. Dishevelled and bare chested, he decided it would be better to avoid the authorities and disappear into the throng. As he approached the crowds at the cross-roads beside Konstanzer Strasse U-Bahn Station, a teenager jazz band struck up, their shiny saxophones, trumpets and trombones reflecting the late morning sunlight. There was something unusual about the band's appearance until Guy realised they all wore black armbands, as did many runners in solidarity with the nine-eleven victims. Beyond the band alongside the route a group of smiling volunteers handed out plastic cups of cold water to runners who took eager gulps before chucking the empty cups down onto the tarmac. Onlookers ignored Guy and continued to blow their whistles as the column cantered along, up to ten runners deep in places. Some had their names printed on running vests which prompted the public to call out in encouragement:

'Wunderbar Klaus!' someone shouted. 'Bravo Anna! Weitermachen!' yelled another.

Alongside the runners a BMW saloon with a large electronic *Timex* display fixed to the roof rack gave the running time, and it occurred to Guy that he might step out from under the red and white tape and thumb a lift, but he looked and felt a physical wreck and thought better of that idea. Marshals were everywhere, easy to make out in yellow jackets labelled front and back with the word *ORDNER*, and a couple of green and white vans were parked beside a team of Polizei near the U-Bahn entrance. Security was much tighter than normal in the wake of nine-eleven and he recalled David had said something about one or two last minute changes to the route. If Guy was to avoid being noticed by the Polizei there was only one thing to do - rather than run away, he should just run.

Under the hot sun the column of runners seemed endless and the spectators continued to wave and clap, oblivious to the shirtless blond athlete in their midst. Music and shouts magnified against the walls of apartment blocks and shops amplifying the festive atmosphere. Guy nipped under the tape and joined the multitude of competitors. He soon worked out he was the only topless runner, he was not wearing a black armband and as far as he could tell he was the only one who limped. Above the clapping and whistles he picked out some of the spectators' comments.

'Er hatte eine harte Zeit,' something about being given a hard time.

Others poked fun at his unkempt appearance, 'Seltsame Stück!' *Strange hunk!*

Towards the north end of Konstanzer Strasse the crowds had thinned as most onlookers were concentrating on the next leg of the route, the tree-lined Ku'damm. Guy looked around and for the first time he saw bunting across the street with the same message in several languages: 'Laufen für den Frieden' *Run for Peace*. With less spectator noise he also heard the scuffle and crunch of hundreds of runners' feet on the sea of discarded plastic water cups. The stench of human sweat wafted on the light breeze and Guy was sure that his own body was a contributor.

There was no sign of David, one needle in a haystack full of needles. The column veered to the right onto the Ku'damm accompanied by the increased clamour of hundreds more spectators. Guy was in a lot more pain and the gun metal that rubbed his private parts scarcely helped. He decided he should grab the chance to extract himself, and manoeuvred to the right of the route alongside the kerb until he came to a junction signed *Schlüter Strasse*. He was about to peel off when a marshal in her yellow jacket on the street corner called to him.

'Bist du ein Läufer?' *Are you a runner?* She pointed. 'Wo ist Ihre Läufer Nummer?' *Where is your runner number?*

'Stuff it,' he thought and accelerated past the startled woman causing his cut ankles to hurt like hell. He sprinted round the corner into Schlüter Strasse and ran smack into a team of six armed Polizei standing in a row beside their green and white Volkswagen parked sideways-on in the middle of the street. He might have bluffed his way had it not been for the marshal who hurried towards the group and gesticulated.

'Warten hier!' One of the Polizei grabbed Guy by a wrist and looked shocked at all the caked blood.

'Nein, nein! CHRIST! You're hurting me!' The officer released his hold and clasped Guy's shoulder instead. He eyed the officer's pistol holster which suddenly reminded him of the Ruger handgun in his trouser pocket and for which he had no permit. He did not understand the conversation that took place between the route marshal and the Polizei but he did understand the stare he was being given, a stare that said: 'What is this battered, cut, bruised, unshaven, topless Dummkopf doing on the marathon route with no official entry number?'

Guy also knew that Germans can be hard taskmasters when it comes to red tape and rules, even harder when it comes to firearm regulations, so it was not clever to hang around. It was vital to get away fast. He told himself to get his skates on.

PART THREE

BERLINER MORGENPOST

Monday 1st October 2001

Violent Clash at IT Firm

Berlin Polizei are mystified by three members of staff at Grishin Informatik GmbH who fought each other yesterday in a vicious quarrel at the firm's premises in Westfälische Strasse. The men are being treated in the Park-Klinik at Weissensee where their injuries are not considered life threatening.

The Polizei are appealing for witnesses, as there are strange aspects to the incident. Firstly it was a Sunday and the fighters, the CEO and two security guards, had somehow managed to lock themselves behind a door that was bolted from the outside, yet none has given a satisfactory explanation.

Second, the emergency services received a call for help from the CEO's mobile number, but his phone was nowhere to be found when the ambulance crew arrived at the scene. Again, no justification for this peculiarity has been offered.

Finally, in the cellar, scene-of-crime officers had discovered a mallet, nails, barbed wire and they were especially puzzled by human excreta all over the floor, although initial investigations suggest that the sheer pain from one victim's broken shin bone might account for the unfortunate mess.

It is not yet known whether the injured will press charges against each other. Polizei Kommissar Stefan Borchardt commented, 'We have officers waiting at the bedsides of the injured who are under sedation, but they will be asked to make full statements as soon as their condition improves.'

CHAPTER 25

The food and wine were out of this world, but throughout the meal Raymond's complexion matched the white table cloth.

After being escorted to their table they had browsed the menu over a half-bottle of Krug Grande Cuvée. Both ordered the same starter, caviar and blinis accompanied by white Pouilly-Fumé. For the main course Raymond forced down small pieces of beef tenderloin while Rudi Galler tucked in to a filet mignon de veau. Their main dish was washed down with 1975 red Château Lafite, although it was Rudi who drank most of it. Raymond took token sips, unable to cope with much alcohol and preferring chilled mineral water instead. He declined dessert when Rudi ordered strawberry soufflé.

During that indulgent lunch both men conversed politely - topics like the alpine chalet owned by Rudi who throughout that morning must have noticed his client's reserve. Raymond reproached himself for buying such an expensive lunch in the wake of his step-daughter's memorial service. He was also concerned about his professional reputation if Alex leads Capsella-Biotech astray and trades on the margins of acceptability. Rudi must have wondered why Raymond seemed distracted and upset, maybe his client was anxious about the safe arrival of the enormous deposit expected soon. Their pre-lunch meeting at the offices of Jacob & Cie had been pure routine, when Raymond formally authorised the investment allocation for his hundred million US dollars.

Raymond had not mentioned his bereavement or his action plan, except over coffee he said to Rudi that his next stop was Berlin.

'Why the Grey City?'

'Eh?'

'A nickname for Berlin, like Big Smoke for London.'

'Oh,' said Raymond, 'it's business. Herron International has an important client there. You'll know who.'

Rudi smiled and drank the last of his coffee. He paused at the ringtone from his host's jacket pocket. Raymond looked at the caller's identity displayed on his phone. He felt a jolt in his chest and became short of breath. Other diners turned and watched him grip the phone like a life-line, until he looked around like a stricken passenger desperate to escape from a sinking liner, his startled face as pale as a corpse. He pushed back his chair, marched briskly from the restaurant and made for the street. Rudi looked puzzled and embarrassed as other diners gaped. Before he had the chance to go after his client, Raymond had climbed into a taxi and was gone.

It did not occur to Rudi that he would end up paying for one of the most expensive lunches he had ever eaten, or to ask himself if he would ever see Raymond again.

In the back of the taxi Raymond looked once more at the caller's identity on his phone. The ringing persisted. Someone must have found the mobile that was now transmitting presumably having discovered Raymond's number stored in it. Either they genuinely needed to contact him or it was a cruel hoax. The taxi had already passed the Botanical Gardens and was heading along Gessner Allee on the right bank of the River Sihl, before Raymond's shaky hand raised the phone to his ear and he took the incoming call.

That evening at Kloten Airport Raymond sat in the departure lounge and waited to board the last flight from Zurich to Berlin. He was not bothered that his action plan was now dead in the water. Joyous news. He was over the moon.

Around twenty minutes after leaving Berlin Tegel he looked left out of his taxi window. Across the Platz der Republik he could see the Reichstag, the restored German Parliament with its glass dome. Dusk was approaching and the building was lit up, and in an odd way the dome's round shape reminded Raymond of Seroxat pills, his antidepressants. For the first time on that trip he realised he had forgotten to pack them, but concluded there was not much he could do about it. The taxi turned left through the floodlit Brandenburg Gate until the driver slowed along Unter den Linden, a famous boulevard. Batches of metal crush barriers were stacked on both sides and litter collection vans seemed to be everywhere.

'Was there a festival today?' he said to the taxi driver.

'Der Marathon. Tausende von Menschen.' *The marathon. Thousands of people.* The driver pointed out the 'Run for Peace' signs. They turned right into Friedrichstrasse and finally stopped in Mohrenstrasse where Raymond checked in to the five star Berlin Hilton. Before German reunification it was known as the Domhotel, *Cathedral Hotel*, a flagship for western tourists visiting the former Eastern Bloc. Now, almost twelve years after the Berlin Wall opened, as Raymond settled into his suite he thought how this sector of the city and its many hotels were transformed beyond recognition.

With a light step he went down to the hotel bar. After the gargantuan lunch in Zurich he was not very hungry but needed a celebration drink, and ordered champagne. Uplifting news can alter a person's perspective on life, and whereas lunch with Rudi had been a trial Raymond's mood was now positive despite the lack of anti-depressants. Perhaps *Dark Cloud* was in remission and if it took champagne instead of Seroxat to repair his brain's limbic system, the part that controls mood, he would not complain.

As the alcohol took hold his mind moved up a gear, to the extent that he felt more relaxed about Herron's pre-war flirtation with US sterilisation programmes. Previous misgivings now gave way to the thought that eugenics was not such a dirty word. Surely it was early eugenic studies that enabled scientists to research how a genome could be engineered, to improve human health or enhance the lives of children otherwise condemned in the womb? Take the IBEC system, landmark technology that reconstructs the building blocks of life and could deal with things like poverty or the effects of climate change. Science was already creating genetically modified crops to tackle global hunger, and Raymond beamed to himself at the prospect of IBEC also treating a range of diseases such as cancer, cystic fibrosis, even HIV. Despite ethical questions, people would have to understand that the IBEC genie was emerging from the bottle with the potential to save millions of lives.

After dark in his suite he stared through the tinted window at the illuminated French and German cathedrals overlooking the revamped Gendarmenmarkt. He was flush from the Dom Pérignon and had ordered a snack of smoked salmon on toast. With his own reflection in the large window superimposed on the view outside, his image appeared to float in mid-air near the two cathedrals. Raymond stared at his gravity-defying figure, finely dressed with both arms to the side, when his reflection was joined by a little girl in a pink dress who appeared from nowhere and took hold of one hand. She looked up with a smile as familiar as her head of chestnut hair. Did he hear her say *Hello Pop,* or was this a dream? He looked straight at her reflection and felt how wonderful it was to be with her again. All of a sudden the girl became an adult, slim and elegant. She tossed her head and parted the same chestnut hair with her hands. Raymond was about to reach out to the woman when her image faded away. He smiled. It was her voice. They were together once more. He was sure of it.

CHAPTER 26

'In Ordnung! Mit mir!' *It's okay! He's with me!*

Guy instantly recognised the lilting voice from behind. Relieved, he pushed the Polizei officer's hand off his shoulder and swung round. He stared intently beyond some bystanders in the direction of the familiar tone.

'Mein Trainer.' *My pacer.* David trotted up, puffing. His cheeks were pink and he looked supremely fit. 'What the bloody hell's going on?' He gaped first at the group of Polizei, then at Guy, then back at the Polizei again. 'Any of you lot speak English?'

'I do,' said Guy in desperation.

'I know that, you twat!' David eyed Guy up and down, visibly shocked by his friend's appearance. 'I was asking these other blokes.' The senior Polizei officer nodded.

The marshal looked away from David, shrugged and wagged her finger at Guy before turning to the Polizei officer and said, 'Er ist kein Läufer.' *He's not a runner.*

The officer looked at Guy and said, 'You are not supposed to be running.'

'He's my pacer,' said David.

'That's right,' Guy nodded, conscious of his own gungy appearance.

'Show me your pacer's registration card.'

'Er, I must have lost it.' Others in the Polizei team exchanged knowing looks.

'Then you cannot run.'

David smiled and patted Guy's arm. 'Don't worry mate, you've been a fantastic help. I'll be fine on the last leg of the route. See you at the finish.' He winked. 'Brandenburg Gate, don't forget.' He ran back towards the Ku'damm and called back over his shoulder to the Polizei team, 'Auf Wiedersehen!' *Goodbye!*

While the others stood and stared at David for a few seconds, Guy did not even hesitate. He half sprinted and half hobbled in the opposite direction down Schlüter Strasse, taking care to avoid a queue at an ice cream stall. He headed straight towards the corner of Olivaer Platz where he paused long enough to look back and shout an anglicised 'Owf vee-dah-zenn!'. His inquisitors' heads spun in his direction as he continued on his way. Minutes later he came to Adenauer Platz bus stop where he boarded the first bus to roll up, which happened to be a number 109.

Although it was never his custom to pray, after the previous two days' experiences Guy now prayed that nobody would trace him back to his hotel room. The proprietor of the Gasthaus knew little about his two English guests, Herr Shepherd and Herr Bond, except on their last visit they paid their bills in cash without a quibble, and one of them had now walked into reception looking like an all-in wrestler who had lost a tough bout.

Guy was in pain, exhausted and hungry. He was a bit more comfortable once he had taken the gun from his pocket and placed it in the bedside locker. He took his wallet and Alex's cell phone from his trousers and dropped them on the bed. The phone was a Nokia, the same make as his own, so he could charge it up while he stripped off his trainers and filthy trousers, shoved them into the bottom of a chest of drawers and slid it shut. Carrying a dirty handkerchief he padded nude into the en-suite bathroom and stepped on the pedal to open the waste bin. The clang of the metal lid against wall tiles startled him for a second. Still jittery, he threw away the unsavoury handkerchief and removed his foot and the bin's lid clunked shut. The metallic sound made him think of the gun, which could possibly be discovered by an over-zealous chambermaid. He returned to the bedroom, grabbed his suitcase and placed it on the bed. He took the gun from the bedside locker and put it into the suitcase then shut the lid. He lifted up the suitcase and positioned it on top of the wardrobe. When Guy went back to the bathroom he caught a whiff of his own body odour, and understood why the Polizei were not keen to chase him. He shut the en-suite door which had a full length mirror fixed on the inside, and stood in front of it to examine his cuts and bruises. It made him realise why David seemed so taken aback an hour ago. Thank God David spotted me in Schlüter Strasse, he thought, grateful that his friend must have sensed a problem and provided a much needed distraction. He felt a pang of guilt that he was not at the Brandenburg Gate to congratulate David at the finish line, but there were other priorities. He stepped into the shower and adjusted the hot tap, but his unhealed cuts were so sore that he cried out when the sharp needles sprayed. His shouts grew louder when he applied soap and shampoo, 'Aaghh! God that stung! Shit! Fuck!' But he persisted. His wounds seeped blood and the reddish water swirled around his feet before it disappeared down the plug hole, like an abattoir.

When the draining shower water faded to pink Guy knew that the bleeding had slowed. Perhaps clotted bits of blood had initially made things look worse, but Christ, he had had enough of the stinging and more than enough of the sharp throb in his testicles. He stepped out of the shower and without bothering to dry himself dripped his way back into the bedroom and grabbed some handkerchiefs to wrap around his ankles and wrists. With all four handkerchiefs secured, he went back into the en-suite to swallow a couple of paracetamol tablets, brush his teeth and to shave while his body dried off. He was desperate for sleep and he knew that the paracetamol would knock him out unless he kept going. He dressed in chinos, a polo shirt and a pair of flip-flops, taking care not to aggravate his cuts and bruises. He texted David's mobile number to say he was back at the Gasthaus. He left the phone charging on the bed, picked up his wallet and limped out to buy sausage and chips.

'All right, mate?' asked the gap year lad who must have remembered Guy from his previous visit to the bratwurst stall. 'You don't look too good. Everything okay?'

Guy nodded. 'Never felt better. I'll have one bratwurst with pommes frites and mayonnaise, please.'

'Awesome. One bratty coming right up.'

The only other person there was the German stall owner who stood behind the counter lowering a basket of frites into boiling fat and tending to a row of sausages that sizzled on the grill. Guy, intrigued by the boy's ethnicity, asked him where he was from. His name was Brian, he lived in Croydon, the only son of a Turkish father and an English mother. He had been offered a place to study catering at Croydon College the following September and was now on his gap year.

'Why Berlin?' asked Guy.

'I studied German at school and I've got relatives here,' Brian replied. 'And it's not too far from home.'

'Home for you is Britain presumably?'

'Definitely not Turkey. If I go back I'd get nobbled for national service.'

'Go back?' Guy raised his eyebrows, just about the only part of his body that did not hurt.

'I was born in Istanbul. The family left when I was two years old.' Brian smiled and squirted mayonnaise onto Guy's bratty and chips, and passed the food to him on a plastic plate.

'Thanks, Brian.' Guy handed over some deutschmarks and started to eat. He nodded at the stall owner then looked back at Brian. 'Do they work you hard?'

'Ten hour shifts, six days a week. But it's good pay and I get Tuesdays off.'

'Laid-back Tuesday,' said Guy with a grin.

'Actually I call it Backstroke Tuesday,' said Brian. 'It's my weekly swim in the Wannsee.'

After Guy had eaten he went back to the Gasthaus bar for a couple of beers, made his way upstairs and swallowed two more paracetamol tablets. The cocktail of food, alcohol and painkillers finally did it for him and he crashed out on his bed. He slept through the knock on his bedroom door later in the day. In fact it was evening before he woke with a start and cursed as he sat up. 'Ouch!' His wrists and ankles stung and his upper body ached as did his most vulnerable regions. After taking several seconds to come to and work out where he was, he turned and looked at the time on the cell phone. Quarter past eight. He wondered how David was.

David answered the knock almost immediately. 'Guy! I got your text. Where the fuck've you been these last two days?' He had long since showered after the marathon and stood at the entrance to his room wearing only boxer shorts.

'Hi David. How did you get on?'

'Christ, what the hell have you been up to? When I spotted you with the Polizei I thought you'd taken part in a boxing match. You're a complete wreck!' He pointed at Guy's face. 'Who gave you that bruise on the cheek?'

'We need to talk, David.'

'We need to get you to a doctor. Let's call a taxi to take you to hospital...'

'No!' Guy brushed past David and tenderly lowered himself onto a wicker chair. He winced.

David pushed the door shut. 'Why not? What happened to you?'

'That's what I want to talk about.'

'Every time I tried to call, I only got your voicemail.' David sat on the bed.

'My phone's been nicked.'

'Well, I tapped on your door earlier this evening but there was no answer, even though the bloke at reception said you were here.'

'Sorry David. It was my first proper sleep for two days.' Guy paused a while then gave David a steely glance. 'So, what's your time?'

David looked at his wrist watch and said, 'Twenty past eight...'

'I meant running time, you pillock!'

'Oh!' David smiled. 'Three hours forty-five, and I'm done in. It was bloody hot and I've got this huge blister.' He turned and lifted up his right leg to show Guy the sole of his foot. 'Still, I've raised over five thousand pounds for Nacro.'

'Congratulations.'

'Thanks, but I've been worried sick about you.' David sat on the single bed. 'For the last time, what happened?'

'Alex Grishin and two other Russians tried to torture me and do me in.' Guy watched David's mouth drop open. 'They achieved their first objective, but failed at the second.'

'Christ, go to the police Guy.'

'Wait. There's more. I wanted to kill those Afghantsi shits, but didn't. I succeeded spectacularly in torturing them. I expect they're in hospital now.'

'Why didn't you call for help? What if the police find out and charge you for assault?'

'David, I don't believe the police will.'

'Why?'

Guy reasoned that Alex Grishin and his two minders were in a weak position. If they ever led the authorities to Guy they would incriminate themselves, surely too big a risk. He told David about his horrendous ordeal in the cellar at Grishin Informatik GmbH.

'They're a bunch of fucking psychopaths, David.'

'They?'

'Yes, all three must have served in the Soviet occupation of Afghanistan. Remember Alex's blog on *MindCrusade*? Captured by the Mujahidin and witnessed all sorts of horrors and torture? This weekend they cheerfully tried to make me suffer what they must've seen all those years ago.'

'I could crucify the bastards,' said David.

'They literally tried to crucify me, and seemed to enjoy it at first.'

'Jesus. How did you stop them?'

'I kicked Alex in the nether-regions and fought my way out,' said Guy. 'When I left they were still conscious and screaming. I don't give a toss about their wounds, but I did call an ambulance.'

'I thought your mobile had been stolen.'

'I borrowed Alex's.'

'No wonder I didn't recognise the caller's number when you texted me today.' David sighed and shook his head. The two were silent for a short while.

'You know what David? That blog at *MindCrusade* was right, it needed a single trigger to fire them into a frenzy.'

'What was the trigger?'

'Me. I know too much. They'll want me out of the way. Permanently.'

'Oh Christ. What do we do?

'Put on our thinking caps.'

'Lord help us,' said David. 'What's more, I'm supposed to be back at work the day after tomorrow.'

'I'm sure that's me.'

After a late breakfast they had gone up to David's room, where he now held a copy of Monday's *Berliner Morgenpost* and pointed at photo coverage of the Berlin Marathon.

'It's a blurred, distant shot, and impossible to make out your entry number,' said Guy, 'it could be any one of hundreds of male runners your age.'

'If it's not me then someone did a bloody good impersonation, look, he's wearing the same colour top.' David put the newspaper down on the table. 'Also I recognise the blonde girl in front of me dressed all in white…'

'Okay, David, you're famous at last. Well done.'

Earlier David had nipped out to buy some newspapers containing reports of a fierce brawl in the offices of Grishin Informatik GmbH. Guy tore out a couple of these articles and strolled over to the bratwurst stall, told Brian he was producing a documentary for

British radio and asked if the lad could translate the text. Brian spoke good German and was glad to help. He explained that the first article began with the headline *Violent Clash at IT Firm* and described how three members of staff at Grishin Informatik had fought each other in a vicious quarrel.

The next article focused more on the nature of the injuries sustained from the fight. Again, Brian translated the report that said Alex must have broken one man's leg, after which the second man had nailed one of Alex's hands to a wooden beam. Finally, Alex must have grabbed a piece of barbed wire with his free hand and gouged out his attacker's eye. The report speculated as to why the three men chose not to press charges and made, in Guy's view, the idiotic suggestion that the punch-up might have been a settling of old scores.

'Even if only one of them presses charges, that puts all three of them in the frame,' said Brian as he handed both articles back to Guy. 'Intriguing isn't it?'

'Why?' asked Guy.

'Well, if they've been under sedation since they were admitted it means they must have forgiven each other in the ambulance on their way to hospital. Will they feature in your documentary?'

'What documentary?'

'You said you're a radio producer.' Brian gave Guy's weary body a sceptical look.

'Yes, of course. It's er, an intriguing case as you just said.'

'Why not visit them? Walk into the hospital with a parcel of fruit and some flowers, pretend you're a concerned relative or friend. Get a scoop.'

'There's an idea. Thanks Brian.'

It was agreed that David should return to London as originally planned. He had explained that he dared not risk getting closer to Guy's troubles or the plight of certain staff at Capsella-Biotech. One spell behind bars was more than enough, a once-in-a-lifetime experience that he refused to repeat even for Guy.

'For God's sake come back to London, Guy. You're in danger.'

'I can't.'

'You bloody can. Give the police an anonymous tip-off.'

'Then what? Beat a hasty retreat?'

'Guy, this is not about you or your pride. You've discovered what Capsella are up to, now it's time for the authorities to take over.'

'You've forgotten something. If pressure is put on Alex Grishin it's highly likely Raymond will be exposed.'

'In which case he deserves it, doesn't he?'

'I'm not sure he understands the extent of Capsella's plans. He obviously knows about the scheme to sell IBEC to Iraq, if nothing else. Even so, if I expose Raymond it means I betray Jessica. I can't do it.'

'Then don't. Sod the lot and come back to London.'

'You don't get it, do you David? Whatever the police may discover Alex will cover his tracks. He'll hide

Capsella's Middle East connections and his contacts will evaporate.'

David raised his hands. 'Job done then. If the authorities keep a close watch on Capsella, Alex and his crew would never dare step out of line. Game over.'

'Wrong. Alex is mentally ill, greedy and ruthless. He stands to make millions by selling the formula of an anthrax phage to Iraq. I bet the money will come from Saddam's off-shore billions. That's only the start, Alex doesn't care two figs who else buys the product provided his Swiss bank account swells.'

'I know what I would do. Use Raymond. It's his firm that bankrolls Capsella.'

'Don't worry, I'll make use of Raymond but not in a way that puts him in danger. I suspect he's unaware of the anthrax phage, but dazzled by the megabucks he'll get from selling what he thinks is a relatively harmless IBEC system to Saddam and others. At least that's my guess.'

'You think Alex has misled Raymond?'

'I do. Raymond is blind to the danger of a rogue state misusing genetic science, such as eugenics or lethal bio-weapons.'

'Does that make Raymond less guilty?'

'No,' Guy hesitated, 'but I'll be in a stronger position if I can make Raymond an ally. He's too big a figure for Alex to write off, whereas it'd be easy to dispatch me and make it look like an accident.'

'Good luck then.' David sounded unconvinced. 'There's not much more I can say.'

'There's one thing more you can do, though. That pedigree website you unearthed…'

'You mean *MyPedigree*.'

'That's the one. When you get back could you research the Grishin family? I can't get that photo of the house in Podbielski Allee out of my mind.'

'I certainly can. Give me Alex's cell phone number in case I need to call you.'

Guy was surprised that David had not asked him the most obvious question of all about the telephone numbers stored in Alex's cell phone. They could provide a behind scenes glimpse at Alex's affairs, and Guy intended to make full use of them. He accepted it came at a price because he no longer possessed his own phone and was unable to find out who might be trying to contact him. He forgot that with some mobile providers you can key into your own voicemail using a different handset.

While David caught his afternoon flight back to London Guy made arrangements to stay on at the Gasthaus. As an additional precaution he also made sure the Gasthaus proprietor would not reveal to anyone that an Englishman named Shepherd was still booked in. Günter Blum was an affable hotelier in his late sixties who spoke pidgin English. Günter also appreciated how cash transactions reduced his tax liability. His two British guests had not only settled up in cash last time round, but one of them had just done so again. In addition, Herr Shepherd now asked to lengthen his stay and slipped

Herr Blum a couple of fifty-euro notes in return for anonymity. It seemed like a fair deal.

With a shifty sideways glance Günter secreted the two notes into his trouser pocket and asked if there was anything else Guy needed.

'A good doctor.'

Günter gave his worn out guest a sympathetic look.

'I don't just mean a doctor who's good at medicine.'

'Was ist los?' *What's going on?*

'I've been badly cut and need antibiotics. But I must be treated by someone who, let's say, will keep their mouth shut. Discretion. Medical confidentiality and all that. Do you know anyone?'

'Ja. Mein Bruder,' said Günter with a genial smile.

'What?'

'My brother has, how say in English? Ein Klinik.'

'It's the same word, clinic.'

'Ja. Clinic near Pankstrasse U-Bahn. North of here, I show you on zee map.'

Günter called his brother, Dr Manfried Blum, to fix an appointment. That evening a cream Mercedes saloon pulled up at the Gasthaus. As the journey got underway it became clear that the taxi driver thought Guy was a sightseer, and provided a running commentary as they passed locations popular with tourists. Guy raised his eyes to the taxi's ceiling a few times. His body hurt, he was fed up and he did not understand German. He let the driver prattle on no doubt hoping for a decent tip at the end of the guided tour. As the driver said, 'Nächsten

247

wir Unter den Linden gehen,' they passed the Berlin Hilton where Guy was astonished to see someone who could have been Raymond or maybe Ben stepping out of a taxi. With just enough time to work out it was more like Raymond in such an immaculately tailored suit, Guy's taxi turned into Friedrichstrasse and continued towards Unter den Linden. He thought of telling the driver to turn round, but hesitated. He did not want to miss a hastily arranged medical appointment that should alleviate his pain. Even so, despite everything on his mind he noted the whereabouts of the Hilton.

For the rest of the drive Guy ignored the driver and thought about the three Afghantsis now under police surveillance in a Krankenhaus which, Günter had explained, did not mean a home for cranks but was German for hospital. Guy faced no immediate threat while the men were under hospital arrest and, apart from Günter, David and Brian at the bratty stall, nobody else knew where Guy was staying. The situation could get more dangerous once any of the injured are released, if only on police bail. The broken shin and the spiked eyeball would involve major surgery and a slow recovery, so the two crazed thugs were safely out of the way. Alex, however, was a less serious case and after surgery to his hand he may not stay for long in hospital.

Tyres rumbled on the cobbles as Guy's taxi pulled up beside the kerb just a short distance from Pankstrasse. He got out of the vehicle, handed some money to the driver and with a wave of one hand signalled him to keep the change. The quiet, musty atmosphere he recalled from his previous visit to the area was broken only by the distant sound of rapper music from an outlying block of flats.

Dr Blum's premises was on the fourth floor of a period residence that must have been one of a few surviving buildings from the final onslaught of World War Two. Guy pressed the button on the entry phone, and waited. When a female voice said, 'Wer ist da?' Guy felt the hairs rise on the back of his neck, only days ago he had heard a similar greeting.

'Herr Scott. My appointment with Dr Blum.'

'Kommen Sie bitte!' The lock buzzed and Guy pushed open the door. He got to the fourth floor where he held open the lift door for a woman he assumed was a departing patient. At the reception desk an assistant greeted him. The faint smell of clinical disinfectant reminded him of his dentist's surgery in London, and he feared that his treatment from Dr Blum would be more painful than recent treatment to his teeth.

'Do you speak English?' he asked the receptionist.

'Of course.' She indicated a waiting area and handed him some paperwork. 'Here is a form to fill in your personal details. It's in both languages. Dr Blum will be with you shortly.'

With an assurance of same day payment Günter's brother had agreed to this short notice appointment, the last slot that evening, in the name of a 'Herr Scott' and he had readily accepted the request for absolute discretion. Guy filled in the form which included tick-boxes to indicate previous illnesses and injuries. He gave his full name as 'Herr Guy Raymond Scott' together with other false details that included the first line of his real home address, followed by the town of Macclesfield in the county of Cheshire. He finished off the bogus address with a concocted post code. He was truthful about his own blood group, O Positive, and about not being on any prescribed medication at the time. He was able to tick 'no' in most of the medical history boxes. He spent a few minutes thumbing through a local journal with articles and pictures of the weekend's marathon, and as far as he could tell none of the photographs included a topless blonde Englishman. There was nothing of David either. His reading was interrupted by the assistant. 'Herr Scott?' and he heard a door click as it opened. He looked up and saw a man in a white jacket and a stethoscope around his neck standing in the door frame of the surgery.

CHAPTER 27

Raymond telephoned his twin brother about the momentous news. 'It's on NBC at three o'clock,' he said. 'Berlin's an hour ahead, it'll be four o'clock here.'

'Time to celebrate.'

'Quite. The chances of something like this happening must be tiny.'

'To think only yesterday I dreamed about the little girl in that pink dress she used to wear,' said Ben. 'Remember it?'

'Yes. The same image came to me last night.'

'What about Guy Shepherd, is he in the picture?'

'I hope so. I've left him a voicemail message.'

When Raymond put his phone down he texted Guy asking him to call back, and included details of the NBC bulletin. Alone in his hotel suite Raymond switched on the television and tuned in to NBC. He looked at his watch. In Berlin it was coming up to four o'clock in the afternoon; on the east coast of the US it would be nearly ten in the morning.

Deputy Inspector Tolan Stevens' ambition had always been to follow his father and join New York City Police Department. A diligent police officer, after ten years on the beat Tolan Stevens was assigned to the Organized Crime Control Bureau where he earned respect for his thorough investigative work. He never enjoyed facing microphones and cameras but press conferences went with the job, and there was inevitable media interest in stories as newsworthy as this one.

Stevens gripped a thin folder in one hand as he guided a middle aged woman through a side door into the police press room and up two steps to a raised platform. He and the woman sat side by side and adjusted their eyes to the bright lights. Projected onto a large screen behind them was the photo and name of the subject of the day's story. Stevens and his companion sat behind an oblong wooden table and looked apprehensively at the cluster of microphones. The photographers clicked away for a few moments before Stevens opened his folder, leaned towards the mikes and called for quiet.

'Hello everyone and welcome to today's press conference regarding this remarkable case of a comeback from the grave. I'm Deputy Inspector Tolan Stevens, beside me is Doctor Naomi Borlick and you already know the name of the person whose picture you see behind us.' Dr Borlick smiled while Stevens frowned nervously at the reporters and journalists. 'After making a short statement we'll invite questions from the floor, one at a time.'

Stevens recognised some of the people in the press room, The New York Times and Daily News along with many others. Apart from NBC, major broadcast networks such as Fox News and CNN were also present as were several local radio reporters with whom he had established mutual trust over the years.

In the Berlin Hilton Raymond's hands trembled as he pointed the remote handset at the TV to turn up the volume. He did not want to miss any of what was to follow.

'As you know,' Stevens began, 'on Saturday New York Police Department were informed that an unconscious adult in their early thirties had been admitted to New York University Downtown Hospital in Lower Manhattan. The ambulance crew that brought in the patient did not know who had reported the casualty, however, it seems the injury was caused by a short piece of insecure scaffolding that fell onto the patient. On arrival at the trauma centre and in a mild coma, the casualty was not yet in a fit state to assist our enquiries for obvious reasons.'

Stevens paused, aware of the total silence, and signalled Dr Borlick it was her turn to speak. She leaned forwards as the cameras zoomed in on her.

'Intravenous drugs were administered in an attempt to bring the patient round from the coma,' she said. 'On Sunday afternoon the patient, a British citizen, stirred and showed signs of consciousness, responded to further stimuli and finally awoke at five-thirty in the afternoon. The only remarkable feature about the case so far was the injured person possessed no personal effects except for business cards describing her as a freelance journalist.' She was interrupted.

'Have you searched the sidewalk where the ambulance crew first arrived?' one reporter asked.

'Yes we have,' Stevens replied, 'but please let us finish our statement before we take any more questions.'

Dr Borlick resumed. 'Further medical tests showed that the victim had ingested an amnesic drug that blanked out the memory of preceding days, and was unable to explain how or why the accident occurred. When the injured person stated their name, the hospital authorities were stunned because it matched that of a Brit reported missing and presumed dead after last month's nine-eleven attacks.'

In Berlin Raymond took a handkerchief from his trouser pocket and wiped the damp from his eyes.

At the New York press conference numerous reporters raised their hands in the air.

Dr Borlick looked at Stevens who returned to the notes in his folder.

'One moment, please,' he said. 'We are appealing for any witnesses to last Saturday's incident to come forward, including the unknown person who telephoned the emergency services. The number to call is shown on the front of this table.' He pointed. 'We hope today's press conference will jog someone's memory, and appreciate the interest shown by you media guys. Now it's time to take your questions.'

Hands shot up and Stevens pointed at a face he knew from the New York Post.

'When will we get the chance to question the patient?'

Stevens moved the palm of one hand towards his companion.

'She'll stay in hospital for a couple more days, but thankfully it looks like her injury isn't too serious,' said Dr Borlick. 'I understand that another press conference may be held if she agrees to take part.'

Stevens nodded. 'We'll need to interview her before then to obtain a full statement,' he said.

Several hands were raised again but a reporter from NBC called out from among the crowd, 'Can the casualty remember what happened to her at the World Trade Center on the eleventh of September?'

Dr Borlick replied, 'No she can't, because she wasn't there.'

'How could she know she wasn't there if she's lost her memory?'

'She's unable to recall the past few days, but remembers what she was doing before that.'

Stevens pointed to a woman from the Daily News. 'Helen, you have a question?'

'Yeah, thanks. If your patient wasn't at the World Trade Center on the morning of nine-eleven, why did everybody think she was there?'

'She had an eight-thirty appointment in the North Tower,' said Stevens, 'and everyone on that floor of the building was obliterated by the hijacked plane. It was assumed that our patient had perished along with all the others.' He paused for effect. 'However, there was a big misunderstanding.' Stevens spoke with slow emphasis. 'Hers was an evening appointment, so she never went to the meeting in the North Tower on that terrible morning.'

In his hotel suite Raymond stared wide-eyed and open-mouthed at the television screen.

In New York there was a hum among the reporters and some of them talked softly into their cell phones. Stevens pointed to a reporter from a local radio station and said, 'Peter, you have a question.'

'What's the last thing she can remember?'

'Four or five days ago she recalls eating some corn flakes,' said Dr Borlick.

'Whereabouts?'

'She couldn't tell us the address, her mind's still a little hazy.'

'Do her family know what's going on?'

'Yes, she's made telephone contact with her British relatives.'

'She's also been in touch with her work colleagues,' said Stephens.

'How did they all react?' shouted someone.

'At first they thought she must have risen from the dead, then they were overjoyed.'

'When will she reunite with her family?' asked a different correspondent.

'Soon we hope.'

'We wonna be there when it happens.'

'Look out for the next press release,' said Dr Borlick.

Stevens singled out another questioner.

'What was she doing in New York before her accident?'

'She was here on business. She works in the fashion industry.'

'Why did she carry business cards showing she's a journalist?'

'That's one of the reasons we want to interview her.'

Another reporter cut in, 'Why did the patient take an amnesic drug?'

'She can't remember ever taking the drug. To her it's as if it never happened,' said Dr Borlick.

Stevens pointed to a shrewd reporter he knew from the New York Times who asked, 'Deputy Inspector Stevens, as a crime investigator why are you assigned to this case? Where's the element of criminality?'

Stevens bit his lip.

'Pieces of scaffolding don't drop from the sky just like that,' said the reporter, 'and why did Dr Borlick refer to the casualty as a 'victim' just now? Do you think she may have been assaulted?'

It was the one question Stevens had dreaded. He looked at Dr Borlick. Before the press conference he had asked her to avoid giving a detailed description of the patient's head wound. 'Our clinical examinations are ongoing...' she began to ramble but was saved by the same reporter's next intervention.

'Was the victim forced to take the amnesic drug by any chance?'

The room fell completely silent.

'We believe so,' said Stevens and quickly took the next question.

The session continued for another five minutes or so. Stevens ended by reminding the correspondents to pick up a press release at the exit. On no account should any of them try to contact Ms Parry, and details of the next press conference would be circulated in the usual way. In the meantime all media enquiries should be directed to the press office of New York Police Department.

As soon as they were clear of the press room Stevens turned to Dr Borlick and said, 'Well done Naomi.' He was thankful that what really happened to Jessica was never mentioned. Well, not this time.

In the Berlin Hilton Raymond pressed the red 'off' button on the remote and heaved a sigh. From the moment he took her phone call in the Pavillon restaurant all he had wanted was to see her, hug her and ask heaps of questions. He yearned to do so in New York but when she learned he was in Switzerland she pleaded with him to wait a few days for her to join him there. While his rocky emotions bounced from shock to disbelief to sheer wonderment, she assured him that she was not too badly hurt but, after her ugly ordeal, she needed to get away from the Big Apple and distance herself from Alex Grishin's cronies. She had promised to update her step-father as soon as they were together again, and that Zurich would be fine. Raymond replied that he was about to travel to Berlin.

'Christ Pop, you're not planning to meet up with that Grishin bastard are you?'

'Yes, I need to discuss business matters...'

'Don't go near the man. It was thanks to him I've been incarcerated here ever since my business trip.'

'WHAT?!'

'Pop, I can't say any more now. Please. I've got medics buzzing around telling me to take it easy and police coming and going with their questions.'

'You're in hospital Jessica, you need family support.'

'I'm fine. Really. There's to be a press conference because people think I'm a nine-eleven survivor.'

'You are a survivor and you're alive. That's all that matters. Does Guy know the latest?'

'I've left him a voice message.' She then gave Raymond details of the press conference, and promised to call him again as soon as she had booked a flight to Berlin.

It seemed bizarre. How could Alex have had anything to do with Jessica, and what exactly did she mean by 'incarcerated'? The two must have come across each other in New York, perhaps there had been some kind of quarrel... He would have to wait to find out, unless he could get in touch with Guy who might know more. But if Guy knew what had happened to Jessica surely he would have told someone – he was supposed to be in love with her. At the memorial service in Ashworth church Guy looked utterly distraught, his grief was genuine. Raymond wished Guy would respond to his latest text, and to Jessica's message for that matter.

He wondered where Guy was. Jessica was probably asking the same question. At that point Raymond suddenly recalled his last conversation with Alex who said after he had talked with Guy he *got rid of him* and *he won't trouble us any more*. Ominous remarks, now wide open to interpretation.

After sending another text to Guy's cell phone he considered contacting the police. He soon dropped the idea, at least until Jessica joined him. Raymond was not yet aware that Capsella-Biotech's Chief Executive and his thugs were being treated in a Berlin hospital, but he did know that Alex was capable of bringing Raymond down with him.

Apart from his expected huge profit on the side, Raymond's company had financed Capsella-Biotech which was about to sequence the entire human genome, a landmark step in the history of science. He told himself that nothing and nobody should get in the way of that, not even Alex whatever his faults and whatever private wealth his other schemes would generate. There were so many questions, and the people to answer them were Jessica and Alex. And Guy. He was stuck until his step-daughter could get to Berlin and he was bored stiff in the Hilton Hotel. He longed to be at home by the trout lake with Jessica and his dogs. He decided to go for a wander, somewhere quiet. He went down to the hotel lobby and asked if there was a lake they could recommend for a stroll and perhaps a bite to eat.

'Anywhere by Havel Lake is nice,' came the reply. 'Try the Wannsee, it's only about ten kilometres from here.'

'I know where that is,' said Raymond. 'I've been past it but never stopped. Can you recommend somewhere for a meal?'

He was given details of a couple of waterside restaurants.

On route to the Havel he imagined the wild celebration among Jessica's work colleagues. Who says miracles never happen? An apt question because a second miracle of sorts was looming, unless it was another of Raymond's dreams. His taxi slowed in heavy traffic as it approached Podbielski Allee U-Bahn station and came to a halt in the queue. Just as the traffic started to move again Raymond could have sworn he saw him walking away from the U-Bahn entrance. Or was it him? Raymond was puzzled by the man's slight limp and the wrist bandages but the face was unmistakable. It <u>was</u> him in a blue polo shirt and plain chinos. Guy stood at a junction for a moment then set off along Podbielski Allee and was soon out of sight.

'What the fuck? Guy?' said Raymond, then louder, 'Stop the taxi, I need to get out!'

'Hier kann ich nicht halten!' *I can't stop now*. The taxi driver pointed at a man in uniform in the middle of the road who was waving them on. 'Polizei!'

'Pull up, please!'

'Moment, bitte.'

A minute later the driver turned off and stopped at an entrance to Kaiser-Wilhelm Platz, a small park. Raymond cursed as he got out of the taxi and paid. He hurried back to the kerbside where he had seen Guy and looked left and right.

Podbielski Allee was the suburban equivalent of a dual carriageway, a leafy avenue that cut straight through a fashionable part of town. Bordered by trees on both sides, there was also a turfed central reservation with its own double row of trees that divided the traffic. Raymond stood at the same junction where he had seen Guy, the one place in the avenue with less greenery and open to the sun's evening rays. The rest of the avenue was in the shade making it difficult to identify individual pedestrians. In the distance he could just make out a bus stop and a person in a dark shirt and beige trousers who boarded a bus that drove away.

'God, how could I be so stupid,' muttered Raymond. He fumbled for his cell phone and called Guy's number. 'I should have done this in the bloody taxi.'

'Hi. This is Guy. Please leave a message and I'll call back. Thanks.'

'I wish you would call me back, this is Raymond on the evening of Tuesday the second and I've just seen you in a road called...' he paused to glance up at the sign, 'Podbielski Allee, however you pronounce it, and I'm outside a bar with tables and red sunshades. I presume you've heard the incredible news about Jessica. Return this call Guy, I think I've a big problem with Alex Grishin. For God's sake, don't have any more to do with him.'

CHAPTER 28

Over breakfast on Tuesday Guy already felt the healing effect of the painkillers and medication. The previous evening's treatment had been lengthy and cost a lot. When Guy presented his wounds there were no awkward questions, although Dr Blum's eyes betrayed a suspicion that there had been a punch-up of sorts. To begin with Guy's urine and blood samples were handed to a nurse while he was asked to strip to his underpants and lie on the surgical bed. The doctor examined the gashed wrists and ankles, and injected local anaesthetic into the wounds.

Before the anaesthetic took hold, the doctor checked over Guy's head and face and worked down.

'No breakages so far,' said Dr Blum, 'Consider yourself lucky.' His English was better than his younger brother's. As the doctor fingered the neck glands Guy asked, 'Have you and your brother always lived in Berlin?'

'Yes, apart from a medical stint I did abroad.'

'OUCH!'

'Sorry, I have to check your ribs, some of them are bruised and we better take a chest x-ray in case of any cracks. You may need to wear an elasticated chest bandage.' He paused. 'How are your arms and ankles now? Can you feel this?' He touched the gashes and Guy did not flinch. 'Good, I'll get to work on them in a moment.'

Guy wondered whether the Blum brothers had ever been members of Hitler Youth, but he decided to avoid that question.

Dr Blum placed the palms of his hands onto Guy's abdomen. At first it tickled and made him giggle, until the doctor pressed harder and then he yelped.

'You must have been hit hard, but I don't think any tissue has been torn. You obviously keep yourself very fit.' Dr Blum placed his stethoscope onto a desk. 'You said that your testicles had suffered a blow. Slip off your underwear please and I'll take a look.'

Guy tightened his fists and screwed up his face while his scrotum was fingered.

'They're quite swollen, although it looks like your inner thigh took some of the impact. As did your penis.' After about a minute the doctor let go and Guy breathed out. 'I'll prescribe you a steroid lotion to reduce the bruising and prevent infection. Apply it twice daily, including beneath the foreskin. No sex for at least two weeks I'm afraid. Sorry.'

'Hardly a problem.' Given the way Guy felt that evening he would not have been bothered if told to abstain for months.

The cuts and gashes on Guy's limbs were jagged and looked sceptic. He could not feel the scalpel's incisions when the doctor opened his wounds to drain the pus. After a thorough antiseptic clean-up the cuts were stitched and bandaged.

'I'll give you painkillers and antibiotics to last two weeks. Don't bath or shower for the next week, just give yourself a basin wash. If you're still in Berlin after seven days you can have the wounds checked here and we'll replace the bandages. Otherwise go to your doctor at home.' He picked up the form that Guy had completed earlier.

'You're from Macclesfield?'

'Er, that's right.'

'Small world. That's where I did part of my training in psychiatry, on secondment at the old county asylum. I think they closed it a few years ago.'

Guy changed the subject. 'Hence you speak such good English. Um, what about my stitches?'

'They'll melt in two or three weeks.' He put down the form. 'Right, we'll soon be finished. Put your underwear and trousers back on while I find out if the test results are ready, then we'll x-ray your chest.

The consultation ended when Guy was given the all clear with his urine, blood and the x-ray. The clinic had its own pharmacy where Dr Blum personally dispensed the medication. When Guy departed he felt like a trussed turkey with the elastic bandage fastened around his torso, but Dr Blum had assured him it would reduce the stabs of pain and help heal the bruises around the rib cage. He also gave Guy several clean spares.

With his ankles still numb from the anaesthetic Guy tottered a bit. He took a taxi back to the Gasthaus where he would look at Günter Blum in fresh light.

A family of four entered the breakfast room as Guy poured himself a second cup of coffee. He took little notice of them and even less notice of the newspaper carried by the mother with its headline 'Mordversuch: Drei Männer Angeklagt' - *Attempted Murder: Three Men Charged*. She folded the paper and laid it flat on a breakfast table and joined the rest of her family who were helping themselves to the buffet at the far end of the room.

Guy took Alex's mobile from his pocket and scrolled through the stored phone numbers. Most were listed in abbreviated format that Guy could not fathom, but he easily worked out what was meant by RH-pers and RH-work because he recognised Raymond's phone numbers. He scrolled down to see whether the name Samir featured in the list, but it was not there, or so it first appeared. Guy scratched the back of his head and tried to recollect Samir's first name. He remembered it began with a 'K' – Khaled or Kareem, something like that. He scrolled back up the list and found the letters 'KS' next to a phone number that began with '964-1-7'.

Guy left the dining room and went to reception to borrow a phone directory. As he searched for international dialling codes he wondered how many people might try to call Alex, unaware of his new situation. Meanwhile he ran his index finger down the international list to discover that the 'KS' number was the international code for Baghdad. 'Mr Samir I presume,' thought Guy.

He got a sudden jump as Alex's cell vibrated. The screen displayed the words 'Number Withheld'. Christ, who can this be? Guy pressed the green button and said, 'Hello?'

'It's me.'

'Who?'

'Me! David. Who do you think?'

'How was I supposed to know? You withheld your number.'

'Sorry, I forgot, it's how my phone's programmed.'

'Next time use a code word or something, okay?'

'Fine. I just wondered how you were. Seen a doctor yet?'

'You bet. It was Günter's brother. Stitches in the wrists and ankles. A chest bandage. Painkillers and medication. No sex for two weeks.'

'I can think of worse things,' said David. 'Look, last night I started on the *MyPedigree* website. It's a bit slow, but has a lot of info. A kind of genealogical Friends United.'

'Reunited,' said Guy.

'Whatever. It's got loads of Grishin's listed, so my work's cut out.'

'Try whittling them down to Grishin in Berlin, or Grishin Podbielski Allee.'

'Sure. Remind me how your family name's spelt?'

Guy spelled out 'Schäfer'.

'You wanted me to use a code when I next call you on Alex's mobile.'

Guy thought for a moment. 'Strewth, erm, how about *Genome* or something?'

'Will do. Sorry I startled you just now.'

When he returned to his room Guy found that the bed had already been made, so the first thing he did was to check that the gun was where he had left it. His breathing faltered as he re-lived the moment the weapon was pointed at him. 'Saved by the piss pot,' he said to himself. He recalled aiming the gun at Alex and trying to pull the trigger, and wondered how it would have felt to kill the person who resembled his father. He knew he should get rid of the gun, but to hand it in would prompt tricky questions, even prosecution, whereas to throw it away would be irresponsible. Another option was to discard the bullets and send the gun anonymously to the police, too risky, so he decided to keep it hidden in the suitcase.

He tried to concentrate. Capsella-Biotech's bid to patent specific genes seemed a non-starter. Alex was fairly confident it could be done, but the notion of holding intellectual property rights over a living organism seemed ludicrous. IBEC, whatever that stood for, was some kind of genetic editing tool that had been successfully patented because the device was a human invention, not a life form. He then reminded himself it was always possible that the Human Genome Project might win the race to complete the full sequence, even though Capsella appeared to have the advantage with its new Spectra machines.

Guy needed to work out where he fitted in and what to do. If there was any chance of stopping the sale to Iraq, perhaps he should contact Raymond who appeared to be in Berlin. Then there was Brian the gap year lad's suggestion to pay a hospital visit, when Guy could try to reason with Alex - chancy, but not Guy's first attempt to sell an idea or plead a case to change a person's mind, something business people did all the time. Maybe he could find a way to obtain assurances from Mr Samir. Guy was sure he had the man's right phone number although he did not know his actual location.

Guy had to decide his highest priority, and one technicality outweighed all else: Alex could cancel his cell phone account any time and render the device useless, so it was essential for Guy to milk the account while it remained active. He lay back on the bed in his room and fiddled with the phone when he realised that previous calls would be logged on it somehow, but when he found the log he soon grasped there was not much he could do with the data. For example on certain dates calls had been made to, or received from, RH-pers and KS, but so what? It revealed nothing specific, however Guy then had another idea and punched the air in glee. He clicked a button to get into Alex's voicemail and waited. After a few seconds a recorded voice said, 'Please enter your PIN.' *Shit!* He got a similar result with texts. No access to what could have been enlightening saved messages.

In order to phone Samir, Guy was more likely to get through if the call appeared to come from a recognised mobile number. He knew he should sound out Raymond first but time was against Guy. He had no idea whether Samir spoke anything other than Arabic, however that fax to Alex was in English so with any luck language was no barrier. As he held Alex's phone he hesitated. He wanted Samir to think the call was from the Grishin mobile, so it was vital to get on with it but he had to work out what to say. The only solution was to pretend that Alex wanted Samir to know he was in hospital.

'It'll get the conversation going,' thought Guy, 'unless Samir has already spoken with Alex in hospital, in which case I'll just hang up.'

CHAPTER 29

It was all over the news on Wednesday third October, with the *Berliner Zeitung* headline 'Von Den Toten Zurück' – *Back From The Dead* above a photo of the New York press conference.

Raymond sat in the lobby of the Hilton Hotel and glowed. Although his German was limited he scanned the article. There was one reference to Jessica's mother Dame Elizabeth Parry, but he was relieved his own name did not feature. For once he felt proud and happy but he also had to be patient. Jessica would contact him later that day to say when she was due to arrive in Berlin.

He thumbed through the newspaper to pass the time, and was about to swap it for a British paper when a shorter article caught his eye. It referred to Capsella-Biotech, Dr Grishin and something about a hospital. He took the paper to the information desk where a member of staff translated it. 'Good God,' he thought to himself in his suite several minutes later, 'charged with attempted murder?' He now knew the story as portrayed by the press, but nothing about Guy's contribution to the carnage. Although Raymond felt he should speak with Alex, he had promised to hear Jessica's account of her ordeal first. His thoughts were stalled by his cell phone indicating a call from Alex's mobile.

'Hello? Alex?'

'It's me. Guy.'

'WHAT? Why are you using Alex's phone? Where the hell are you?'

'Good questions. I'm not sure how much longer this phone will work, I must be quick. Are you still in Berlin?'

'How did you know I was here? What are you doing in Berlin? Did you get my message…'

'I should ask you the same things for God's sake. Raymond, it's urgent. Can we meet up?'

'Of course. I'm at the Berlin Hilton in Mohrenstrasse, it's easy to find.'

'I know exactly where you are, see you there in an hour.'

When Guy got to the Hilton he was taken straight to Raymond's suite. Their handshake had the warmth of a father and son reunion. Guy said that he was mighty glad to see Raymond as they had a lot to talk about. To Guy's initial surprise Raymond said how exciting it was about Jessica.

'What do you mean?'

'You got my voice messages I presume?'

'No, my phone was nicked. I used Alex's.'

'Jesus Christ, you mean you don't know?'

'Know what?'

'I sent you texts and messages, the press conference and everything.'

'Raymond, stop telling me about your bloody messages and just say what this is about. Please.'

'Oh my God. You really haven't heard, have you?'

'Heard what for fuck's sake?'

'Jessica's alive, Guy.'

Guy turned white and sat down on an armchair. Raymond repeated: 'Jessica's alive.' He paused while Guy began to weep. 'It's headline news, back from the dead they say. Something awful did happen to her around the time of the nine-eleven attacks but she was never in the World Trade Center that morning.'

Raymond continued to talk even though he could tell Guy struggled to take it in. 'She told me Alex Grishin had detained her, and she's been in hospital with some sort of concussion. That's all I know. She flies to Berlin in a day or so when we'll hear her full story.'

Raymond opened the mini-bar and took out several miniatures of Jack Daniel's and poured the contents into two glass tumblers. He gave one to Guy who was trying not to sob. Raymond walked over to a table and picked up the *Berliner Zeitung*. 'There you go,' he said and handed him the paper.

Guy wiped away the tears. On seeing Jessica's picture he gave a wide smile. He put the paper down onto a coffee table as Raymond sat in an armchair opposite him.

'I'd love to call Jessica,' said Guy.

'Whenever you like, but it's early in the States. Have lunch here first.'

They talked for over two hours like old friends who had not seen each other for ages. Guy asked whether Ben and Jessica's colleagues had heard the latest, and Raymond assured him that they had. Guy said that the three Russians had taken his cell phone, preventing him from accessing his voicemail, including messages from Jessica. He then described how earlier he sneaked into Capsella's premises at Wannsee, discovered faxes from a man called Karim Samir and found a photo of his family's property in Podbielski Allee.

'That's the same road where I saw you yesterday,' said Raymond.

'I went to the house in search of any connection with Alex, but there was nothing out of the ordinary.' When Guy asked about the numbered bank accounts in Zurich and the DNA editing product, Raymond side-tracked by explaining that IBEC stood for *Identical Bacteria Enzyme Corrector*, advanced gene therapy invented by Alex and his team and completely separate from the Human Genome Project. When asked how the IBEC system was being funded Raymond sighed.

'I may as well tell you, bugger it,' he said. 'Alex is using the Spectra 6500 computers.'

'The sequencing machines?'

'Yes. Two hundred, to speed up the process…'

'You mean three hundred?'

'Er, no. That's the whole point. There are three hundred machines in total, but you and others don't know that the other hundred installed at Alex's Westfälische Strasse office are there to develop IBEC as a commercial product.'

At last Guy had got it: Herron International had financed all the new computers, a third of them siphoned off for Alex and Raymond to create a separate money spinner for their personal gain. Guy asked Raymond if he knew about something called a phage. Raymond was puzzled and simply shrugged. He listened intently as Guy described his conversation with Alex at Grishin Informatik last Friday, his sickening treatment there and how he fought his way out.

'The water boarding sounds terrible,' said Raymond. 'I'm so sorry for you. Your escape must have felt like payback time.'

'Well, I got even,' said Guy. 'Anyway, on my way to a doctor I saw you outside the Hilton. Sorry, I should've stopped but I had to get these wounds cleaned up.' He held up one wrist and the other hand pointed at his ankles. 'Not that my injuries are anything like as bad as my revenge on Alex and his cronies.'

'It was in the papers, the police assume they tried to kill each other and they're charged with attempted murder. What state are they in?'

Guy explained how their injuries ranged from nasty to horrific, with Alex least badly hurt having suffered a punctured hand. Guy said that the shock would have subdued all three of them for a while.

'Take my advice and assume nothing,' said Raymond, like a self-styled expert on the persistent nature of Post-Traumatic Stress Disorder. But he was astonished when Guy described his telephone call to Karim Samir. 'How did you make contact with him?'

'Easy,' said Guy. 'I used Alex's cell phone to dial his number and introduced myself as Dr Grishin's assistant called Scott.'

Raymond raised his eyes to the ceiling and shook his head.

'On the spur of the moment it was the only name I could think of,' Guy said with a smile. 'It's quite clever actually. Scott is a first name or a surname, take your pick.'

'Spur of the moment is your life story, Guy. For once, why can't you think things through before you act?'

'I had no choice! Alex could close his cell phone account at any time. I had to make the call immediately.'

'Fair point.' Raymond thought for a moment. 'Were there any incoming calls for Alex?'

'No, apart from one misplaced call from my flatmate. Other callers may have left voicemails but I can't access those without Alex's PIN.'

'Anyway, you told Mr Samir that your name was Scott?'

'That's right. He speaks good English. I told him that after an accident Dr Grishin was in hospital and had asked me to make it known he'd be out of contact for a few days at least.'

'What did he say?'

'He thanked me for letting him know, and I used the opportunity to ask him if he had anything to report to Dr Grishin.'

'And?'

'Samir had hoped Alex would provide an update on the delivery of the IBEC programme and the phage formula so he could arrange the so-called Zurich payments.'

Raymond blushed. After a pause he side-tracked once again and said, 'You'll have to explain what's meant by a phage.'

Guy repeated Alex's explanation of a phage, of Iraq's attempt to develop an antidote to anthrax bio-weapons and the Russian research into a man-made virus that destroys bacteria. He ended by saying he believed Saddam Hussein was prepared to pay squillions for the technology for reasons more sinister than self-defence.

Raymond remained silent and rubbed his chin. 'Christ almighty,' he whispered, 'I didn't know Alex had such a lethal product up his sleeve.'

'How much did you know?'

'The money was payment for the system that edits DNA.' He took his hand away from his chin. 'I was certain that international sales of IBEC would rocket as soon as the human genome had been sequenced. But now I see why Iraq offered to pay such a high premium. Anthrax. My God.' Raymond leaned back and held his hands over his face. 'What have I done? Where does this leave me?'

'Look, others have messed up as well. Take me, the idiot who got your step-daughter involved. And we still don't know exactly what happened to her in New York, how much she knows and who else she might have told. I'm so incredibly sorry for all my screw-ups.' Guy stared at Raymond for a while and then said, 'There's also Alex's half-baked scheme to patent certain genes.'

'How did you know about that?'

'In Alex's paperwork there was a copy of his presentation to the IGSA conference.'

'Jessica went to that, it didn't go down well with the audience. Personally I think it's absurd.'

Guy stood. 'One thing's for sure. Beating ourselves up won't achieve a thing.'

'True. How did you leave it with Samir?'

'He asked me if his meeting was postponed.'

'What meeting?'

'Apparently he was due to meet Alex tomorrow at nine-thirty.'

'Tomorrow? That means he must be in Berlin already.'

'Or on his way. He's agreed to meet us at the Eierschale tomorrow morning.'

'Where's that?'

'The restaurant-bar on the junction of Schorlemer Allee and Podbielski Allee where you spotted me yesterday. He'll be there at nine-thirty.'

After lunch Guy remained in the Hilton suite to call Jessica. Raymond went for a stroll in bracing wind up Friedrichstrasse and along Unter den Linden where he browsed window displays and upmarket boutiques. Past the old opera house he noticed something out of place for a boulevard of linden trees, a tall pair of hawthorns with fresh new berries that heralded the coming autumn. Between them was a bench where he sat for a short while and watched people and traffic. He began to feel cold so he moved on until he came to a coffee salon where he ordered hot chocolate. He placed his hands on the steaming cup. Throughout the whole saga he had dug a deep hole for himself. It was not clever to assume Alex originally approached the Iraqis only to arrange the first IBEC deal, even though his Russian connections made the client easily accessible. If it ever got out that Sir Raymond Herron had indirectly used his company's funds to help Iraq develop bio-weapons, he would be more than ruined. He would be totally destroyed.

His hands shook as he sipped his drink. He wondered how much Jessica knew, whom she may have told and what her reaction would be when she finds out how he had behaved. He was appalled by what had been done to Guy, though he admired how he escaped his tormentors. He wondered what harm may have been done to Jessica and the part played by Alex, and Raymond decided it was mainly his own fault. Although Guy had interfered and used Jessica, it was Raymond who had made it possible for them to get to know each other in the first place. In business dealings up to now he had never felt shame but he knew he would feel it when he reunited with Jessica - he could feel *Dark Cloud* lurking.

Raymond also knew he was unlikely to get Alex to cooperate or be less devious, but after hearing Jessica's version of events he would have to communicate with the man somehow. He drank the rest of his chocolate and made his way back to the Hilton. He entered the suite and found Guy with his hands in his pockets gazing out of the window at the Gendarmenmarkt.

'How did it go?'

Guy turned round, a sparkle in his eyes. 'She's on the mend. We had a long chin-wag.' He smiled. 'It was incredible to hear her voice again, like being in a fantasy world.'

'When can we expect to see her?'

'She's ignored all medical advice to convalesce and booked herself onto a flight from JFK on Saturday, she'll get here on Sunday morning.' Guy hesitated for a moment. 'She asked whether I had watched the press conference about her. Of course I said no as I never got her message. My phone's probably in a skip somewhere near Grishin Informatik.' He looked resigned. 'There's something else. Jessica thinks at the press conference the police glossed over their suspicion that she was drugged and assaulted.'

'I got that impression, but when we last spoke she didn't elaborate.'

'You should know the truth, even if it's worse than you imagined. Jessica was drugged and she was assaulted. She knows why but hasn't told the police.'

'Christ. She must be bloody scared of something. Or someone. Is anyone being charged?'

'No. Unless Jessica names people there's not a shred of evidence to prove any wrong doing,' said Guy. 'Suspicion is one thing. Proof is another, and Jessica can't or won't provide it. The hospital has confirmed she had amnesia which means she can genuinely claim loss of memory. Her reappearance after everyone thought she was dead makes a great media story, but she's not adding to it. She promised to tell us more when she's in Berlin.'

'I can't wait to see her.'

'Neither can I. But we've got things to do before then. Like buy a pay-as-you-go phone. Then let's share what we know about Jessica's trip to New York, I'm afraid I've a few confessions to make.'

'Fine with me.'

'Most importantly, we should work out what line to take with Karim Samir tomorrow morning.'

'I agree. Nip out for your new phone, and when you get back we can discuss tactics over a bottle of plonk.'

While Guy went to buy a mobile phone Raymond called Room Service and ordered a bottle of red house wine. He drank his first glass and made a decision utterly out of character, prompted by the whisky and wine perhaps. He picked up the telephone and called Ben. Their conversation lasted about twenty minutes when they discussed arrangements for Tuesday the ninth. The plan would enable Raymond to avoid tricky explanations yet keep up appearances, and he judged Ben more than capable of taking on the job. Given the exceptional circumstances Ben did not even ask to mull it over and immediately accepted. Raymond gave him instructions to collect the necessary paperwork from Ashworth Manor, and they agreed to speak again in a couple of days.

CHAPTER 30

At eight-thirty on Thursday morning Guy and Raymond met for breakfast at Eierschale Restaurant-Bar. It was a clear day with a slight chill in the air. They sat at a table under a red sun umbrella in a corner of the garden terrace where they could not be overheard. Both men were dressed in unmistakably different styles: Raymond's bespoke suit was tailored in the finest Savile Row navy cloth, while Guy wore a shiny grey two-piece bought off-the-peg in a hurry the previous day. Over fruit juice, Brötchen and coffee they reviewed the agenda for their imminent meeting with Karim Samir.

'I can't tell you much about him, he's Alex's man,' said Raymond. 'Some time ago Alex cultivated a high ranking member of the Russian Military Attaché's staff here in Berlin who arranged the introduction.'

'It's like something out of the Cold War,' said Guy. 'Remember John Kent spotted Alex at the Russian Embassy?'

'You're well versed in John's report. You never gave it back, where is the bloody thing?'

'It's safe Raymond. You have my word.' He winced and swallowed a couple of painkillers.

Raymond sighed and looked at his watch. 'When Mr Samir arrives are you still okay to start the talking?' He sounded nervous.

'Sure. I'll make the introductions as it was me who approached Samir. Even though you two haven't met he'll know who you are, which should boost my street-cred as Alex's so-called messenger.'

'I hope to God you know what you're doing.'

'Stick to the agreed line, that Alex is too ill to receive visitors so he asked us to relay any messages about IBEC.'

They had established what line to take after their visit to Alex at the Park-Klinik the previous evening. On the advice of Brian the gap year lad they arrived at the hospital clutching flowers and a basket of small fruit easy to eat with one hand - strawberries, apricots, grapes. Hospital staff did not question who they were but explained the patient was in police custody. There was no mention of the other two casualties.

When they arrived at the ward, Guy pressed a buzzer and a voice told them to push and enter. They walked down a corridor with part-glazed doors on one side. Their footsteps tapped on the linoleum floor and there was a smell of disinfectant. Outside one room an armed police officer sat at a table reading a book. As they approached him they saw Alex in hospital pyjamas propped up in a single bed in the room. Perhaps Raymond's tailored suit gave away his nationality as the officer addressed them in English.

'Can I help?'

'We hope so,' said Raymond.

Guy looked through the glass pane and saw Alex turn his head. 'We wish to visit Dr Grishin.'

'Your names?'

Before Raymond could open his mouth Guy said, 'Mr Herron and Mr Scott.'

'Some identity?'

Raymond produced his UK driving licence while Guy pretended to pat his pockets and fumble around. 'Oh dear, I've left everything at the Gasthaus.' He studied the officer's face, glad to see he was not from the team he met at the marathon the other day.

The officer looked at Raymond's licence, handed it back and said, 'What is your connection with the patient?'

'We're friends,' said Guy.

'All right. Let me examine those items.' The officer made a cursory search of the flowers and the fruit and when he was satisfied he picked up a clip board and wrote down the names given to him. He told them to keep their visit short and opened the door to let them in.

They entered the room and noticed the officer leave the door ajar. Guy placed the flowers on the window sill.

'What a surprise,' said Alex in a vindictive tone.

'How are you?' said Raymond and put the fruit down on a bedside table for Alex to reach with his good hand.

'Bedbound on strong antibiotics.' He held up the bandaged hand. 'This was operated on but it's infected. They operate again tomorrow. So, you've come to wish me well?'

'You could say that,' said Raymond as he stood to one side of the bed, 'nobody should have to endure the painful ordeal you've experienced.' He glanced at Guy who stood on the opposite side of the bed. 'Nor should anyone suffer the torture you and your thugs inflicted on Guy if his story's true.'

Alex pulled a face at Guy. 'You interfering little shit…'

'Enough! Listen. Guy's in the picture so I can speak plainly…'

'Keep your voice down for Christ's sake,' Guy hissed, 'the bloody door's open.'

Raymond dropped his voice to a near whisper directed straight at Alex. 'You're plainly off your rocker. The sale of the gene editing system will make us both very rich, yet you've gone behind my back and crossed too many boundaries.'

'What boundaries?' Alex scowled and gestured with his undamaged hand.

'The anthrax phage for a start.' Raymond spoke so quietly that he almost mouthed the words. He glanced through the slit in the doorway. The duty officer was preoccupied with his book. 'If that's the real reason Iraq is paying such a high premium, I want no part in it.'

This was the moment when Guy realised he had gained an ally and began to feel proud of his former boss for taking a stand. It would surely make it easier for Jessica to forgive Raymond. Guy's other thought was that with any luck Jessica might forgive him too.

Raymond said, 'Plus, whatever you did to Jessica was shameful. She arrives in Berlin any day, and has quite a story to tell.'

'Your daughter's another interfering so-and-so. Why did you send her to follow me…'

'She's only my step-daughter Alex. You have my word, I never sent her anywhere to do anything.'

'On the spur of the moment she rocked up of her own accord to snoop? Who the fuck are you kidding?'

'It was my fault,' said Guy. 'I'm to blame.' He could feel his temper approach boiling point. 'She was in New York on business and I asked her to attend your presentation to the IGSA Convention.'

'Whatever.' Alex shrugged. 'I had no idea who she was at the time so I told my team to keep her silent and out of the way.' He looked up at Raymond. 'When I found out she was your step-daughter I gave immediate instructions for her release and make it look as if she'd had an accident. She's not badly hurt. What's the problem?'

'You fucking sod!' Guy lunged at Alex and grabbed his bandaged hand.

'AAGH!'

'Thanks to you we all thought Jessica was killed at Ground Zero, you stinking pile of Russian shit…'

The police officer entered. 'What is this? I thought you were friends of the patient.'

'Yeah,' Guy replied, 'and friends sometimes quarrel don't they?'

'Pull yourself together!' It was Raymond. 'Take your hands off Dr Grishin right now.'

Guy let go of Alex's hand and stepped back. The officer eyed the three of them for a few seconds. 'I think you've had enough time here…'

'Give us just a few more minutes,' Guy said. 'I promise to stay calm.'

'Is that all right?' The officer looked at Alex who nodded.

'Five minutes.' The officer went out and returned to his book but this time left the door wide open.

'I'm sorry,' said Guy. He lowered his voice. 'Look Alex, you and those other two fuckheads now face serious criminal charges. You cannot continue as top man at Capsella-Biotech.'

Alex ignored Guy and looked at Raymond. 'If I can survive being forced to watch my comrades being disembowelled by the Mujahidin, I can cope with this minor inconvenience.'

'Christ, you need help,' said Raymond. 'This is not some minor blemish, you could spend years behind bars.'

'Too bloody right…'

'Shut-up Guy,' said Raymond. 'Let's stick to the point. Alex, we're meeting Karim Samir tomorrow when he'll want to know that delivery is on track.'

'You can tell him the work is on schedule.'

'I'll tell him the IBEC programme is held up. His reaction should be interesting.'

Alex glared at both men. 'I know exactly how to extricate myself from here. It's one of several lines of defence that I've set up over the years.'

'I don't know what you're on about but don't threaten me,' said Raymond quietly but forcefully. 'Whilst you and those other two Afghantsis fester under arrest you have no freedom to communicate.'

'I'm at liberty to talk to the police at any time.' His eyes focused on Guy. 'I can piss all over you if I want. One word from me and you're in deep shit, you arrogant cunt.'

Guy glared back at Alex and spoke to him in an intense, measured tone. 'And one sour word from me to the police or to Samir will land you in even deeper shit, comrade. What's more, I suspect the Iraqi's won't like being double crossed either.'

The police officer entered. 'That's enough. You must leave. Thank you.'

Outside the isolation room Guy asked to speak with the doctor handling Alex's case. Raymond appeared a bit puzzled by the request. They were directed to a staff area on the same floor.

'What the hell are you doing?' Raymond asked as they walked towards a young man seated behind a desk.

'Our friend Dr Grishin must receive the best possible care, don't you agree?'

'This is pushing our luck isn't it?'

Guy smiled at Raymond then turned his attention to the man they were approaching. 'Do you speak English?' asked Guy.

'Certainly. How can I help?'

'We're concerned about Dr Grishin, a patient under arrest. Could we speak with his doctor?'

'You're speaking to him.'

'Oh. Are you the surgeon?' Guy looked at the name badge pinned to the doctor's breast pocket: *Andreas Richter*.

'No. There's an orthopaedic consultant who's already operated on the patient and will do so again soon. I'm responsible for his post-operative care.'

'Okay, well, we're worried about Dr Grishin's frame of mind. He's under huge stress and we think he needs psychiatric help.'

'Being under arrest must cause a lot of stress,' said Dr Richter.

'I understand,' said Guy, 'but we've done some research. He once fought in Afghanistan with the Soviet army. He suffered terribly as a prisoner of war. A few years ago he was diagnosed with Post-Traumatic Stress Disorder and I believe it's come back to haunt him...'

'I knew nothing about that. Let me think. Take a seat over there and I'll find out whether one of our psychiatrists is available.'

Raymond nodded. 'Thank you Doctor Richter.'

'I'm Andreas. We're informal here.' He smiled and picked up a telephone handset.

Twenty minutes later Guy and Raymond found themselves in a consulting room together with Andreas and a bespectacled middle-aged psychiatrist, Jan Baumann.

'It's late and you're lucky. I'm not always here at this hour and I only have a few minutes. I understand you're concerned about one of our patients. What can I do for you?' Another English speaker, like most Germans.

'It's about Dr Grishin who's under arrest in this hospital,' said Raymond.

'He's not the only one under arrest,' said Jan, 'we've got two others here as well.'

'I'm referring to the one in the isolation unit on this floor.'

Jan Baumann smiled. 'They're all in isolation units on this floor. Andreas tells me it's the one with the pierced hand.

'That's right.' Guy spoke to Jan for the first time. 'He suffers from what we call Post-Traumatic Stress.'

'I know the condition.'

'We think it caused the vicious fight that brought him and his two colleagues here. From what I've gathered, Dr Grishin's two men fought alongside him in Afghanistan. We're convinced they endured hideous combat trauma that caused their mental state.'

'That must have been some time ago,' said Jan, 'but it's well known that Post-Traumatic Stress can kick in many years after the actual event.' He paused to remove his glasses, twiddled them in his hands for a few moments and then said, 'I'd be happy to get my team to interview the three men, although I understand the other two have more serious injuries so we should let them recover a while longer. But we can talk to Dr Grishin in a day or so. Depending on how it goes, there could be follow-up sessions.' He replaced his glasses. 'In the worst case and only if necessary we may have to refer one or all of them to a mental health institution for specialist counselling. I hope that sounds helpful.'

'It certainly does,' said Raymond. 'Thank you.'

'These things can take time, remember. I presume they all have medical insurance?'

'I expect so,' said Raymond, 'but if there's a problem here are my credentials.' He produced a business card from his breast pocket. 'I can pay a substantial deposit now if you want.'

'That won't be necessary Mr...' Jan inspected the card, 'sorry, Sir Raymond.'

'Call me Raymond.' He smiled. 'I can be informal too you know.'

They all shook hands.

Raymond invited Guy back to his Hilton suite for supper, lamb chops and sauté potatoes on a bed of caramelised onions, accompanied by a red Rioja wine that helped them unwind. Guy explained why he had asked Jessica to attend Alex's speech at the IGSA Convention in New York.

'I now realise it was stupid, but I seriously believed she could gather information without getting into danger.'

'When Alex talked this evening about Jessica he said that she'd snooped, whatever that entailed,' said Raymond. 'She must have gone beyond what you asked her to do. I suppose you can't be blamed for that, but I still chide you for involving her in the first place.'

'You're right and I'm very sorry.'

'Put that aside, we'll soon learn from Jessica exactly what happened. She's alive and unharmed, more or less. That's all that matters.'

Towards the end of their meal Guy posed a question. 'Where do you stand?'

Raymond put down his knife and fork. 'In what way?'

'At the moment you have two standpoints, one as Chairman of Herron International that funds a genetic sequencing programme, the other as a private individual who's used company funds to bankroll a new editing system that'll make you a killing on the side.'

'I'm in business to make money. Always have been.' Raymond picked up his wine glass. 'When Alex first introduced me to Capsella I trusted him and his company to win the race to sequence the human genome. I still believe in the potential benefits of such a landmark scientific achievement. You must know what also drives me…'

'Dame Elizabeth?'

'Exactly. Her life was cut short by a disease that could well be eliminated by genetic science.' He took a sip of wine. 'When I became aware that the IBEC system could edit genes, I was excited. At last I could take revenge on Huntingdon's as well as make a killing as you say, at the same time.'

Guy nodded as if he understood. He had finished his meal and was lining up the cutlery on his plate.

'Then Alex told me of a client in the Middle East seriously interested in the IBEC product and prepared to pay a massive sum for it. The amount was mind-boggling, and would secure my and Jessica's future.'

'My question is more about where you stand now, Raymond.'

'I feel unbelievably guilty about the pain you've suffered. And about whatever was done to Jessica.' Raymond's voice was anguished. 'Iraq must never get hold of bio-weapons but it looks like they might unless you and I can stop this deal.'

Guy talked about a possible agenda for their meeting with Mr Samir the next day, and eventually they agreed which points to raise.

'I still don't get it,' said Raymond as the Eierschale waiter cleared away the breakfast things. 'If Alex wanted to tell the police you attacked him and his two henchmen he'd have done so by now. Assuming he daren't say more than he already has, why's he so confident he can escape his predicament?'

'I don't know. It sounded like he's got contingency measures to bail him out of his present situation.' Guy shuffled his chair a few inches further into the shade to protect his eyes from the rising sun's rays. The same waiter returned to wipe the table and then moved away. Guy reckoned they were out of hearing range, even so he lowered his voice. 'What I do know is, if any one of us squeals we'll bring down the whole house of cards. You and I won't squeak because we want to protect Jessica as well as ourselves. She won't say anything that incriminates you or me. And Alex won't utter a word against us in case we hang him out to dry.'

'It gives us a hold over him,' said Raymond.

'True, but he's demented beyond reason. Post-Traumatic Stress Disorder requires specialist treatment so let's hope Alex gets it in spades.'

'We'll have to broker a deal with him. God knows how.' Raymond looked at his watch. 'Let's think about that after we've talked to Mr Samir. He'll be here soon.'

He was mid-thirties and around five foot ten inches tall. With dark hair and brown eyes, a tanned face and a neatly trimmed moustache, he was very much the ladies' man from a traditional upbringing. His paternal grandfather had worked with the Indian Civil Service during which time he fell in love with a British woman, a social 'faux pas' in those days although not entirely unheard of. They had a daughter who married an Egyptian businessman called Hasani Samir, and Karim was the youngest of their four children. After he graduated in economics at Cairo University he worked for his father's electronics business as an export agent, and it was there that he started to build a network of lucrative government contacts in the Middle East. By the time he was thirty Karim had left his father's firm and set up his own import-export agency supplying electronic components to the defence industry. One of his clients was the government of Iraq and he was always on the lookout for new merchandise otherwise difficult to obtain, for which he charged the highest price. His masters in Baghdad facilitated smooth business transactions, providing him with military contacts and neutral venues for discreet meetings, thus he was introduced to the Russian Military Attaché in Berlin where he met Dr Alexander Grishin.

Karim Samir walked towards Raymond and Guy dressed in brown suede shoes, flannel trousers and a neatly pressed shirt with an open neck that exposed thick chest hair, carrying a small leather briefcase. Raymond later admitted that he initially thought it was Omar Sharif with whom he had once played bridge.

'You must be Sir Raymond and Scott?' Samir sounded on his guard.

Raymond and Guy stood up. 'That's us,' said Guy. 'Good morning Mr Samir. My name's Scott and this is Sir Raymond Herron.' Samir placed his briefcase on the ground and shook hands with them.

Guy offered him a chair. 'Can we get you some tea or coffee?'

'Coffee, thank you.'

'I'll do the honours,' said Raymond. He got up to find the waiter and ordered a fresh pot of coffee for three. When he returned a few minutes later Guy and Samir were talking about the attractions of life in Berlin.

'It's a wonderful centre for the arts,' said Samir, 'On my last trip here I went to a classical evening at the Philharmonie, it was magnificent. I'm also fond of architecture, the renovated Parliament Building never ceases to fascinate me.'

Raymond sat down and joined in the conversation. 'I know, the glass dome is splendid. I saw it floodlit on my way to the Hilton Hot…' The toe of Guy's shoe jabbed his shin under the table. 'Er, I mean, on my way to the place where I'm staying.' He switched to the main topic. 'Now, we have some business matters to discuss don't we, Guy?'

'Oh?' Samir's voice was sceptical, on his guard again. 'I thought your name was Scott.' He looked towards Guy and then back at Raymond. 'What's going on?'

'Scott is my surname,' said Guy as his shoe poked Raymond's other shin. 'I'm Guy Scott. Sorry for any misunderstanding.'

Samir looked dubious. 'Show me proof of identity.'

The charade was almost identical to the one they performed for the police officer at the Park-Klinik the previous evening. Raymond produced his business card and vouched for Guy who again fibbed that he had left his belongings back at the Gasthaus. Samir took Raymond's card and seemed reassured. He nodded and said, 'Dr Grishin spoke highly of your financial expertise, Sir Raymond. And I hear you were recently awarded your knighthood.'

'Call me Raymond, it's better to be informal don't you think?'

'No I don't,' said Samir with a straight face. 'Formality is a sign of professionalism and good manners, Sir Raymond.'

'Well, quite.' Raymond adopted a sombre tone. 'Mr Samir, may I see your proof of identity?'

Guy intervened. 'That won't be necessary.'

'Not necessary perhaps, but perfectly in order.' After Samir produced his business card he asked after Dr Grishin. Guy explained how Alex had accidentally fallen off a step and impaled one hand on the pointed end of a metal guard-rail. The wound had since gone sceptic and required further surgery.

'That's not what I've heard,' said Samir. 'Yesterday I read a local newspaper report about a fight when Dr Grishin was arrested.'

Raymond frowned and looked anxiously at Guy who said, 'Absolutely. There was a scuffle and that was when Dr Grishin fell onto the guard-rail.'

'I see.' There was a pause while Samir eyed the other two. 'Is he allowed to receive visitors?'

'No,' said Guy, 'that's why he's asked us to talk with you.'

'In that case how did you acquire the mobile phone you used to call me? Surely you took the phone from Dr Grishin in the hospital.'

'Ah, well, we were allowed to visit him just the once for business reasons, we got special permission from the police. A one-off.' Guy paused. 'Since then he's taken a backward step. The wound's gone sceptic and he's sedated part of the time.'

Samir's face remained expressionless. 'Which hospital is he in?'

'It's in the Pankow district,' said Guy.

'Whereabouts?'

'Near a lake,' said Guy.

'Which lake?'

Raymond cut in. 'The Weissensee.'

'What's the hospital called?'

'The Park-Klinik,' said Raymond.

'Of course. I remember now, it was in the newspaper.' Samir looked at Guy. 'Now, tell me about work in progress at Capsella-Biotech.'

'Dr Grishin wanted me to ask you for an update on the financial side of the deal.'

'Why? There's no change. Fifty per cent on delivery of the IBEC programme and the other fifty when Baghdad successfully applies the formula.' Samir looked at Raymond. 'I have the Swiss bank account numbers and the currency will be in US dollars, as agreed.'

Guy looked at Raymond who swallowed hard and said, 'Mr Samir, there may be a slight problem with the IBEC system.' Samir gave him another dark stare. 'You see, the team at Capsella-Biotech now think that the formula could be flawed. Some recent tests have shown inconsistencies that must be resolved before any clients buy the product.'

'Will it take long to resolve the inconsistencies?'

'That's what Dr Grishin wanted us to explain,' said Raymond, 'it would seem that it's a bit of an open book until further trials are carried out.'

'This is news to me. When did these issues arise?'

Guy coughed. 'The initial research was conducted on plants such as Capsella Rubella or Red Shepherd as we say in English. I presume you already understand the IBEC process? A molecule of bacteria is carried by an enzyme to faulty sections of DNA, where it acts like a cutting tool to edit the mutations.'

Samir nodded.

'However,' said Guy, 'the enzyme that carries the adapted bacteria fails to function in certain types of living organisms. Please don't ask me to explain the bio-chemistry because, believe me, I can't.'

'Nor me,' said Raymond.

'Dr Grishin wanted me bring you up to date with the situation.' Guy picked up the coffee pot and refilled Samir's and Raymond's cups leaving only a dribble for himself.

'My client's position is clear and always has been,' said Samir. He stirred his coffee. 'With no product there will be no down payment. Meanwhile Capsella-Biotech will continue to shoulder all development costs, obviously.'

Guy noticed the look of disappointment on Samir's face. Or perhaps it was fear. As a go-between Samir would have to convey this news to his clients. He would certainly be frustrated by delays to his own fee payment. Guy wondered what commission Samir charged the Iraqis. Ten per cent? Twenty?

Samir then dropped a bombshell. 'I understand that IBEC is patented. If that's true how can there be inconsistencies or flaws?'

'Dr Grishin is convinced that he is dealing with a minor technical flaw. It shouldn't take long to rectify,' said Guy.

Samir frowned and dropped a second bombshell. 'I will arrange to visit Dr Grishin myself,' he said.

'Don't do that,' said Guy testily, 'he really is very unwell and I doubt the police will allow you to see him.'

'I must try,' said Samir. 'If I'm to keep my client on side I need to provide technical explanations for any delay to the deal. I'm surprised you can't give me more details Mr Scott. You're supposed to be Dr Grishin's assistant.'

'Look, I've got your contact details,' said Guy, 'let me obtain a report from one of the scientists working at Capsella-Biotech and I'll forward it to you.'

'Don't bother. I'll ask Dr Grishin to arrange that when I next see him.' Samir pushed back his chair and stood. 'Thank you both for your time,' he said as they all shook hands, 'enjoy the rest of your stay at the Berlin Hilton, Sir Raymond.'

When they were alone Guy turned to Raymond. 'As soon as Karim Samir visits Alex he'll twig we told him a pack of lies.'

'We've got to stop Samir,' said Raymond. 'And fast.'
'How?'

Raymond looked thoughtful. 'I know,' he said, 'find a good reason to persuade Dr Baumann and the police to prevent further visits until Alex has undergone psychiatric assessment. Unless you can think of anything else.'

'No I can't, but I can think of another thing you should do. Move out of the Hilton. Samir knows you're staying there and I'm not sure how much I trust him. I'd be happier if you remained incognito like me. I could book you into my Gasthaus.'

'Okay,' said Raymond, 'what about Jessica? She thinks I'm at the Hilton…'

'She can stay at the Gasthaus too if there's room.'

Günter Blum was pleased to make two additional rooms available to Raymond and Jessica. The unoccupied bedrooms on the top floor had shared facilities only, so it was agreed that Raymond would have the room occupied until now by Guy who then moved up a floor. He was happy to use a communal washroom, and sure that Jessica would not mind either. While Guy returned to the Gasthaus to book the extra accommodation Raymond went back to the Hilton to pack his things and check out. In his suite he telephoned the Park-Klinik and spoke with Jan Baumann. It turned out to be straightforward once Raymond explained that Dr Grishin's work colleagues were eager to visit and discuss business. Jan agreed it best to block all future visits especially from the workplace, to relax the patient as much as possible. Raymond was told not to worry, Jan would make sure the police were given the appropriate instructions on medical grounds.

To kill time before Raymond arrived at the Gasthaus Guy ordered a beer and sat at an outside table in the centre of the forecourt. He wondered how Raymond had got on with his call to Jan Baumann. It also occurred to Guy that even if Mr Samir was unable to visit Alex, all he had to do was call Capsella-Biotech and ask to meet one of their technical staff and if so, nobody could prevent it. Given the venomous nature of the clients, hopefully only a few select members of Alex's staff were even aware of the IBEC product, and they would never discuss it without Alex's personal authority.

Guy took a sip of his beer. His pay-as-you-go buzzed with a text from David who now had Guy's new phone number. The message said: *Re: Grishin family. You won't believe what I've found. Call me ASAP. David.*

CHAPTER 31

When Raymond got out of his taxi at the Gasthaus, the first person he saw was Guy at an outside table with an empty beer glass on it. Shaded by a sun umbrella he was twiddling with his pay-as-you-go phone.

'Hello Guy. Good news from the Park-Klinik.' Raymond and the taxi driver walked across the forecourt. The driver dumped Raymond's luggage onto the ground and went back to his vehicle without a word. 'The police have been told on medical grounds Alex mustn't have visitors.'

Guy looked up and grinned. 'Brilliant. How did you get them to go along with that?'

'Simple. I asked Jan Baumann,' said Raymond. 'He agreed it best to keep the patient calm before the second operation on his hand, and before a psychiatrist starts on him.'

Guy pushed back his chair, stood up and put the new phone into his trouser pocket. 'Here, I'll help carry your things and collect your room key.'

'This is kind of you Guy.' They both stood in Guy's old room. 'I didn't expect you to move out on my account.'

'No worries. This room's more convenient, being on the first floor and having an en-suite,' said Guy. 'Okay if I take a bit of down time? My flatmate wants me to phone. He's found out something about Alex.'

After Guy closed the bedroom door Raymond unpacked. With everything in place he wondered where to put his suitcase and looked at the top of the wardrobe. Another suitcase was there. He assumed it was Guy's and shoved his own suitcase under the bed and as he did so he looked around and compared the sparse furniture with the opulence of his Hilton suite. At least here there was a desk and the room also had an internet modem socket.

He plugged in his laptop, logged on to his Herron International email and saw over twenty new messages. Eleven were from William Vinson who had copied him in on routine client correspondence. None required immediate action. Two emails were from Raymond's PA with diary requests for December and January so he clicked 'accept'. Another two came from unknown senders - probably spam, a downside of this awesome technology – which he deleted. The others were condolences from people yet to learn of Jessica's miraculous return. Raymond would reply later to avoid a volley of congratulations and requests for more information. Instead he went to his personal email account with its anonymous address known only to Ben and Jessica who had each sent him one message. Ben's confirmed he was definitely up for it next Tuesday if his services were still required. He had asked Raymond's housekeeper for the paperwork, and all he needed from his twin brother was the script.

Raymond opened Jessica's message, written after her second interview with Deputy Inspector Tolan Stevens who had asked her to attend a follow-up press conference:

'The media are lapping up your 'back from the dead' story,' Stevens had told her.

'I don't care. The answer's no,' said Jessica, 'they can write what they like for all I care.'

Stevens persevered. 'They just want to ask a few questions that's all. You never know, it may jog the memory of someone who can help our enquiries.'

'I want to leave New York and return to my relatives.'

'There's another thing,' said Stevens, 'reporters were hoping to capture the moment you reunite with your family.'

'Why the hell do you think I'm leaving this city as soon as I can?' Jessica was adamant. 'Forget the idea.'

Stevens shrugged. 'I suppose there's no law to make victims talk to the press.'

'I'm a victim now am I? I thought it was a loose piece of scaffolding that caused my injury.'

'You know damn well that's not true.'

Jessica said nothing.

'Why won't you make a full statement? You were assaulted…'

'I lost my memory. I've nothing more to say.' She gave Stevens a wan smile. 'Sorry.'

Stevens shook his head and sighed. 'Forensics say the back of your head must have been struck by a softer implement, a truncheon maybe.'

'Beats me. I don't remember.'

'The scaffolding never so much as touched you, Jessica.'

Raymond was interrupted by knocking. He turned and squinted at his bedroom door. 'Come in.'

Guy entered clutching his laptop. 'Look what my friend's found.' Guy walked over to the desk. 'I'd never have believed this for one single fucking instant,' he said and placed the laptop in front of Raymond. 'Christ. Read this. It's from David.'

'He's your flatmate, right?'

'Yep. A bloody good researcher too.'

It took Raymond several minutes to study David's explosive email while he murmured 'strewth' and 'crikey' in a low voice. When he had finished he looked up at Guy with astonishment in his eyes.

'This changes everything, Raymond.'

Dr Borlick had already given Jessica the all clear to leave hospital provided she felt up to it. The police could not pursue the case without fresh leads, there was no evidence to incriminate anyone and they could not justify holding Jessica in the US against her will. In hospital she had borrowed a laptop computer from a staff nurse and wrote to Raymond's private email address:

From: J. Parry
Sent: Thursday 04 October 2001 18:21
To: Pop_TroutLake
Subject: Capsella and me

Darling Pop,

At last a chance to drop you a line. Sorry for being evasive when we spoke but I'm under pressure on several fronts, when all I want is to be with you. And Guy.

Hope you got my flight arrival time - 08:30 Sun 7th Oct.

I'm sickened by what happened to me here in NY and dismayed that you might be remotely connected with any of it. My emotions are still wobbly but in the next day or so I'd like to get things off my chest and lessen the blame game when we get together in Berlin.

Hope it's okay if I send you a narrative shortly? Please understand I will not throw accusations at you or Guy, it's simply my side of the story. Looking back some of it was probably my fault anyway.

I'll be in touch again soon.

Feel free to show this and any of my messages to Guy if you want.

Fondest love,

J xx

From: Pop_TroutLake
Sent: Thursday 04 October 2001 22:11
To: J. Parry
Subject: RE: Capsella and me

My dearest Jessica,

Wonderful to hear from you but so very sorry for all you've been through. If it's easier to write down your own version of events, please do. I check my emails daily.

This whole saga has really got to me. To make things worse I've left my Seroxat pills at home. Dark Cloud is lurking. Let's agree not to play the blame game. Please.

Longing to see you again. Will be at Tegel airport on Sun. Guy will be there too - presume that's all right!

With much love,

Pop xx

Raymond received Jessica's narrative on Friday evening, sooner than expected. She began with stuff her step-father already knew, that Guy had persuaded her to attend the IGSA annual convention where Alex Grishin disclosed how Capsella-Biotech enhanced its own genetic sequencing with data mined from the Human Genome Project. She had also witnessed the audience's hostile reaction especially when Alex revealed Capsella's plans to obtain gene patents.

Later that day she had overhead a conversation between Alex and one of his colleagues, and a word sounding like 'anthrax' together with a reference to Alex's hotel room number - 1227. If something sinister was going on Jessica thought she should inform Guy. There was not much to go on except for one word she may have misheard, or heard out of context. However Jessica decided to forage for more evidence, and one word she had not misheard was Alex's room number.

Common sense told Jessica to stay within the law so the problem was how to ferret and not get caught. It did not take long to think of a solution that was simple if not entirely ethical.

The Roosevelt Hotel concierge rang Alex's room to say a journalist was in the lobby asking to interview him and could they show her up to his room. In mid conversation the receptionist put her hand over the mouthpiece and told Jessica that Dr Grishin said such requests should be made to the press officer at Capsella-Biotech.

'Tell him I've a deadline to meet with *The Independent* and I was fascinated by his presentation today.'

The woman spoke again to Alex. Again she placed her hand over the mouthpiece and said, 'Handouts were available after his speech. You can pick one up tomorrow morning.'

'I'm not here tomorrow. I've got other bus... I mean more interviews to do. Can I have an appointment with him? Please?'

The woman talked to Alex for a moment longer then put the receiver down. 'I'm sorry ma'am, Dr Grishin insists you liaise with his press officer.'

Bugger, she thought. The next day was tied up with final preparations for her fashion show. But then she had another idea. After thanking the woman at the concierge she took the lift up to the twelfth floor and walked past Alex's room in the vain hope of staging a 'chance' meeting by accidentally-on-purpose bumping into him. Jessica strolled backwards and forwards along the landing several times but Alex did not appear. She began to think she should take a chance and knock on his door when a cleaning trolley emerged from an adjacent room. Jessica turned away and pretended to adjust her hair at a mirror over one of the half-circular tables positioned at intervals along the landing when the chambermaid knocked on the door of room 1227. There was no answer. Jessica watched the woman produce a master key and wheel her trolley into Alex's room leaving the door wide open.

After a couple of minutes Jessica stole towards room 1227 and peered inside. There was a double bed which the chambermaid had already 'made down' for the night - a pointless luxury Jessica always thought - a desk by the window, two arm chairs and a large television screen. At the far left corner a door was open and the sound from within indicated the chambermaid was cleaning the en-suite. Jessica took a few steps into the room. She saw an assortment of paperwork on the desk and could not resist the urge to get closer. She crept towards the other side of the room from where she could see the chambermaid wiping the sink. Unfortunately the chambermaid saw Jessica's reflection in the mirror, stopped cleaning and turned round.

'It's, er… I'm Mrs Grishin,' Jessica stammered. The chambermaid looked puzzled, perhaps she did not speak much English. 'I shan't be a moment,' said Jessica and glanced at business cards on the desk. She took a card, held it up and said to the chambermaid, 'Found it!' She quickly left the room and took the lift down to the lobby where she made straight for the revolving door onto Madison Avenue.

Raymond took a break from reading Jessica's email. He made his way down to reception and out to the forecourt for some fresh air. He sat at the table with Guy's empty beer glass on it. Guy had made a proposal that unsettled him at first but the more he thought about it the more sense it made. David's discovery might also make it possible for Guy to see Alex again even though other visitors were barred. He sat thinking for a few more minutes until Guy joined him.

'You okay?'

'I'm reading Jessica's account of her time in New York but I don't think I can continue. It weighs heavily.'

'Raymond, it weighs on me too and I haven't even seen her message yet.'

'I'll forward it…'

'Fine, but read all of it first. Jessica wouldn't have sent it if she didn't want you to know what happened.' Guy paused. 'I've just spoken with Andreas Richter. He took some convincing, asking why we didn't tell him on our last visit that we were more than just friends of Dr Grishin.'

'Correction. It's you who's more than just a friend. I remain a business contact. Anyway what matters is how did Dr Richter react to your request?'

'Andreas said in the circumstances I could see the patient on my own, but only after the second operation on the hand and to keep my visit short. He will tell hospital staff and the police to exempt a 'Mr Guy Scott' from visitor restrictions.'

'That's good.'

'I also asked Andreas about progress with Alex's mental state, and the first psychiatrist's session will be after his operation.'

Guy stayed outdoors while Raymond got up from the table and went back to his room and his laptop. He overcame his instinct not to reopen Jessica's message and continued reading how, armed with Alex Grishin's contact details, Jessica had secured an evening appointment with Dr Grishin the day before Fashion Week. Capsella-Biotech's Press Officer, Emma Gough, had been surprisingly helpful.

'Sure you can interview him. Which newspaper did you say?'

'I'm researching a piece for *The Independent*.'

'British?'

'That's right.'

'What's your editorial line?' Emma asked.

'Our readers will be fascinated by the speed at which Capsella claims it can sequence the remainder of the Human Genome. I'd like to ask about that and your plans to patent certain genes.'

'You know there's been a press release?'

'I'd like to probe a little deeper,' said Jessica.

'Dr Grishin cannot provide any technical details, understand?'

'Of course. I'm interested in his views on the future impact of his ground breaking research.'

'Okay,' said Emma, 'you're in his diary for the evening of Thursday the sixth. Ten o'clock in the lobby of the Roosevelt. Do you know where that is?'

Early on Thursday morning on her way to Fashion Bound's final preparations for the fashion show, Jessica stopped at a booth with a machine that made instant business cards. She keyed in bogus text to pass herself off as a freelance reporter, pressed the 'print' button and in less than three minutes ten neatly formatted cards dropped down to the dispensing tray. Each one had the words *Jessica Parry* in bold font on the centre line and *Independent Journalist* underneath, while her home address and cell phone number appeared in plain font lower down. She picked up the cards and put them into her handbag and continued her journey.

That evening after Fashion Bound Ltd had rounded off a successful day of rehearsals Jessica went to the Roosevelt. She soon found Alex, sitting at the same table where he and the other man had held the dubious conversation she overheard two days before. She walked up and introduced herself.

'Dr Grishin? Hi, I'm Jessica Parry. I recognise you from the IGSA conference.'

He stood. They shook hands and Jessica handed over her fake business card. When Alex offered her a drink she asked for still water. He signalled a waiter.

'Take a seat,' said Alex. 'You're writing for *The Independent* I believe.'

'That's right,' said Jessica as she sat down.

'How can I help?'

Jessica said she was researching material on the Human Genome Project and was fascinated by Dr Grishin's presentation to the IGSA Convention. Her readers would be interested to know why Capsella-Biotech seemed to put commercial consideration before public interest by refusing to share its findings.

'You must have heard my answer to that question at the conference,' said Alex. 'Unlike the official Project we receive no public funding and we never signed the

1996 Accord.' The waiter arrived with Jessica's chilled water and black coffee for Alex.

'Don't you risk unnecessary duplication?' Jessica asked.

'Possibly but our approach is fundamentally different.'

'In what way, Dr Grishin?'

'Call me Alex.'

'Alex. How do the two approaches differ?'

'The public project ploughs its way through the entire Human Genome to cover absolutely every letter of DNA from beginning to end, including all the junk. Roughly three billion letters. The data is uploaded onto a website called *GenBank*.'

'Why can't Capsella be part of that process.'

'In a way we are,' said Alex, 'we can access *GenBank* data like everybody else. Capsella is acquiring the most powerful sequencing computers on the market to map DNA faster than the public project.'

'Another thing I don't understand. The first draft of the sequenced Human Genome has already been presented in public, like that news clip with Bill Clinton and Tony Blair. Yet there's still a need for more sequencing.'

'True. Quite a lot of junk DNA was excluded at the time of the announcement which highlights the difference between Capsella-Biotech and the public project.' Alex paused and Jessica gave him a fixed stare. 'The public project appeared as good as almost done but it still had swathes of DNA letters to complete. Our sequencing machines will work faster and my team will use the *GenBank* data to fill any of our gaps. It's a win-win.'

'Is junk DNA important?'

'Very. At first everyone thought it was unwanted garbage but scientists now believe it performs a number of vital functions, some yet to be identified.'

'Can I ask you about your firm's plans to patent certain genes? The proposal caused uproar at your presentation. Was this a commercial decision?'

'All our decisions are commercial. This is no exception. If we patent a relatively small number of genes it gives us market share.'

'Market share or a monopoly?'

Alex said nothing and glared at Jessica.

Jessica took a gulp of water and crossed her legs. 'Will it actually work? How can you patent a living organism? It's not as if a gene is a new invention is it?'

'We've already filed some gene patent applications. Let's wait and see.' Then Alex dropped a big clanger. 'We were delighted to get the IBEC patent…'

'The what?'

'Oh… it's a product that, um, makes changes to DNA…'

'Really? How interesting Alex, tell me more. What does IBEC mean?'

'It's commercially sensitive.'

'Not now you've got a patent number, anyone can look it up. At least tell me what IBEC stands for.'

'Identical Bacteria Enzyme Corrector.'

'You said it makes changes to DNA. How?' Jessica thought of the overheard conversation. 'Is it an editing tool?'

'You seem to know already.' Alex sounded suspicious. 'Yes. It's a product that edits DNA.'

'And who will you sell it to?'

'Client information is definitely sensitive,' he replied.

'I meant what kind of client. Companies? Institutions? Governments?'

Alex flinched. 'Look, I can't elaborate. You wanted to ask me about the impact of our project to sequence the Human Genome, can we stick to that?' He took a sip from his coffee cup.

'But it's all linked isn't it? Capsella-Biotech, a private company, aims to win the race to sequence the Human Genome and sell a product that edits it. Amazing. This will make a great article…'

'Steady on,' Alex looked worried. 'What conclusions will you draw?'

'You may have guessed I'll trash the notion that Capsella can patent a few genes.'

'Nyet! That's unreasonable!' Alex dumped his coffee cup down on the saucer. The cup handle broke off. 'You don't know if it's possible or not.'

'No, but I can guess. I could also guess the kind of client who'll buy IBEC.'

Alex put the broken cup handle to one side and spoke in a monotone that reinforced his Russian accent,

'Instead of offering opinions why can't you fucking journalists base your articles on facts for a change?'

'I'd be delighted. But I need to know more about how IBEC works if you want a fair hearing.'

'I'll show it to you. Emma Gough will give you a call. How much time do you have left here in the States?'

Raymond folded down the screen of his laptop. He had a strong intuition about the direction of Jessica's story. Worst of all, it was Guy who had set her up. She went to New York to organise a fashion show, not chase news stories from traumatised molecular biologists. Yet by doing Guy a favour she must have got carried away after picking up snippets of information.

Guy knocked on Raymond's door and opened it. He poked his head round. 'Sorry to butt in,' he said, 'I left my suitcase here, can I grab it?'

Raymond nodded. Guy walked over to the wardrobe and was about to reach up for his case when Raymond asked him if there was any more information from David.

'No. In any case he's already done enough to get me into a tizzy.'

'Keep your composure Guy. We could use David's discovery to our advantage if we're to sort out this mess.'

'How would you feel in my position?'

'It's impossible to undo the past, I've had to learn the same lesson.'

'Fair enough, but it feels like I've been set up…'

'*SET UP?*' Raymond raised his voice. 'Look who's talking!'

Guy went red. 'Christ Raymond, I'd no idea Jessica would come to any harm. Lay off will you?'

Raymond looked uneasy and raised his hands in submission. 'Take your suitcase and clear off,' he said, 'while I force myself to read the rest of Jessica's story.'

'Please yourself,' said Guy. He reached up and snatched at his suitcase. He lost his grasp and it slid off the top of the wardrobe onto the floor. The lid sprung open and Raymond turned in surprise at the metallic thump as the gun dropped out.

'What the hell's that?' said Raymond.

'What's it look like, someone's toothbrush?'

'I meant where the hell did it come from and what was it doing in your suitcase?' said Raymond.

'It belongs to Alex and his two Afghantsi friends. They tried to shoot me. I tried to shoot Alex but the safety catch was on.' Guy picked up the gun with one hand and held it with his forefinger on the trigger guard and the barrel pointed down. 'I've never fired the bloody thing but I sure as hell didn't want to leave it with those demented bastards.'

'But it's against the law to possess…'

'SHUT UP! I won't take lectures from you about staying within the law,' said Guy as he placed the gun on top of a chest of drawers. 'You can keep the fucking thing.' He stomped out of the room carrying his suitcase.

Raymond sat and stared at the gun for a considerable length of time.

It took Raymond a while to return to Jessica's narrative, like a reluctant schoolboy tackling his homework. He was saddened by that last exchange with Guy who was obviously stunned by the information from David. It stunned Raymond too. In his depressed state he felt there was something pre-ordained about Alex's gun, so he placed it out of sight in the bottom of the chest of drawers. Eventually he summoned the will-power to return to his step-daughter's email where she wrote that her second meeting with Alex Grishin was set for Monday the tenth of September. By then Fashion Bound Ltd had packed up after its successful show at Fashion Week, but Jessica had stayed on for her sponsorship meeting scheduled for the following evening with Maynard Baker Securities.

At nine o'clock that Monday morning Jessica handed in her key card at the Carlyle Hotel, and as arranged walked over to a small coffee table furthest from the concierge. It was an area out of view of CCTV cameras, which explained Raymond's query about what she had done in the thirty minutes between moving away from the registration desk and leaving the main entrance at nine-thirty. Jessica described how she was greeted by one of Alex's colleagues whose voice she immediately recognised as the person who had spoken with Alex on the other side of the pillar in the lobby of the Roosevelt. He must have been in his late thirties and wore a linen jacket over an open-necked blue cotton shirt. He eyed up Jessica for a few seconds then introduced himself as Rob Butler, head of research for the IBEC project and appointed by Alex to escort her to Capsella's premises. After they exchanged business cards he told Jessica there was no need for her to bring anything, and she joked that all she had was a notebook and pen.

Outside the Carlyle Hotel they walked along Madison Avenue past a building fronted with scaffolding to a company car that would take them to Capsella's laboratory in Broad Street, Newark. Forty minutes later they arrived at a copper glazed tower block overlooking Newark Military Park. They entered the lab and were greeted by Alex who invited them to sit in front of a TV monitor. Rob explained to Jessica that to save time, instead of a live demonstration of the IBEC system he would play an edited recording of an experiment that used a mutated version of a plant called *Capsella Rubella* filmed through an electron microscope. Jessica had no idea that she was about to watch a video of the actual demo seen by Raymond a while back. The monitor screen flickered for a few seconds as Rob began to talk Jessica through the process. She looked at the images while he explained how a pre-programmed molecule of bacteria was carried by an enzyme to the target sequence of the plant's DNA. It then cut in to both strands of the double helix, deleted the defective DNA and allowed corrected versions to be inserted.

'What do you think?' said Alex when the video ended.

'It's amazing,' said Jessica. 'How did you hit on the idea?'

'Several years ago I asked Rob Butler and his team to research ways to improve gene therapy, to make the outcomes more certain. It grew from there.' Alex looked at Rob who nodded and smiled.

'Team work at its best,' Rob said modestly.

Alex turned towards Jessica and invited her to join him for coffee and ask any other questions. Rob excused himself, he had another meeting, so he shook hands with Jessica and thanked her for her interest and said he looked forward to reading her article. When they entered Alex's office Jessica took in the view through the window. The *Wars of America* bronze sculpture stood proudly in the park below, while a grimy Baptist chapel did little to enrich the setting. They sipped their coffee with Alex seated behind his desk and Jessica on a chair opposite with the notebook on her lap. She began by asking him where he thought the IBEC editing tool would lead – an open-ended question. Alex replied that the ultimate goal was the elimination of all diseases with genetic traits that pass down generations, animals as well as humans.

'And plants,' Jessica reminded him.

'Yes, plants,' said Alex. 'You know, after tests on plants we applied the IBEC process to mice, we're confident that one day it will be used on humans after clinical trials.'

'Wow.'

'Wow indeed, Ms Parry.' The tone of Alex's voice changed. 'There's something else that wows me, too.'

'What's that?' Jessica noticed Alex lower his right arm and lean slightly to one side as if to press something under his desk.

'You're a fucking fraud.'

Jessica stiffened. 'What?'

'What kind of set up do you think I run here? You must reckon we're a bunch of second rate amateurs.'

'I don't know what…'

'Don't give me that shit!' Alex stood up. 'You might think my Press Officer is a sucker but I assure you Emma Gough knows her stuff.'

'I asked her for this appointment and…'

'Yes, and Emma checked you out. Writing an article for The Independent? My arse. One call to that newspaper confirmed they've never heard of you.'

Jessica turned deathly pale. 'I'm a freelancer, The Independent is a prospective client, I…'

'Anyone can say they intend to write for a publication. That's not the same as being commissioned to produce an article.' She did not reply. 'Ever heard of search engines?' Alex leaned forward and placed both hands on the desk. He looked straight into Jessica's eyes. 'There's a certain Jessica Parry who heads up a London company called Fashion Bound Limited. A coincidence? It didn't take much for Emma to learn that the cell phone number you gave her matches the contact number of the Director of Fashion Bound.'

The office door opened and a brute of a man entered, dressed in the uniform of a security guard. Jessica's hands began to shake.

'Your other slip-up was to have no email address on your business card. It's something journalists usually provide, but you didn't.' He paused to look up at the guard then returned his gaze to Jessica who started to cry. 'I'll give you one chance, and one chance only, to tell me what you're up to before I and my friend fly off the handle.' He stood straight and folded his arms. 'We've got very short tempers.'

Jessica trembled. She dropped her notebook on the floor as one shaky hand took a handkerchief from a pocket to dab her eyes. 'I… I… was concerned about a certain remark…'

'What remark?'

'It was after your conference presentation. I happened to be in the Roosevelt Hotel when I overheard you talking with Rob Butler. One of you said something about anthrax…'

'Did we? What possible interest could you have in that?' For a second time that morning she did not reply. 'Speak up young lady. As I said, you only have one chance.' The guard took a couple of steps in her direction. She shuddered while Alex continued, 'And why attend my presentation when you're supposed to be a fashion show producer? Answer me!'

Jessica could not keep the tears back. She drew in a deep breath and looked at her feet. 'I've been interested in genetics ever since my mother died of a terrible illness that passes down the family. I've read about the Human Genome Project and I'd also heard about the work of Capsella-Biotech. When I learned you would speak at the

IGSA Convention while I was in New York I decided to attend.' She wiped the tears from her cheeks and looked up at Alex. 'By chance I overheard you and Rob Butler talking in the hotel lobby, like you had discovered something, possibly the misuse of genetic science. I wanted to find out more.'

'Had you got away with your ruse and found out more, what would you have done?' Alex's tone signalled his surprise at the naïvety of her confession.

'I… well… who knows, I might even have written an article for…'

'Bollocks. You're an intelligent woman, people don't gather information without a serious reason.' He waited for her to speak. She looked at him but said nothing. 'Who are you working for?'

'Nobody!'

'I don't believe you.' He looked at the guard and said, 'Hold her below decks. You know where I mean.' He turned his back on Jessica and paced towards the window. The guard took one of Jessica's arms and pulled her from her chair. He rummaged through her pockets and took out her cell phone and a Cath Kidston wallet.

'Christ! Who the hell do you think you are?!' she yelled as she was dragged towards a side door designated as a fire escape. 'You can't do this to me!'

Dark Cloud descended. On the verge of tears Raymond had read enough of Jessica's narrative. He forwarded her email to Guy with a brief covering message: *Here it is. I can't read any more. Over to you.*

CHAPTER 32

Guy rose early on Saturday. He went for a jog, slower than usual and with a slight limp but comfortable enough thanks to the chest bandage. Normally he alternated between a steady pace and the occasional two hundred meter sprint, a sequence that helped him to shake off stress and clear his mind. Today he avoided the sprints, kept to a gentle stride and covered about eight kilometres. He started out feeling more disgusted than stressed by David's disclosures, but the exercise helped.

Back at the Gasthaus out of breath and caked in sweat he stripped, gingerly removed the chest bandage and wrapped a towel round his waist. His ribcage ached. In the men's, as instructed he gave himself a stand-up wash at a basin. If someone walked in while he was admiring his reflection in the mirror that was their problem, but in the event Guy was not disturbed. Back in his room he put on a clean chest bandage before slipping on a t-shirt and shorts. When he re-read David's revealing email he noticed a new message in his inbox with the subject: *FW: Capsella and me*. It was Jessica's personal story forwarded by Raymond. Guy scrolled down her message and was surprised by its length, she must have wanted to set things straight before reuniting with her step-father. It would take a while to read and he dithered, he had other priorities.

First, to prevent the Iraq deal it was vital to stop Samir. To find out if Samir had tried to bluff his way to contact Alex, Guy could call the hospital or ask the duty police officer who recorded visitor's names at the door to Alex's isolation room. Second, he must confront Alex with the astonishing genealogical material from David. Third, he thought of the value to science if Capsella-Biotech would share its technology and genomic data with the Human Genome Project - in other words join forces. The big question was how to achieve it.

With Alex due for surgery that afternoon Guy decided to ask the Park-Klinik for an appointment. He phoned the hospital, reminded them he was exempt from the visitor ban and arranged to see Dr Grishin at eleven o'clock on Monday the eighth. Given Guy's particular connection with Dr Grishin the hospital staff also revealed that a businessman called Karim Samir had indeed asked to visit the patient, but the request was turned down.

Data-sharing would require Raymond's full cooperation. When both men sat down to breakfast later that morning Guy asked how he had slept. Raymond said that he neglected to bring some pills with him, it had been a fitful night and he was glad when morning finally came. He seemed to have forgotten about the gun in his room; at least he did not mention it.

'You look ill Raymond, what's the matter?'

'I feel like a dark cloud, gloom everywhere...'

'Cheer up, we're seeing Jessica tomorrow,' said Guy. 'That's positive, surely?'

'Never forget, you and I are involved in something that's hurt her.'

'She's good natured. She'll forgive…'

'Have you read her email?'

'Not yet.'

Raymond looked dejected. 'I'm ashamed, Guy…'

'You must shine a light through that gloom, for Jessica's sake.'

'It's uphill work. I'll try.'

'Good man,' said Guy. 'Look, I've been in touch with the Park-Klinik, they told me Karim Samir tried to visit Alex. They refused his request which means your ploy worked, well done.'

'Glad I've been of some use.'

'I visit Alex on Monday. You can guess what I'll talk about, it'll be a complete surprise to him.'

'As it was to you,' said Raymond.

Guy excused himself and went upstairs to Jessica's email.

Back in his room Guy read how Jessica overheard 'anthrax' at the Roosevelt Hotel; and how she posed as a journalist to arrange a meeting; Alex's reaction when Jessica trashed the notion of gene patents; his gaffe about the patent for IBEC and his suspicion when Jessica hinted she had heard of it; her grasp of the obvious risks if Capsella controlled the Human Genome and owned a system that edits it. Guy was riveted by Jessica's description of the IBEC video, but his t-shirt became damp with sweat when he read how Alex accused her of fraud and had her removed. No wonder the narrative had upset Raymond.

'Time for a break,' Guy murmured as he closed the laptop screen. He turned and looked out at the constant drizzle that spattered against the window pane. The view was uninviting and he was glad he had jogged earlier when it was dry. He leaned back to stare up at the ceiling, hands clasped behind his head. Raymond's loss of self-esteem puzzled Guy who could not work out whether it was shame or something that lurked deeper. He recalled Raymond's remark at breakfast about forgetting some pills - sleeping tablets or a stronger substance?

Over the next few minutes it really struck home: in less than twenty-four hours Guy would actually see Jessica. The pleasing thought that she was booked in to the next-door room reminded him to take his daily medication and apply the steroid lotion lower down, before he returned to her story:

The door slammed and a key turned. She was alone. For a while Jessica paced up and down and her footsteps sounded off the walls to convey a hurried sort of nervousness. She was not used to this kind of treatment and there was a side to her hosts that made her skin crawl. She juddered at the thought of them and at her own foolish lack of caution, but as soon as the alarm is raised surely it would just be a matter of time before she is found?

Over an hour had passed when the thug who confiscated her mobile phone and incarcerated her came back into the room carrying a bowl of cereals and a spoon. The man neither spoke nor looked at her as he placed the bowl on a table, turned and left. There was another distinctive click as the door was locked once more from the other side.

Abandoned again, she perched on the edge of the table and eyed the cereals. Bloody cornflakes. She had no appetite but sheer boredom prompted her to eat a solitary spoonful; she left the rest to go soggy in the milk.

She knew that these people were way ahead in their quest. They held the key to vital information that would be sought by thousands of organisations and perhaps millions of individuals. They could hold the global community to ransom like a new brand of medical fascism. The final solution.

'They haven't any right to do this, and they know it,' she thought. 'Why else have they incarcerated me here?'

By the time he finished Jessica's chronicle Guy was puzzled yet reassured by her civilised treatment in captivity. She was vague about the final days before her release, no doubt as a result of memory loss; perhaps he could talk to her about that when they were together again.

Her flight was thirty minutes late when it landed at Tegel Airport. Raymond spent the time drinking coffee and listening to jabbered flight announcements while Guy looked around a souvenir stall. They now peered anxiously over the heads of passengers towing their luggage out of the arrivals gate.

'Where is she?' said Raymond, 'I hope she caught the flight…'

'It's all right,' said Guy who did not look at Raymond but gazed at the multitude, 'she'll be here. I promise.' Then he spotted her and pointed at the queue. 'There she is!'

'Where? I can't see her.'

'Over there,' said Guy, 'behind that tall girl in the red blouse.'

The two men waved and she waved back. Moments later they embraced.

'It looks like another war has started.' Guy pointed at a television screen fixed to a wall. They were in the Kaffee Salon on Unter den Linden that Raymond had visited the other day. *Operation Enduring Freedom*, the US invasion of Afghanistan had launched that morning with an air assault and covert operations on the ground.

'Dear God, why?' said Raymond.

'To topple the Taliban,' said Jessica.

'Getting rid of the Taliban is one thing,' said Guy. 'It could leave a dangerous power vacuum.'

'I'm sure the US has a post-war reconstruction plan,' said Raymond.

'Oh?' said Guy. 'I reserve judgement…'

'Come on!' Jessica tried to be jocular. 'This is a celebration brunch…'

'Quite right!' said Raymond who sounded happier.

'This is a great way to chill,' said Jessica. They were seated at a circular table and tucking in to a buffet of fruit, meats, cheeses, fresh bread and coffee.

'Did Alex's mob feed you all right?' asked Guy.

'Not too bad, but I got sick to death of cornflakes,' Jessica replied.

The two men exchanged puzzled glances.

'Don't worry,' she said, 'I'll tell you about it later...'

'We've already read your email,' said Raymond.

'Most of your email,' said Guy. Jessica looked from one to the other.

'Well, yes. Most of it.' Raymond reached for a slice of Parma ham.

'I hope you didn't mind,' Jessica's eyes started to water. 'I wanted to give you my story then let you pose the questions.' She wiped her eyes with a handkerchief but managed a smile. 'Even if they're only about the frigging cornflakes.'

Polizei Kommissar Stefan Borchardt was assigned to handle the case. Put another way he demanded to handle it and nobody queried his motives. He was an experienced officer credited with numerous murder and assault investigations, and the fight between the three Russians at Grishin Informatik GmbH seemed just another criminal incident. His initial report did not speculate why the Chief Executive and two bodyguards had lashed out at each other, but concentrated instead on the facts. Speculation was a perk indulged by the media, not the Polizei.

Borchardt was mulling over information from Alex as he walked out of the isolation room and shut the door behind him. The officer on guard duty stood up, but

Borchardt gestured he should sit down again and paced along the disinfected corridor towards the secure double doors. It had been a very profitable meeting with Alex who was now calmer. The next task was to prepare a convincing interim case report for his superiors. He reached the end of the corridor and was about to press the button on the wall to unlock the door when through the glass he saw a blonde man, probably in his early thirties and wearing a blue open neck polo shirt, about to ring the buzzer. Borchardt turned to the officer on guard outside Alex's room who signalled it was all right to let the man in.

'Guten tag,' said Borchardt who noticed that the man clasped a single sheet of paper in one hand.

'Gooten targ,' said the man in a pitiful accent.

'Report to the officer on duty by that table.' Borchardt spoke English with cold authority.

'Thank you.'

Borchardt noted the power-house physique of this good-looking visitor, but he was puzzled by the slight limp. Perhaps the man was a gymnast with some kind of training injury.

Guy's first impression of Borchardt was of someone in his fifties, tall and heavy, going bald with puffy cheeks and a muzzle nose. Unattractive and unfit maybe, but from their brief exchange he was a person with clout. Guy made his way towards the small table and gave his details and the contents of his pockets to the duty officer. He asked about the man with the raincoat and was told he was a senior police officer who had just interviewed Dr Grishin.

He entered the isolation room with an intimidating expression on his face; it was hard to acknowledge a lineage he would have preferred to disown.

'Does the name *Eberstadt* mean anything to you?' said Guy. He leaned against the window sill with one hand in his trouser pocket while the other clasped the sheet of foolscap. He stared straight at Alex who was sitting up in bed.

'Should it mean anything?' It turned out that Alex's second operation the previous day only required local anaesthetic and the procedure was a success. The cleansing of the infection and the painkillers must have put him into an agreeable frame of mind, or so Guy thought, unless something else had lifted Alex's mood.

'I meant do you recognise the name?'

'Of course.'

'In that case you should read this.' Guy walked over to the bed and placed the paper in Alex's good hand. He went back to the window and leaned against the sill, conscious that he was no longer bothered how the invalid might react to the news.

Alex gave Guy a wary look before he turned his attention to the sheet of paper and started to read. After several minutes the studious look on his face turned to bafflement and then bleak mirth.

'Welcome to the fold, cousin. Who gave you this?'

'David Bond, a friend. He researched it on *MyPedigree*, a family history website.'

'Never heard of it. How do you know this information is accurate?'

'It's accurate all right,' said Guy. 'You'll be surprised how many subscribers upload all kinds of information including distant family and acquaintances. From there it wasn't difficult for David to cross-reference and join up dots. He's also applied to public records for the relevant certificates. There's no doubt at all.' He paused. 'Cousin.'

David had unearthed information about two sisters who spent their formative years in Berlin during the early twentieth century. Miriam and Adina Eberstadt, three years apart in age, grew up in a house in Podbielski Allee, a smart suburb of the German capital. Both girls had emigrated after marriage. Miriam became Frau Schäfer and moved to Britain with her husband Carl and their son in the nineteen thirties. Later known as Miriam Shepherd she was Guy's great-grandmother. Adina on the other hand lay low in Berlin and outlived her parents to survive the war. Penniless, she did menial jobs until 1950 when she took an administrative role in a government department of the newly formed Deutsche Demokratische Republik. There she met and fell in love with a Soviet liaison official, Mikhail Grishin, who worked for the army of occupation. They married and subsequently moved to Leningrad where Soviet citizenship was granted to Adina. A year later she gave birth to a son, Alexander Mikhail Grishin.

'What does this make us?' said Alex. 'Second cousins?'

'First cousins twice removed.'

Several seconds passed until Alex started to chuckle.

Guy was thrown by Alex's manner. Perhaps it was relief following the second operation on his hand that made Alex behave like someone in a gloomy tunnel who finds a distant light. Perhaps the flare-up of his Post-Traumatic Stress Disorder, for which Guy blamed himself, had gone into remission. On the phone the previous evening Guy and Jessica had discussed this possibility given her lenient treatment in captivity, and they assumed there must be a 'flip-side' to PTSD. If it was possible for Alex to alternate between nasty and cool, for now at least he seemed less troubled, quite animated and he livened up the more he talked. Guy wondered if Alex already knew that Jan Baumann's psychiatric team planned to give him counselling while under hospital arrest.

As the only sons of deceased parents and no siblings, Guy and Alex did not have much to say about their immediate families. The one exception concerned Miriam Shepherd who always regretted that after emigrating she never saw her sister again.

'I expect many other families had similar experiences in those days,' said Guy.

'Some a lot worse,' said Alex, 'entire families that ended up in death camps.'

That remark made Guy think of Josef Mengele, the doctor of Auschwitz and one of the masterminds of Nazi genocide, whose medical experiments on twins were sometimes linked to the eugenics movement.

'I need to ask you two things,' said Guy.

Alex gave an uncharacteristic smile. 'Don't tell me. You want an apology.'

'That would be nice, but not what I have in mind.'

'It wasn't on my mind either and you're not going to get one,' said Alex.

Guy walked across the room and sat on the edge of the bed. He stared straight at Alex. 'Actually the things I must ask are more important than an apology.'

Polizei Kommissar Stefan Borchardt sat in his grey Audi saloon parked in a layby near woodland in the Berlin borough of Spandau. He took out his cell phone and dialled a Zurich number.

'Jacob Bank, guten Tag.'

'Can you put me through to Herr Galler?'

'Ihr Name?'

'Code word *Spandau*.'

'Moment, bitte.'

Music came from the bank's switchboard then a man's voice said, 'Galler speaking. Please give me your second code word.'

'*Zitadelle*.'

'And the first and third digits of your ID number, please.'

'Two. Eight.'

'Thank you, Herr Borchardt. What can I do for you?'

'What is the current value of my numbered account?'

'Wait please...' Galler tapped his computer keyboard. 'Nine hundred and eighty-one thousand, seven hundred and six Swiss francs.'

'What's that in US dollars?'

'One moment... six hundred and ten thousand, three hundred and sixty-two dollars. Do you want the break-down?'

'Okay,' said Borchardt.

'In dollars it's one hundred and eight thousand in government bonds, sixty-six in cash and the rest is allocated to your portfolio of Canadian stock.'

'Good. Now listen. In the next few days a large deposit will be paid into my account.'

'How much and in what currency?'

'Two million US dollars.'

'Where will these funds come from?'

'A client of yours who should have sent instructions by now.'

'If they have, I can't say so over the phone.'

'I'm reassured to hear that,' said Borchardt.

'How do you want your funds invested?' said Galler.

'I don't. I need cash.'

'We could put your money into currency deposits or low-risk bonds if you like.'

'Not now,' said Borchardt. 'Later perhaps.'

'As you wish. What code word shall I use to notify the arrival of your funds?'

'Um... Capsella.'

'Capsella? Thank you Herr Borchardt.'

Borchardt ended the call and remained still in the car seat for several minutes. Two million was a lot of money but there were people whose silence he needed to buy. The transactions were always done in cash in hotel rooms about town. His training years ago taught him how criminals avoid a trail: always liaise at random times, always take different routes and always bring the booty in varying designs of briefcase. One other lesson – never threaten the collaborator's career but do threaten what could happen to their family – one squeak out of line was all it would take.

It worked every time.

Guy walked up to the hospital bed to take back the print-out. He was about to put his first request to Alex when he noticed something partly concealed under the pillow that looked like a cell phone. He frowned and whisked the sheet of paper from Alex's hand.

'You're in particularly good form today,' said Guy as he returned to the window sill. 'When do you expect to be discharged from here?'

'I take it that's not one of your important requests,' said Alex. 'I have a psychiatrist's consultation in the next day or so,' said Alex. 'They'll discharge me afterwards I suppose.'

'You're under arrest. When you leave here you'll go to a police cell.'

To Guy's surprise Alex howled with laughter.

'I'm glad you think it's so funny,' said Guy. He suddenly recalled something Alex had said on the previous visit: *I know exactly how to extricate myself from here. It's one of several lines of defence that I've set up over the years.* While Guy contemplated what this meant he turned his attention to the black shape just visible under the pillow. He asked himself why anyone under arrest would risk being found in possession of a phone on the day of a police interview. If that man Borchardt had seen the device surely Alex would now face a further charge. Unless…

'For fuck's sake what did you want to ask, cousin?'

'I'm asking this with Raymond's support. And Jessica's.'

'She's of no consequence,' said Alex.

'Not now perhaps, but she soon will be. She's flying back to New York to spill the beans. Publicly.'

Alex did not flinch. 'She only knows what I'd already announced in my IGSA speech and that'll be published in specialist journals.'

Guy folded his arms. 'That's not the point. It's what she will do in the US that really matters. Which brings me to my requests. We want you to cancel the Iraq contract and merge Capsella's sequencing operation with the Human Genome Project.'

'They're demands, not requests.'

The two men remained silent for a while. Guy walked to the end of the bed, placed his hands on the foot board and leaned forward. 'Look,' he said, 'I know you'll lose a phenomenal sum of money if you let the Iraq deal go, but as I speak Raymond is meeting Karim Samir. I think he'll win over Karim, and you three have one thing in common – your reputations. Put aside the criminal charges you face and think of the contribution to science if Capsella-Biotech's sequencing system could enhance the public Human Genome Project. Doesn't that strike any chord? When we first met you talked about job security for your employees as if they were extended family.'

Alex looked strangely self-assured for someone who faced jail. 'You make it sound so simple, cousin,' he said calmly.

'You're in a real jam,' said Guy. 'Frankly I don't give a toss about our family links which is just one of those coincidences you'd never get away with if you wrote it in a book…'

'I'm not writing a book.' said Alex. 'In case you haven't noticed I've got a lot of other work to do.'

'That's my point,' said Guy, 'where you're going you'll have all the time in the world to write as many books as you want.'

Once again Alex roared with laughter.

'Am I missing something Alex? Why is jail such a joke? My best mate will tell you there's nothing to snigger about in a cold prison cell…'

'Ahah! Would this be your friend Bond by any chance?'

'Oh shit,' Guy looked at the floor and scratched his head. 'Look Alex, I promised David I would never breathe a word to anyone so you better keep your bloody mouth shut. Okay?'

Another roar of laughter.

'You know what,' said Guy, 'you're an arrogant bastard just like my father and I hate your fucking guts!' He made straight for the pillow and grabbed the partly concealed object. 'And what's this cell phone doing under your pillow?'

Alex grinned. The duty officer opened the door and entered the room, stared first at Guy who was holding up the phone and then looked at Alex who continued to grin. For about fifteen seconds the three of them remained motionless like waxworks on display until to Guy's astonishment the officer said nothing, turned round and walked out shutting the door as he left.

'Now who do you think is really in charge here?' said Alex.

Stefan Borchardt started the engine and turned his Audi round. He drove back to his office where he hung up his raincoat and settled down to draft his interim report on what was now known as the Westfälische Strasse case. Although he had no idea how many case reports he must have filed in his career, he was often surprised by the number of times every-day phrases or sentences could be repeated for different situations. However, this report was unlike the others and it required original wording to make it stick.

'Bringen Sie mir einen Kaffee,' he called to an assistant in an adjacent office. He had to establish that Dr Grishin and his two employees had no case to answer and he reckoned with a degree of inventiveness he could drop all charges and maybe shift the blame onto a third party. It was worth all that money to get it right, and who knows, Alex Grishin may even have been telling him the truth.

'Ich bestellte Kaffee!' *I ordered coffee!* As Borchardt shouted the door swung open. A minion brought in a mug of steaming black coffee and placed it on his desk. 'Danke,' said Borchardt. With a wave of one hand he dismissed the junior and set to work.

He finished the report that evening. He wrote that Dr Grishin and his two colleagues were attacked by an intruder who apparently gained entry to Grishin Informatik posing as a genuine visitor. The fact that the incident occurred over a week-end did not undermine this hypothesis - business people often worked during high days and holidays. The report stated that investigations would concentrate on forensic evidence gathered at the scene, and the police were anxious to interview British businessman Guy Shepherd on suspicion of three attempted murders. Borchardt glossed over the withholding of vital information by the victims on grounds of their traumatic experience. With two million US dollars in the pipeline there would definitely be no prosecutions on that score.

The Kaffee Salon on Unter den Linden had become Raymond's preferred watering hole. The weather was mild enough to sit with Samir outside at one of the small tables sectioned off from the rest of the pavement. Samir seemed more at ease, maybe because this was his second meeting with the Chairman of Herron International.

Raymond was sure that this Egyptian intermediary would have checked him out since they last met at the Eierschale Restaurant-Bar.

Raymond had arranged the meeting to discuss tactics and a fresh proposal, an invitation that was readily accepted as he had hoped. He assumed his offer sounded strategic if nothing else and Samir was about to find out what was involved.

'What do you think of *Operation Enduring Freedom* in Afghanistan?' asked Raymond. He raised his voice above the traffic noise. 'Were you surprised by the news?'

'I was. But I don't think it will stop there.'

'How do you mean?'

'President Bush suspects that Iraq might supply Al-Qaeda with weapons of mass destruction. In 1991 George Bush Senior gave Iraq a bloody nose but his son might order a more decisive invasion.'

'Fight against Iraq? Again? I hardly think so,' said Raymond.

'Do you seriously believe the US won't act after what's happened in New York? As long as Bush believes that Iraq supported the hijackers who slammed aircraft into the World Trade Center and the Pentagon, he will want Saddam's blood.'

'So where does this leave you, Mr Samir?'

They talked for a further hour. Although Raymond's latest proposal wrecked his own chances to make a fortune the meeting went better than he dared imagine. He was uncomfortable about the sheer scale of his forfeited profit but at least it would not be an actual loss. By contrast Samir would make less money than planned, but better than no gain at all. It was an attractive proposal and Samir was savvy enough to understand how it could open new channels for his growing business. In fact Raymond's offer was first thought up by Guy who believed it could also enhance Karim Samir's reputation – a useful step for any ambitious entrepreneur.

It had been Jessica's decision to fly back to New York that Monday. As her plane taxied to the end of the runway at Tegel airport she looked at her wrist watch. The local time was seven in the evening, one hour ahead of London where the professional actor only had fourteen hours to go before he would walk on stage.

CHAPTER 33

He got his first glimpse of the Queen from the doorway of Buckingham Palace Ballroom. It felt like waiting in the wings to make his début.

'I'm really quite nervous,' he said to a steward.

'It's quite normal,' she replied with a gentle smile, 'everyone else is, don't worry.'

At the steward's signal he entered stage left along a crimson carpet bordered with gold strips that resembled, he thought, yellow no-parking lines. He halted just short of the dais, beside a Gentleman Usher to the Queen.

The Lord Chamberlain announced, 'To receive the order of knighthood, Sir Raymond Herron, for services to business.' The Gentleman Usher nudged his arm, 'Now sir,' his prompt to walk a few more paces and turn to face the dais. A Household Division band played *The Londonderry Air* as he paused, bowed his head and took three steps towards the velvet investiture stool positioned centre stage, directly in front of the Queen.

He had begun that cool crisp day with an unhurried breakfast clad only in his dressing gown. Afterwards, as he changed into his pressed morning suit, he had started to feel nervy and forgot to put on one sentimental item kept in a small Asprey's box on his dressing table. He had time to spare when the taxi had deposited him in the shadow of the Queen Victoria Memorial, a marble and bronze statue near the end of The Mall opposite Buckingham Palace. The early autumn breeze chilled his face and hands, but he enjoyed the fresh air as he strolled among diplomats, the military, celebrities and public servants; he only recognised a few of them and he hoped to God nobody would mistakenly think they had recognised him. From beyond the wrought iron railings he had watched guardsmen in their bearskins march across the coloured tarmac of the Palace forecourt and take post at their sentry boxes. He dreaded the moment when security staff would inspect everyone's entry passes, but when the gates had opened at ten o'clock sharp he was relieved that they only checked the unique serial number on his pink admission card before he was allowed through. Along with other excited guests he was directed across the sunny forecourt towards the inner quadrangle, observed by discreetly positioned armed police officers.

Inside, stewards had shown the audience to their seats and guided honours recipients backstage to an ante-room near the resplendent Picture Gallery, where Knights Bachelor were advised by a dapper military officer on the protocol for kneeling before Her Majesty. A replica investiture stool was available as a prop for any recipients who wished to rehearse the action, and he took his turn at it.

After he had stepped aside from the stool to make way for someone else he hung around for several minutes, concealing his jitters. To kill time and avoid possible identity muddles, he kept his distance from fellow recipients and at one point pretended to admire some Rembrandts and a Canaletto in the hope that nobody would take any notice of him. Some hope…

'Raymond?'

Oh hell! A tap on the shoulder, a smile and a handshake came from a spruce gentleman who had approached him from behind, 'I thought it was you. Congratulations again. How are you?'

His throat tightened but he maintained his poise. 'Oh, hello old chap. In great shape thank you.' An accomplished actor, his voice and smile betrayed no awkwardness or hesitation. 'What's your award today?'

'Don't you remember from our chat at The Reform last month? My CBE?' The man narrowed his eyes. 'Dear oh dear,' he said, 'you must be anxious today.'

'Well, there's a lot on my mind.' He kept his cool. 'But it's good to see you again.' He smoothed back a slick of hair with the palm of his hand which drew an inquisitive stare from the gentleman. Having played his part to near perfection, one absent item almost gave him away - he recalled the unopened Asprey's box in his bedroom and cursed himself for forgetting to put on his signet ring. Engraved with the Herron family crest, the gold ring was identical to the one that Raymond always wore on his little finger. With a valedictory smile he turned and scurried from the Picture Gallery to join the line-up before anyone else tried to grill him.

The artiste was now poised ready in the wings and it was almost time to go on stage. The general sound of chatter had steadily increased in the adjacent Ballroom as seats filled. The noise came to an abrupt stop when the

Queen entered, attended by the Lord Chamberlain and flanked by two Ghurkha orderly officers. After the National Anthem the band played light background music, and when the clear-cut voice announced 'Sir Raymond Herron,' he had felt that familiar twinge of stage fright, although he knew from professional experience that it would recede.

And now this talented performer was kneeling before the Sovereign. The music continued as the Queen dubbed both shoulders with the sword that once belonged to her father King George VI. He stood and slightly lowered his head to enable the Queen to position the red ribbon and badge around his neck.

As he raised his head the Queen gave him a radiant smile and said, 'I'm very glad indeed to give you this.'

'Thank you, your Majesty.'

'You're in charge of a major finance house?'

'Yes Ma'am, it was founded by my grandfather before the war.' He knew the script.

'Have you always worked there?'

'I trained at a merchant bank before I joined the family business,' he lied.

'One hears the business climate is quite a challenge at the moment.'

'Yes Ma'am, it's possible we could face a recession next year.' Flawless ad lib.

'Well, one must hope it won't happen and things improve.'

'Indeed, Ma'am.'

The Queen smiled once more and held out her right hand, time for him to shake hands again, take three steps to the rear, nod his head and exit stage right. He walked out between the gold 'no-parking' lines of the red carpet and into an ante-chamber where an official helped him to remove the ribboned insignia and positioned it neatly in a red leather box. The official handed the box back to him and said, 'Congratulations, sir. If you wish you can hold this up in front of the photographers outside.'

The charade was almost over. With an enormous sense of relief he hurried past signs that pointed along a gallery lined with magnificent portraits, to the staircase down to the Palace quadrangle and the assembled photographers. At the top of the stairs he heard a clock softly chime the half-hour, and that was when it happened.

'Doctor Blum will see you now.'

'Thank you,' said Guy. He followed the nurse into the consulting room and shook hands with the doctor.

'How is my patient from Macclesfield today?' said Dr Blum.

'Who?'

'You're from Macclesfield aren't you?'

'Oh I see.' Guy blushed. 'Yes, I'm in pretty good shape thanks.'

'You look it. Take off your shoes, lie down over there and the nurse will check your ankle and wrist wounds.' Dr Blum gestured to the surgical bed and remained standing. 'We'll give them a good clean and apply fresh dressings.'

Guy lay down. The nurse removed his ankle dressings and wiped the affected areas with cotton wool doused in surgical spirit. Guy feared it would sting like hell and he winced, but he hardly felt a thing.

'The ankles are healing well,' said Dr Blum. 'Let's hope the same can be said of your wrists.' He then asked Guy how the previous week had been.

With a quick glance at the nurse's cleavage and back at the doctor, Guy was not sure whether the question was a subtle reference to his testicles or to life in general. He stalled for a moment then said, 'I've had a lot on my plate.'

'We'll try not to keep you here too long.'

'That's all right,' said Guy, 'actually I was going to ask your advice on psychiatry, if that's all right.'

'You look sane to me.'

'Seriously, I need advice.'

'Of course.' Dr Blum turned to the nurse, 'Excellent work. You can start on this gentleman's wrists.' The nurse asked Guy to hold up his wrists and rest on his elbows while she set to work with more cotton wool and surgical spirit.

Guy explained that earlier that day he had received a call from Dr Jan Baumann at the Park-Klink, about a patient with Post-Traumatic Stress. The psychiatric consultation with Dr Alexander Grishin had not been a positive experience for either party. Alex refused to cooperáte and would not answer even the mildest questions, preferring instead to abuse his inquisitor. At one stage Alex had growled that he never asked to be questioned by a shrink and in any case who the hell was paying for the session. All Guy could do was thank Jan for the update and ask about the next stage, to which Jan replied there was never even a first stage because patients like Alex can only be helped if they want to be cured, a bit like drug addicts or alcoholics.

Of course Guy knew more than he divulged to Jan. Alex appeared to have the police in his pocket, the only possible explanation for the cell phone under the pillow which nobody under hospital arrest would be allowed to possess. And if Alex could manipulate the police he would no doubt be as arrogant as a bull rhinoceros, so it was not surprising he had shunned the psychiatrist.

'I'm surprised that Baumann breached patient confidentiality,' said Dr Blum, 'telling you such things has professional repercussions.'

'We're family, Alex Grishin is a cousin,' said Guy.

'I didn't realise. How can I help?'

'I was hoping you could come up with something.'

'Oh.' Dr Blum turned to the nurse. 'Thank you Ingrid, the dressings are fine. Could you give us a few minutes alone please?' She smiled and left the room.

Guy sat up and swung his legs off the bed. 'Alex Grishin is a sick man in charge of a vital genetic research operation.'

'That's hardly a crime,' said Dr Blum.

'No, but in another sense you couldn't be more wrong. Can I speak off the record?'

Dr Blum nodded.

'Less than two weeks ago Alex and two of his cronies tried to kill me, but my death was not enough for them, I had to be tortured as well.' Guy pointed at his ankles. 'Hence this treatment.'

Dr Blum looked horrified. 'How did you get away?'

'I beat the living shit out of all three, that's why they're in hospital.'

'What did they have against you?'

'I know what Dr Grishin is up to.' Guy said that the three Russians were veterans of the Soviet invasion of Afghanistan, often referred to as 'Afghantsis'. They worked at Capsella-Biotech GmbH, a firm that claimed it would win the race to sequence the Human Genome as well as own the rights to edit it. The potential profits were vast as were the dangers, one client being the Iraqi government that might use the technology to enhance its bio-weapon capability including anthrax. When Dr Blum asked if the appropriate authorities had been notified Guy replied that there was insufficient proof and matters were too involved. He did not say he was too close to Raymond Herron whose step-daughter was also his girlfriend. Factor in David's discovery that Guy and Alex were distant cousins and it was a sorry mess.

'How do I know you're telling the truth?' Dr Blum rubbed his chin.

'Alex Grishin is deranged,' said Guy. 'He desperately needs help. He's under hospital arrest but I think he's bribed the police to keep the law on side.' He looked straight into Dr Blum's blue-grey eyes. 'I'm not making any of this up, I promise.'

'If Grishin has paid off the police you can be sure there will be no prosecution,' said Dr Blum, 'which means he could go free as soon as he's discharged from hospital.'

'Christ.'

'What would it take to prevent Dr Grishin from achieving his aim?'

'Capsella-Biotech must surrender its data and operating procedures to the publicly funded Human Genome Project. I've an associate who's met an intermediary acting for Iraq who we hope to win over. But I still need to work on Dr Grishin whose terrible ordeal as a prisoner in Afghanistan has warped his mind.'

'You won't turn him round in a day any more than Rome was built in a day,' said Dr Blum.

'Thanks a bunch,' said Guy.

'But I have an idea. It might work, and it will cost you.' There was a twinkle in Dr Blum's eyes.

'I do know someone who's open to paying medical fees,' said Guy, thinking of the Chairman of Herron International.

'Good.' Dr Blum then outlined an idea that astounded Guy. When he had finished he said, 'Right Mr Scott, it's time to examine those testicles of yours.'

In Buckingham Palace he clutched his boxed award and placed his hand on the banister at the top of the stairs, when out of the blue he felt as if he had been struck by an invisible bullet.

'Christ, my bloody head!' In one instant he lurched forward, dropped the red leather box which jettisoned its contents, then he clutched the side of his head with the hand that had been on the banister. The distant sound of band music continued while further down the stairs two be-medalled women stopped, turned, and stared in alarm at the scene above. In a vain effort to steady his fall, his other hand grabbed the first available item which happened to be a tall iron flower pedestal, and there was a loud scrape as metal jarred against the wall. He let out a rasped cry. One of the two women gasped. The pedestal with its disarray of tangled flowers knocked a china vase off a shelf as the whole shebang crashed on top of him at a flat turn a few steps lower down the staircase.

A Palace steward leapt two stairs at a time as she raced down to him. Pieces of broken china crunched under her shoes. 'Holy shit,' she muttered under her breath, then out loud, 'are you all right, sir?'

'I'm a nurse,' panted one of the women who had both rushed to his unconscious body, 'he's bleeding, please call an ambulance.'

'I'll fetch help straight away.' The steward raced back upstairs to be confronted by several honours recipients who stared at the scene below. 'Jeez!' she said to herself, and called over to a colleague, 'John, redirect everyone down the other staircase. There's been an accident.'

'Okay…. ladies and gentlemen please step this way, there's another exit. Thank you!'

People began to drift away, some looked back anxiously over their shoulders but from the far end of the gallery the faint tune of *English Country Garden* indicated that the investiture had not been interrupted, as names continued to be called and honours bestowed. The steward used her two-way radio to summons a first-aider and request an ambulance, then joined the two women who by now had caught their breath and had lifted the pedestal off his body.

'He's still breathing,' said the steward, 'help me get him onto his side so he won't swallow his tongue.' The three had managed to turn him when the sound of rapid footsteps heralded the arrival of the first-aider.

After a few minutes the casualty opened his eyes, murmured something inaudible and tried to move. 'Keep very still, sir' said the first-aider, 'You've had an accident and I need to check you over.' Then he turned to the two women, 'An ambulance is on its way. I'll keep him still until the crew arrive. Thank you for your help ladies, it was so kind of you.'

The first-aider knelt. 'You seem to have come a right cropper, sir, but I'm sure you'll be just fine.' He carried out concussion checks of the eyes, tongue, pulse and limb movements. The first-aider then asked the casualty to use one hand to touch his own forehead, chin and chest which showed he was in possession of his faculties.

He was lucky. Apart from minor cuts and some painful bruises his condition was not serious, although he had been slightly concussed. When he first came round he could recall the Queen's second handshake but he could not remember the instance of his fall. As the investiture came to an end the first-aider boxed up his ribboned award, and paramedics took him by ambulance to St Thomas' Hospital across the river from Big Ben where he stayed for a couple of nights under observation.

The consultant who examined him said that the scan showed no sign of a stroke or heart failure, his blood pressure and lungs were also in good shape, so he must have undergone a strange seizure for which there was no obvious explanation. Advised to take a few days' quiet rest, on the Saturday morning he was discharged with pain killers and a letter for his general practitioner. He clutched the box containing the Insignia of Knighthood and limped out of the hospital into a steady damp drizzle, shuffled to the edge of the pavement and hailed a taxi to take him home.

'Blimey, 'ave you just been mugged, mate?' asked the taxi driver.

'No, thank heavens, but it feels rather like it.'

He climbed out of the dank cold into the warmth of the taxi. Although his body ached as he eased himself onto the back seat, he could feel the weight of deceit fade away. The hospital staff had recorded his real name and details and had not asked any awkward questions, unaware that he had acted as a stand-in two days before. As the taxi weaved its way through the morning traffic, he noticed the day's first edition of the *Evening Standard* on the adjacent seat and he picked it up. He started to read an update on investigations by United States police into the recent death of an American tabloid photo editor infected by anthrax spores sent through the mail.

A few moments later his eye caught a second headline that took several seconds to sink in. He stared at the article in disbelief. 'Oh, God!' he exclaimed to himself and reached into his pocket, pulled out his cell phone and dialled a number with shaky fingers. Nothing happened, he must have misdialled. 'Shit!' he hissed. The taxi driver gave him a curious look through the rear view mirror. He dialled again. 'Oh, God!' he uttered once more and then the number connected. After the sixth ring he was diverted to a recorded message: 'You're through to Sir Raymond Herron. I can't take your call now, please leave your name and number and I'll get back to you very soon.'

'Oh, God!' he said for the third time.

CHAPTER 34

The alarm on his cell phone vibrated. A light sleeper, he opened his eyes and reached down to the floor to turn it off. This was the hardest bit, getting out of his warm bed even though it was already mid-morning, but the snoring from his half-brother in the upper bunk was enough to stop him from drifting back to sleep. He got up, put on his track suit and trainers and picked up a small backpack that contained a towel with a few other belongings and sneaked out of the room. He did not bother to wash but made straight for the front door of the house. It was 'Backstroke Tuesday' and once again Brian Erkan planned to enjoy his only day off in the week.

It was a short walk to the bus stop where he stood in the mild chill that prevailed under a metallic sky. He got off the bus at the edge of Grunewald forest where he jogged six kilometres through pleasant woodland paths to a lonely spot he knew at the edge of Wannsee Lake. 'Backstroke Tuesday' was a loose term because Brian was also keen on the breaststroke, and he liked to practice both. At first the water looked deep and inviting as he put down his backpack and took off his track suit and trainers. He concealed his belongings under nearby shrubs. His blood circulation was good from the jog but when he stood nude by the water's edge the icy dip seemed more forbidding. He looked at a distant orange buoy bobbing on the grey ripples then he ran along a derelict wooden pier and threw himself head down and arms outstretched into the water. 'CHRIST it's cold!' he yelled as he surfaced. After a few meters of breaststroke the initial shock receded and he turned face up to commence the backstroke towards the buoy.

The invigorating swim contrasted with his repetitive job at the bratwurst stall, where the only variety was the quantity of bratwurst he sold and the choice he could offer of mayonnaise or curry sauce. The customers could be quite interesting, only the other day he had chatted with a British documentary producer working on a local crime story. As Brian kicked his feet and swung back his arms he stared at the clouds breaking up to reveal patches of blue sky. Perhaps the day would bring better weather after all.

He reverted to breaststroke and reached the buoy which no longer appeared so small. He trod water while holding on to a piece of old rope hanging from a d-ring. He looked at the distant shore and observed a man walking along the disused pier with a black object in one hand, perhaps a pair of binoculars. Wild fowl watchers sometimes visited the area and so as not to disturb him Brian manoeuvred to the far side of the buoy where he was less likely to be seen and tried some under water swimming. At one point beneath the surface his ears picked up what he thought was the muted 'crack' of a car backfiring, which was odd because there was no main road nearby. Eventually he tired and returned to the buoy to catch his breath. After a few more minutes he swam back towards the end of the pier where he saw what might have been dark seaweed floating in vomit on the surface, but he ignored it and carried on until the water became shallow enough to stand up and wade ashore. There was no sign of any bird watcher.

Brian's flesh was goose pumped and he shivered. He dried himself quickly and put on his track suit. He picked up his backpack and strolled along the waterfront until he came to his favourite breakfast salon, *Gaststube am Wannsee* where he ordered Kaffee and Brötchen. His body glowed from the exercise as he relaxed in the warmth of the parlour with its checked table cloths and a cute waitress. After he had wolfed the bread rolls and hot coffee his thoughts turned to the messy seaweed. It was unusual to find that kind of stuff in a lake and for some reason it bothered him. Without really knowing why, he decided to take another look at it and went back to the pier and realised that the apparent seaweed looked more like human hair mixed with fresh offal. Unless it was something else…

Dr Blum assured Guy that he was on the mend.

Guy's phone vibrated. 'Sorry,' he said to the doctor as he answered the call. 'Hello?'

'It's Doctor Jan Baumann. Is it all right to talk now?'
'Go ahead.'

'My colleagues and I've discussed your cousin and agree it's pointless to pursue his case. He refuses all psychiatric help, it's impossible to do anything for him.'

'I understand,' said Guy, 'what do you recommend?'

'Unless anyone can get through to Doctor Grishin by some miracle…'

'I might know someone,' said Guy, 'can you hang on?' He placed one hand over the mouthpiece and talked with Dr Blum, then returned to Jan. 'Another doctor with experience in psychiatry has agreed to visit Doctor Grishin and give it a go.'

'Who is this other person?' Jan sounded doubtful if not suspicious.

'He's with me now, can you speak to him?' Guy passed his phone to Dr Blum and Jan eventually agreed he could visit Alex.

'It looks like my earlier proposal is about to happen. Dr Baumann seemed unsure about me visiting Grishin, but there it is.' He paused then said to Guy, 'As I said, it will cost.'

'How much do you charge, Doctor Blum?'

'Call me Manfried from now on.' Confirmation as if it was needed that his fee would be big.

The previous evening Deputy Inspector Tolan Stevens had celebrated reaching the age of forty and his body was now paying the penalty for the alcoholic bash organised by his elder sister. He entered the interview room and shook hands with Jessica before introducing his colleague Danielle Hunt. The room looked and smelled like a deserted class at school - tables and chairs neatly positioned at intervals, noticeboards on the far wall. Stevens and Hunt took their seats opposite Jessica at one of the tables.

'Thank you for offering to talk with us again,' said Stevens, 'I hope you're not too jet lagged.'

'That's okay,' said Jessica with a smile.

Stevens placed a small console on the table and drew it closer towards him while his fellow officer sat cross legged with a note pad on her lap and pen at the ready.

'As a matter of interest what made you change your mind?' Stevens rubbed his groggy eyes and glanced at his companion who was all set to jot down any off-the-record information, a contradiction in terms but nobody in the room seemed to care.

'Is´there a law against a change of mind?'

'Absolutely not,' said Stevens.

Jessica bit her lip. 'It's a bit weird actually. While in hospital here in New York I wrote down the sequence of events before and after my incarceration. It was a conciliatory gesture to my step-father and boyfriend, it meant they had the facts before I flew to Germany.'

'Do you have that text with you?' asked Hunt. 'It could speed up today's session.'

'No,' she said. 'I put a lot of thought into the narrative and I don't need notes, I know my story by heart.'

'So, you know it by heart. But why the sudden change of heart? Why wait till now to provide a statement?'

'Two reasons I suppose,' said Jessica. 'First of all, we've come up with a negotiating stance that should speed up the process to sequence the Human Genome.'

Stevens and Hunt gave each other curious glances then looked back at Jessica. 'To sequence what?' said Hunt.

'The Human Genome. The code of life. Some time ago an official project was set up to unravel and map the double helix of human genes. They say it will be mankind's greatest scientific achievement.'

'What the hell has that go to do with you being drugged and assaulted?' said Stevens.

'Quite a lot actually. Secondly, I've compared notes with my boyfriend Guy who was beaten up in Berlin by a bunch of crazed Russian war veterans. One of them was Dr Alexander Grishin who is head of Capsella-Biotech, a genetic research company that could hijack the rights to sections of the Human Genome.'

The two police officers looked intensely at Jessica. After a short silence Stevens asked her what her recent ordeal in New York had to do with the violence she had just described in Berlin, and he got the same response: 'quite a lot actually' but this time Jessica also pointed out that in captivity she had been treated quite well, and she and Guy had concluded it must have been the flip-side to Alex Grishin's mental disorder.

'That's the man whose firm sequences the Human Genome, right?' said Hunt.

'Yes. He's a molecular biologist.'

'If he's off his head how can he hold down a job like that?' said Stevens.

'Because he's not off his head,' said Jessica, 'not in the way you say it. He suffers from PTSD, a recognised mental illness.' They looked at her with blank expressions on their faces. 'I'm talking about Post-Traumatic Stress Disorder.'

'I've heard of that,' said Hunt. 'A classmate's uncle suffered from it after Vietnam.'

'It also happened to a lot of British servicemen who fought in the South Atlantic.' Jessica hesitated then said, 'I guess that goes for a lot of Argentine soldiers as well.'

'According to my friend's uncle they get nightmares and flashbacks,' said Hunt. 'It can lead to heavy drinking, drugs and crime.'

'How can you be so sure that Dr Grishin has this 'PT' whatever you call it?' said Stevens.

'Ask Guy. He got the brunt of it last month. His flatmate did some research and Grishin's mental condition is well documented apparently.'

Polizei Kommissar Stefan Borchardt stood at the water's edge of Wannsee Lake and watched police divers do their work at the end of the dilapidated pier. The area was cordoned off and the forensic team's vehicle and a black van were parked among trees beyond the white tape. The van had no rear windows, it was the type used to convey dead bodies to the pathologist's morgue. A Polizei photographer snapped pictures of the scene and as the body was lifted onto the pier he took closer shots and waited patiently for the corpse to be removed. Borchardt continued to watch and think. It was a gruesome sight but no worse than the many other head-jobs he had seen in his long career. He felt sorry for the unfortunate young

Turk who found the body and who seemed very shaken. Nonetheless the lad had the sense to summons help from a nearby Gaststube where a young waitress had immediately called the emergency services. Over hot drinks and schnapps both witnesses were now in the Gaststube giving statements to one of Borchardt's officers.

A stretcher was carried to the pier by four men whose job was to load the body into the van. One of the divers submerged below the water and resurfaced a few minutes later just as the body was being carried away. The diver removed his goggles, waved and shouted at Borchardt who walked to the end of the pier to speak with him. The diver had found a semi-automatic handgun on the bed of the lake. Borchardt turned and called to the forensic team. A woman in a white protective suit wearing rubber gloves and clasping a plastic bag stepped out of the other vehicle and walked up to Borchardt and the two divers. She placed the gun into the bag and sealed it. Borchardt instructed the divers to conduct a thorough search for any other pieces of evidence. The divers climbed out of the lake onto the pier and adjusted a device used for under-water searches, then re-entered the water with the specialist equipment.

While Jan Baumann's dismissive aside 'best of British' still resonated in his ears Dr Manfried Blum wasted no time in fixing a date to visit Alex at the Park-Klinik. When the hospital staff agreed to his appointment they had refused to admit Guy.

'Why is that?' Manfried was on the phone to a staff member.

'I'll transfer you to the Polizei.' Manfried was put through to the duty officer outside Alex's isolation room.

'We don't know anyone called Guy Scott,' said the officer. 'We were told by Doctor Grishin that someone called Guy Shepherd falsified his surname to gain access to the patient, which is an offence.'

'One moment,' said Manfried. He put the officer on hold and looked at Guy. 'They don't know you. I thought you were the patient's cousin.'

'I am,' said Guy.

Manfried said to the duty officer, ' He's the patient's cousin.'

'They are cousins, but the real name is Shepherd not Scott.'

Manfried relayed that last remark to Guy.

'Oh shit. Look, I'm sorry Manfried. I better come clean. My first name really is Guy, but my surname is Shepherd. I'm Alex Grishin's first cousin twice removed. I've never set foot in Macclesfield. I don't even know where the bloody place is.'

'Can I call you back,' said Manfried to the duty officer, 'in about ten minutes?' He hung up.

'You better tell me what you're up to, Herr Shepherd.'

'Everything I've told you is true, except for my surname and home address.'

'You falsified your medical details…'

'I made a wrong decision, okay? I wanted to cover my tracks so that Alex Grishin and his Afghantsi mob couldn't find me. I was scared for God's sake, the bastards tried to kill me and could do so again.'

'So why did you visit your so-called cousin if your life is in danger?'

'It wasn't in danger while he was wounded and under hospital arrest.'

'But you told me he's got the police in his pocket.'

'I know that now. I didn't know it at the time,' said Guy. 'For fuck's sake if you don't believe me call your brother. Günter has my details, he's even seen my passport.'

'That won't be necessary.' Manfried called the hospital for a second time and learned that Guy Shepherd was wanted by the police for questioning and not permitted to visit Dr Grishin under any circumstances.

'Why do the police want to question him?'

'On three counts of attempted murder. If you know his whereabouts you must inform the Polizei immediately.'

'Er, I'll be in touch if I know anything. Meanwhile I'll make my visit as arranged. See you then.' Manfried put the phone down and looked at Guy. 'Herr Scott... I mean Herr Shepherd...'

'Call me Guy.'

'Guy, it sounds like you're in trouble.'

Tolan Stevens took his eyes off Jessica and reached for the console. 'Well,' he said, 'let's make a start.' He pressed the 'record' button and said, 'Eleven forty-five on October ninth. New York Police Department. Deputy Inspector Tolan Stevens accompanied by Officer Danielle Hunt. Interview with witness Jessica Elizabeth Parry, thirty-two years, resident in London, England. Please tell us what happened after your arrival in New York last month.'

Stevens listened and Hunt doodled on her pad as Jessica gave her account of the events that led to her captivity, including the reason why she attended the IGSA Convention and a rundown of her dealings with Dr Alex Grishin in the Roosevelt Hotel. Encouraged by her interviewers she described the video she watched at Capsella-Biotech's lab, the serious implications of one company holding a licence to sections of the Human Genome as well as the means to edit it, and how Alex had quickly sussed she was no journalist but a pretender.

Both officers nodded sympathetically as Jessica explained that Alex wanted to know who Jessica really worked for, why she had been 'sent' to probe into the affairs of Capsella-Biotech, her fears for the safety of her step-father and boyfriend. She had weighed up Alex's questions and decided to say nothing, except to tell him to sod off.

'Excuse my language,' said Jessica.

Stevens smiled. 'That's okay. How did Dr Grishin react?'

'He shrugged and said it was up to me. I'm not sure he saw me as a serious threat. He didn't look like someone with PTSD. It was as if I was a mere inconvenience.'

'Where you frightened?' asked Hunt.

'More angry than frightened. He then told me that I would remain as his house guest – I think that's the expression he used – until he had completed the first IBEC deal and secured certain patents his firm had applied for.'

Stevens clasped his hands and placed them on the table. 'How were you treated?'

'That was the bizarre thing,' said Jessica, 'I was looked after fairly well. It sucked that I had no phone or TV, just a radio, and the food was dreary.'

'Do you wish to press charges against your captors?'

'No.'

'Why not?'

Jessica said her priority was to protect Raymond from unnecessary stress, he already had enough on his shoulders together with his depressive illness. Added to which it was strange that her captors had not treated her harshly, until the day she was forcibly administered an injection and later dumped in Manhattan to make it look as if she got concussed by accident. Not that any of this could be easily proved, Stevens acknowledged.

'Let's get this straight,' said Stevens, 'you've returned to New York but you won't take legal action.'

'I'm on a mission to offer something special to the Human Genome Project,' said Jessica.

'Okay, so where do we come in?'

'I've decided to do that press conference you were so keen on.'

'Ah. Now you're talking,' said Stevens.

Borchardt sat in his office and looked at his computer screen. His face broke into a smile. The serial number of the Ruger handgun was legally registered in the name of Dr Alexander Mikhail Grishin, member of a Berlin gun club. It would help validate the claim that Guy Shepherd took the gun after he had assaulted Alex and the other two Afghantsis. From earlier discussions with Alex, Borchardt concluded that only two people other than Guy could have had access to the weapon: David Bond and Sir Raymond Herron. David Bond can be ruled out as he had apparently returned to Britain, which left Sir Raymond who must therefore have been the person whose brains were blown out at the end of the pier at Wannsee Lake.

To Borchardt it seemed unfortunate that the deceased had not been executed mafia style because it would have been smart to nail Guy Shepherd for the murder. Forensics had already reminded Borchardt that water can contaminate fingerprints on metal, however he had responded with orders to examine the ammo magazine for any untainted prints. Even so, if Guy Shepherd had an alibi for his whereabouts at the time of the death there could be little to disprove that Sir Raymond took his own life. From Brian Erkan's statement it seemed that the deceased was alone when he

371

stood on the pier with the handgun initially mistaken for binoculars. The Turkish teenager was in tears as he recounted his ordeal but a liaison officer had reassured him that even if he had tried to swim back to the man on the pier it would not have made any difference.

Borchardt felt it was a fair exchange to have deliberately placed the cell phone under Alex's hospital pillow in return for the handgun used by Sir Raymond and now in his department's possession. What he needed to establish was where the deceased had stayed and if there was a suicide note. He set his team to work on it just as his cell vibrated with a one-word text message from a Zurich phone number: *Capsella.*

Brian Erkan was pissed out of his skull somewhere on the Ku'damm, but he did not know precisely where. His blood stream was overloaded with an evening's worth of beer and too many chasers. Passers-by gave him a wide berth as he puked up into a waste bin. He tried to hail a taxi but when the cream Mercedes slowed the driver peered through his windscreen at the unrestrained drunk and accelerated away.

'Fuck you!' Brian shouted and wrapped one arm round a lamp post. 'Kraut bastard!' He stuck two fingers up at the disappearing taxi. 'You try staying sober when you've just found someone's fucking brains floating in the Wannsee!' He leaned forward unsteadily and wrapped his other arm around the lamp post as if to hug it. 'Cunts!' he sobbed at nobody in particular. His shoulders heaved and more bile dribbled from his mouth down the side of the lamp post onto the pavement.

'You look stressed,' said a soft voice from behind.

Brian felt a gentle pat on his back, looked round and said, 'What the fuck do you want?'

'What troubles you?'

'It's none of your bloody business!' Brian's speech was slurred.

'Can I help in any way?'

Under the light of the street lamp Brian gave this stranger the once-over and saw a blurred image of a well-dressed man probably in his thirties with a tanned complexion. 'I just need a fucking taxi!' More bile dripped from his mouth.

'Easily arranged.' The man flagged down a taxi and said to the driver, 'Here's fifty euros. If it costs any more this is my business card. My friend is unwell. Please take him home.'

As Brian was assisted into the back of the taxi he prayed that no more bile would rise from his stomach. He could hardly focus on the Middle Eastern man. 'Christ mate,' he garbled, 'you're cool. Thanks so much. Sorry I swore at you just now.'

'That's okay. You take care,' said the man who shut the taxi door, gave a friendly wave and continued along the Ku'damm.

Brian might have been completely stoned but as the taxi pulled out from the kerb he had just enough presence of mind to think he had encountered a young Omar Sharif. A gentleman anyway, whoever he was.

On his way to the Park-Klinik for his Wednesday morning appointment with the Chief Executive of Capsella-Biotech, Manfried gripped the steering wheel of his car and thought about Guy and how he had come to like this self-assured young man who was not from Macclesfield. Following a further conversation with Guy, Manfried now appreciated the importance of genetic sequencing and editing and the need to make Dr Grishin cooperate. Today's task should be easy enough. Easier than even Guy realised. The easiest twenty thousand deutschmarks that Manfried would ever earn.

Manfried was greeted at the hospital entrance by Jan Baumann.

'Hi. I'm Jan.' They shook hands.

While Manfried was taken up to Alex's isolation room, Jan provided some background to the case. 'As a scientist Dr Grishin is held in high regard. His company does ground-breaking research into genetics and gene editing. He's under police arrest, though I understand the situation might change for the better quite soon.'

'What condition is he in?'

'He's had two operations on his hand,' said Jan. 'It's healing well, no infection. But as you know it's his mental state which is the real problem. It goes back to his service with Soviet forces in Afghanistan where he witnessed unimaginable horrors.'

'I've gathered that,' said Manfried. 'Look, I know there's only a slight chance but if I can just spend an hour alone with him I might get somewhere.'

'You're welcome to try. As I said, best of British.' Jan spoke to the duty officer who did not look inside Manfried's medical bag before he opened the door, and Manfried was introduced to the patient.

Brian's head throbbed as he arrived for work at the bratwurst stall.

'Gute Zeit gestern?' *Good time yesterday?* asked the stall owner.

'Anything but,' said Brian who felt so tender he never wanted to touch another drop of alcohol again. The stall owner shrugged. Getting smashed may have been Brian's way of dealing with such a horrific ordeal but he also needed to talk about his experience. The stall owner was unlikely to be sympathetic so the familiar British radio producer who ambled up to buy bratty and frites was the obvious target.

'Hi! How's the documentary going?' said Brian.

'What documentary?'

'Your programme about those three blokes in hospital.'

'Oh I see,' said Guy, 'it's, er, going fine. And thanks for the tip about taking fruit and flowers to access the hospital patient. It worked.'

'No probs. What can I get you?'

'Bratty and pommes frites please,' said Guy. 'Wasn't yesterday your day off?'

'Unfortunately,' said Brian.

'Why?'

'I had to give a statement to the police.' He scooped a portion of frites. 'I found a dead body in the Wannsee.'

'How awful,' said Guy.

'You can say that again. Mayonnaise?'

'Yes please.'

'They reckon it was a British businessman who must have topped himself.' Brian poured mayonnaise onto the pommes frites. 'He used a Ruger pistol apparently.'

As Guy turned on his heels and raced back to the Gasthaus, Brian stared open mouthed with the redundant plate of food in his hands.

'What are you going to do to me, you cretin?' asked Alex.

Manfried peered through the glass section of the door at the duty officer reading a motor magazine, and drew a curtain around the bed to form an inner sanctuary 'We're going to stay calm and have a chat. It won't take long.' He placed his medical bag on a small table and opened it.

'You might be calm,' said Alex, 'but if you think I'm up for your psychiatric babble you're wrong. Go and fuck yourself. I'm in control round here.'

'We'll see about that,' said Manfried walking slowly towards him with both hands behind his back. 'Now, I want to ask you...' Without warning he leaped forward and produced a swab of chloroform which he pressed hard against Alex's nose and mouth.

'What the bloody...' was all that Alex said. He struggled madly with his good hand for a few seconds and slumped. A minute later Manfried let go and stuck a plaster over Alex's mouth. From his bag he took a cannula and a syringe with no needle but already filled with two milligrams of Midazolam. Often used for conscious sedation, it was an amnesic drug that suppresses the central nervous system and causes patients to have no recollection of their procedure.

Alex's head moved and he groaned. Manfried did not have a moment to lose however the drug had to be delivered slowly. He moved the pyjama sleeve up Alex's arm and carefully inserted the cannula. It had a slot where Manfried placed the nozzle of the syringe and carefully delivered the serum while he watched his new patient relax.

That first stage was a doddle. The next one should be quite easy too.

Guy sprinted across the forecourt and made straight for the entrance. He stopped inside and slammed one hand onto the bell at the reception desk to get someone's attention. Günter appeared from the back office.

'Morgen. Wie geht es dir?' *Morning. How are you?*

'Günter,' he gasped, 'where is Raymond Herron?'

'I last see him gestern, zat is yesterday.'

'Oh Christ. Fuck.' Guy sighed heavily. 'Sorry Günter, give me his room key.'

'Was?' *What?*

'I said 'key'. Der Schlüssel. Now, for God's sake.'

'Ah.' Günter turned and stepped towards a key rack and reached up. 'Here is zee key.'

'That's my key you dolt. I want Raymond's key.'

Günter handed over the correct key then leaned over the counter and watched Guy dash upstairs to the room he had occupied until recently. Guy had one thought on his mind. The gun. He must find that gun. He unlocked the door to Raymond's room and entered.

The room was clean and tidy. Guy glanced at the made up bed. It was unlikely that the chambermaid would have been in at that hour of the morning, so unless Raymond did his own housekeeping the last time the room was tidied must have been the previous day. Guy rummaged through the chest of drawers and searched the wardrobe but he could not find the gun. He searched under the bed and in the en-suite bathroom. Then he went over to the bedside table and pulled out the single draw. No gun, but two envelopes, one addressed to Jessica Elizabeth Parry and the other to Mr Guy Shepherd. 'Oh Jesus Christ,' he muttered. He picked up his letter and sat on the edge of the bed.

Gasthaus Blum
Zehlendorf
Berlin

9th October 2001

Dear Guy,

Never in a million years did I think that a time would come to write my own suicide note, but here it is. At least, here's one of them. The other is more emotional in which I reassure Jessica of my eternal love and respect for her.

I owe you an explanation, Guy. I also owe you my thanks, and not just for the loan of the Ruger handgun...

First, let me say that sixty is quite a good age to go. A few years back I was at the height of my powers but now I've started to plateau. I can't cope with stress. It fuels my depression, the condition I call Dark Cloud that has come into sharper focus with my greed (and since I left my anti-depressants at home). Regret, shame and embarrassment have overcome my desire to live, and I fear my relationship with Jessica is soured for ever.

I want to leave something behind, and here I must thank you Guy for recommending the proposal that I've put to Karim Samir. He is a businessman who gets the wider picture, a quality I admire. He is prepared to act as intermediary to establish a new collaboration between the Human Genome Project and Capsella-Biotech. At a much reduced price of course but I believe Samir will be a reliable go-between and still earn reasonable commission, though nothing like the money Iraq is offering him. He also agrees to broker the sale of IBEC to the scientific community and he warmed to your suggestion to set up a charitable foundation. I'm sure he will meet you after I am gone to progress these initiatives. Please Guy, do me one last favour and follow this up. When you speak with Samir you should find that the US invasion of Afghanistan has altered his thinking, especially given his prediction of further military intervention in Iraq. In short, he is now on our side.

Meanwhile Jessica is in New York to take soundings from the Human Genome Project and pave the way for Samir to offer up Capsella-Biotech's data. She will link up with Samir the moment you give her the word. My passing will be a terrible shock for Jessica but at least she will never have to bear my craving forgiveness. Neither will she have to oversee my decline in old age, another thing that has often worried me.

I have every confidence in you and Samir at the helm of the proposed deal. One day medical science will get its revenge on Huntingdon's Disease, indeed, the global community will get its revenge on swathes of hereditary conditions. Bravo! Meanwhile think of me at last reunited with my beloved Elizabeth.

It has been said when the curtain comes down it's time to get off the stage. In my case I hope to leave the show while the audience want more. One day you and others will judge whether I've achieved that.

Take care of yourself and please look after Jessica.

Raymond

Guy sniffed and wiped a tear from one eye. There was no letter addressed to Ben Herron who had stood in for Raymond at yesterday's Investiture in London. Guy asked himself whether Ben might have picked up vibes of Raymond's distress, or even sensed the instance of his death by telepathic means. Either way, Ben and Jessica must be notified of Raymond's suicide immediately.

As for that Grishin bastard, he was about to find out what it's like to be sedated with an amnesic drug and unwittingly forced to reveal awkward facts such as the scum on his payroll. When it comes to torture two can play at that game especially when the first prize will be Alex's committal to a secure psychiatric ward.

CHAPTER 35

The second New York press conference was hastily convened for the morning of Wednesday the tenth of October. Once again the police press room was laid out with a dais and table at one end, rows of seating for the journalists and floor space for television cameras. Unlike the previous occasion Jessica's image was not on display and the media were informed that this time she would appear in person.

Earlier Jessica almost fell out with Tolan Stevens over the agenda, but they reached a compromise. Stevens had wanted to cover Jessica's captivity, her reaction when she found out everyone thought she had perished in the Twin Towers attacks, and the incredible moment when she reunited with her family. Jessica reluctantly agreed provided she could state that she bore no ill will against her abductors, and spelled out the true aims of Capsella-Biotech GmbH. She would also say that an intermediary will propose a data-sharing deal between Capsella and the Human Genome Project. The proposal would include Capsella's pioneering IBEC system that literally 'edits' genes, a breakthrough in medical science.

Finally, regarding certain claims made by Dr Alexander Grishin at the recent IGSA Convention, Jessica would also unveil information (researched by David Bond) about the growing body of opinion against gene patents. Apparently the US Government was already under pressure to ban all gene patents. What effect such a ban might have on Capsella's future share price was not Jessica's concern.

They were about to enter the press room when Jessica's phone rang. 'Excuse me,' she said to Stevens as she held the phone to her ear and turned away. 'Guy dearest? What is it?'

'Are you alone darling?'

'No. I'm about to start the press conference.'

'Christ. Listen. Don't ask me why, get to some place where you can't be heard.'

'But I don't see why…'

'Just do it.' Guy's voice was emphatic. Jessica dashed to the ladies.

'Hey! Where're you going Miss Parry?' Stevens held out both arms in despair.

This was the moment when Jessica learned of Raymond's death. She never made it to the press conference which was more than a flop - it had to be cancelled much to Stevens' embarrassment but he sympathised after he learned why Jessica had made off in such a hurry.

Ben was not answering his phone when Guy tried to phone him, but later on Jessica received a call from Ben who had just read the *Evening Standard* article about his twin brother's suicide. During their emotional conversation Ben thought it best not to tell Jessica about the spasm that had landed him in hospital for two days.

Borchardt sat at the counter reading a copy of *Der Spiegel* over a mug of coffee and a ham bagel. He often frequented this café for his lunch break especially if he wanted down-time away from colleagues. He was just about to lift the coffee mug to his lips when he received a call from the same cell phone he had smuggled into Alex's isolation room.

'Guten Tag, Alex.' said Borchardt.

'Good day Polizei Kommissar Stefan Borchardt.'

'Wer ist da?' *Who is this?*

'Does Jacob Bank in Zurich mean anything to you?'

'What?' He went pale and stood up.

'Does the figure of two million US dollars ring any bells?'

Borchardt's heart beat faster. 'What do you mean?'

'I think you know precisely what I mean. If you don't want your corrupt dealings to hit the morning newspapers you better meet me at the lobby of the Berlin Hilton in two hours' time.'

'Who the hell are you? Some gutter journalist?'

'The Hilton in two hours.'

'I can't,' he said lamely, 'I've got a meeting with my superiors…'

'How about the name Rudi Galler? And your account number four-two-six-eight-one-six? You don't want that splashed across every newspaper in Europe do you, Polizei Kommissar Borchardt?'

He began to sweat. 'Where did you say? The Hilton?'

'The Hilton. Two hours from now. And bring Doctor Jan Baumann with you as well.'

'Who?'

'Don't give me that shit Polizei Kommissar Borchardt. You know exactly who. And I don't care if he's in the middle of a life-saving brain transplant, if there's no Doctor fucking Baumann with you in two hours' time, you won't get a second chance.'

Borchardt clenched his fist and crashed it down towards the counter but he missed and sent his bagel flying. 'Whoever you are I'll get you for this…'

'Temper, Borchardt.' The barely familiar voice was smooth and cool. 'Don't be late. I'll wear a red scarf and carry a copy of *Computer Bild*. You and Baumann are to carry copies of the same magazine. My code word is *Zurich*, yours is *Jacob*.'

'If you seriously think you can get away with…'

'Listen, asshole. I've prepared duplicates of a press release about you and a big, big corruption scandal. They're in sealed envelopes, one held by a lawyer and the other by a media contact who'll publish the story unless he hears from me in three hours from now. I suggest you don't try anything.' The phone went dead.

Between them Manfried and Midazolam had done a superb job. In the twilight world induced by several minutes of conscious sedation Alex had responded to all of Manfried's questions. Even though Alex was partially sedated and despite the amnesia that would follow, physical force was used to question him. By the time the chloroform wore off and Alex came round the Midazolam had been intravenously delivered. Manfried held up Alex's bandaged hand and jabbed it with a screwdriver. Thanks to the sticking plaster on Alex's mouth his scream was no more than a deep throated whine like the distant screech of car brakes, whereupon Manfried told him he could either cooperate and answer questions or face more unbearable pain. Alex frantically nodded in agreement.

'One sound from you that alerts the duty officer outside,' Manfried had whispered, 'and my screwdriver goes straight through this juicy hole in your hand.' He jabbed his patient once more to reinforce the point. 'Understand?'

With tears in his eyes Alex winced, whined and gave another frenzied nod. After the plaster was removed he disclosed the names of corrupt professionals and public servants on his payroll. Manfried recorded the session on a Dictaphone which he gave to Guy who immediately recognised two names: Doctor Jan Baumann who was supposed to oversee the efforts to interview Alex, and a senior officer called Stefan Borchardt who was the police spokesman quoted in news articles about the fight at Grishin Informatik and the body in the Wannsee. Other information from Alex revealed that Borchardt held sway over a network of corrupt officials, there were details of Borchardt's Swiss numbered account into which two million had been paid and the name of one of the bank's client relationship managers, Herr Rudi Galler. A few moments later Alex succumbed to the delayed sedative and fell asleep. When he awoke half an hour later the first person he saw was Jan Baumann. Manfried had gone.

I know exactly how to extricate myself from here. It's one of several lines of defence that I've set up over the years. At last Guy understood: Alex's insurance policy was to have Borchardt and others in his pocket, and perhaps Borchardt himself had made certain it was he who handled Alex's case from the outset. It would explain the recent deposit of two million.

Guy stood in one corner of the lobby at the Hilton. The comic thought occurred that after Alex came round from the amnesic drug he would not recall any of his tortured exchange with Manfried. Alex's accomplices could never accuse him of knowingly betraying them. At the appointed time Guy held his copy of *Computer Bild* in one hand and looked towards the hotel entrance as Alex's two co-conspirators walked in, carrying copies of the same journal. Guy had already met Jan who now looked awkward and shamefaced, so the other person had to be Borchardt whom Guy recognised from their chance meeting in the Park-Klink. After they exchanged code words Guy led them to a small meeting room he had hired.

The only refreshments on the table were two glasses of lukewarm tap water.

'Sit down,' said Guy who remained standing and removed his scarf. He sensed a degree of animosity between the two men. 'Let me remind you both, if I don't contact my media associate within the hour, the press release goes out. You'll be ruined.'

'We know,' said Borchardt. 'We're not going to top you.'

'You would if this was a dark alley somewhere,' said Guy.

'Are you trying to tell us there is no press release after all?'

'No, I'm saying I know the sort of people I'm dealing with. A pair of worthless two-faced bastards with no decency, no morals and no sense of justice.'

'Cut out the sermon.' Of the two it was Borchardt who did all the talking so far. He took a sip of water. 'What do you want from us?'

'I want both of you to do something useful for a change.' He pointed at them. 'How's that sound?'

Borchardt looked at Baumann. 'This is all your fault Jan you stupid idiot, why the fuck did you let Doctor Blum into the isolation room?'

'If I'd refused Blum's offer of professional help it would have looked suspicious,' said Jan.

'You should have stayed with Grishin, not left him alone with…'

'SHUT UP!' Guy yelled and they fell silent. 'I asked you, how does that sound?'

Jan looked up at Guy and said, 'What do you mean?' He nervously picked up a glass tumbler and swallowed all the water in two gulps.

'If you do exactly as I say not a word will ever be uttered about the bribes you so readily accepted from Alexander Grishin. I couldn't give a toss about your sodding numbered accounts in Switzerland, provided you agree to spend the money in the way I'm about to tell you.' Guy paused to look at the puzzled expressions on both men's faces. 'Look, there's something much more powerful and important at stake. Think of this as your contribution to medical science. There'll be no reward for you except my pledge of silence and, as long as you always respect that, there'll be no earth shattering press release to torpedo your happy retirement. If anyone so much as lays a finger on me, any of my friends or colleagues, my German lawyer has instructions to open a sealed envelope with a duplicate press release and you two mother-fuckers will go behind bars.' Guy beamed at the two men. 'What do you say?'

'Where's your proof?' Borchardt's voice was calculated, almost smug.

'A witness has made a Dictaphone statement.' Guy skipped saying that it had not been made under oath.

'You don't give us much choice,' said Borchardt. Tell us what you have in mind.'

David Bond walked up to a news stand and selected the same edition of the London *Evening Standard* that Ben had found in the taxi on his way home from St Thomas' Hospital. Like Ben, David read the story about a US tabloid photo editor killed by anthrax spores. Then he came across the smaller article about the Chairman of Herron International LLP, Sir Raymond Herron, whose corpse had been recovered from a lake in Berlin. The German police were no longer treating his death as suspicious and British consular officials were in touch with his family about repatriating the body.

When David phoned Guy to find out more, he also learned about a plan to have Alex banged up in a secure psychiatric ward.

'How the hell will you achieve that?' asked David.

'I've got friends in high places,' said Guy. 'It's partly thanks to Günter Blum's brother.' Guy did not elaborate.

'What happens now?'

'I'm trying to get myself out of trouble.'

'What's new?'

'I mean it. The Polizei want me for questioning in connection with the injuries suffered by those three Afghantsi brutes.'

'Oh God. I knew this would happen…'

'I'm hoping that with Alex in a secure ward he'll find it impossible to manipulate his police cronies.'

'Will that make any difference?'

'I hope so,' said Guy. 'A corrupt police officer and an equally corrupt doctor have just received an offer from me that they can't refuse. Don't ask for details now, but it should protect me as well as let Karim Samir launch a new era for Capsella-Biotech.'

'Bloody hell,' said David, sounding unsure what to make of this latest development.

'Meanwhile I feel safe staying at this Gasthaus,' said Guy, 'and Günter Blum remains discreet provided I keep giving him extra money.'

'That can't go on for ever,' said David. 'Anyway, I've some news. An email from the records office in

High Holborn confirms the relationship between you and Alex. Certificates are in the post.'

'Happy families,' said Guy.

'Talking of which, how's Jessica?'

'She's back in Berlin. I'm desperately sorry for her. She had to identify Raymond's body, a terrible ordeal given the facial injuries. In the end it was a burn mark on his hand that clinched it, but the authorities insist on a confirmatory DNA test. Ironic isn't it?'

'They can't use Jessica's DNA, they weren't blood relatives,' said David. 'She was only Raymond's step-daughter.'

'I know. Ben has offered to provide a DNA sample.'

Guy then explained that the British consular staff needed Jessica's address during her stay in Berlin so, to avoid compromising Guy, she had booked out of the Gasthaus and moved into the Berlin Hilton on Mohrenstrasse. David then heard how Guy had broached the subject of money with Jessica and found her hugely sympathetic. Apart from Manfried's fat fee, Guy was clocking up considerable personal expenses during his stay in the city. When he gently broached the matter with Jessica she offered him money from her trust fund. Guy had raised an eyebrow and thanked the gods, as well as Jessica – until then he never knew there was such a fund.

'Jessica's been incredibly brave,' said Guy. 'Obviously she couldn't accomplish all she intended in New York, but I'll ask Samir to pick up from where she left off.'

'Can I do anything at this end?'

'Not now thanks David, I'll get back to you when I know about their return to London.'

'Whose return?'

'Jessica and Raymond,' said Guy. 'I expect Jessica will accompany his body once it's released, and presumably Ben can meet her at Heathrow.'

'I understand,' said David.

'By the way, you did a great job researching the campaign against gene patents. Well done.'

'My pleasure. Mind you, the information took me quite by surprise.'

'Me too,' said Guy. "I better hang up, I've got stuff to do like offer Karim Samir the chance to negotiate a workable gene deal. Wish me luck.'

CHAPTER 36

'I am sorry to hear such tragic news,' said Samir. 'Why take his own life?' He and Guy were at the Berlin Hilton in the same room used for the meeting with Borchardt and Baumann.

'At first he was unaware of Dr Grishin's, how can I say, more underhand dealings,' said Guy. 'The reality came as a shock. Sir Raymond also suffered from depression. Have you seen the news report?'.

'No, Mr Shepherd. But I have looked for news of Dr Grishin's progress, and it's gone quiet. I'm forbidden to visit him at the Park-Klinik.'

'You've got me to thank for that, Mr Samir.'

'Why?'

'Dr Grishin and I are related. We're first cousins twice removed.'

Samir gave Guy a perceptive stare. 'I didn't know that.'

'Neither did I until recently,' said Guy. 'It alters my approach to Dr Grishin. Let me explain.'

Guy described Capsella's refusal to share data from its sequencing of the Human Genome. When he referred to the new product that edits genes and the anthrax phage, Samir admitted he thought they were intended for defence purposes only. Samir looked astounded when Guy told him that a doctor and a police officer had been persuaded to detain Dr Grishin at the Park-Klinik, pending his committal to a secure ward in a psychiatric clinic.

'It's necessary I assure you,' said Guy. 'Dr Grishin is mentally ill and needs specialist treatment.'

'How did you get the police officer and doctor to agree to this?'

'I made sure they had no alternative,' said Guy. He did not describe the arrangement whereby these two venal profiteers had precisely one week to sort things out. Their task included dropping all charges against Alex and the other two Afghantsis who were still seriously ill in hospital, and for whom Guy did not care a jot. It was also a condition that no charges would ever be pressed against Guy. To make it work there were others who would be bribed by Borchardt and Baumann, hence Guy's earlier instruction to dig deep into their own ill-gotten funds. No doubt Rudi Galler would be on hand to assist them.

'Shortly before his death Sir Raymond indicated that he trusted you to steer your business in a different direction,' said Guy.

'My contacts in Iraq do not believe that the US would ever invade their country,' said Samir. 'The last time I spoke with Sir Raymond Herron I told him that since *Operation Enduring Freedom* I now think otherwise.'

'The US will invade?'

'It's likely. I believe history will show the nine-eleven attacks to have been Saddam Hussein's death warrant.'

'Yet you've been happy to sell defence products to Iraq…'

'How could I have known the nine-eleven atrocities would happen?'

'You and your agency have sold weapon components to Iraq for years. Suppose Saddam had sponsored the terrorists who hijacked those three American planes? What are your thoughts about the victims?'

'Some may disapprove of Saddam's régime. Nevertheless Iraq is a sovereign state entitled to protect its borders.'

'Every act of violence has its victims, you know that, Mr Samir. Don't you have a conscience about Iraq's treatment of dissidents for example?'

'If I hadn't provided the Iraqis with defence equipment, somebody else would have.'

'So it's somebody else's problem, is it?'

'I did it to grow my business,' said Samir.

'Not for the money?'

'It was never just about the money. Since childhood I've had big ambitions. I've recruited a great team, developed contacts and built an impressive franchise. The last thing I want is for it all to crash, even if I have to turn my back on the Iraqis.'

'I'm glad to hear that,' said Guy. 'It's why I've asked the Chief Operating Officer of Capsella-Biotech to join us today. And the acting Chairman of Herron International. They'll be here any time now.'

Lina Rothstein was a dynamic business woman well respected at Capsella. Appointed as the company's Chief Operating Officer three years ago, she took her role seriously and expected others to follow her example. Her mantra was to value each and every employee, never take criticism personally, listen to advice from mentors, and build consensus rather than go it alone; someone with femininity matched by strong emotional intelligence.

When Guy went to the hotel lobby he found Lina talking with William Vinson, the hastily appointed acting Chairman of Herron International LLP. They were sitting in armchairs by a window where sunlight streamed. They vaguely knew each other from occasional telephone conversations, although most dealings between their two companies had been handled by Raymond and Alex until now.

They both stood as Guy approached. He walked up to Lina and shook her hand. She was gracious and put him at ease.

'It's good to meet you.' Guy smiled at her.

'And you too,' she said. 'Has Mr Samir arrived?'

'Yes, he's here.' Guy turned to William. 'Sorry for the short notice.'

'Not at all. Thanks for sending the list of today's discussion points.'

'Let's go to the meeting room,' said Guy. 'Have either of you have met Mr Samir before?'

They shook their heads.

Rudi Galler was at his desk in the Zurich branch of Jacob Bank. He still smarted from the embarrassment of Sir Raymond Herron's sudden departure from the Pavillon restaurant the other day, and from the humiliation of being left to pay for the hugely expensive lunch. He wondered why he had heard nothing more from Raymond who had promised to provide updates on the timing of his imminent sensational deposit.

Raymond's existing funds were in an 'execution only' numbered account which means that the client relationship manager, in this case Rudi, could only invest the funds as directed by the account-holder, Raymond. As a contingency Jessica was a co-signatory of the same account, should anything ever happen to Raymond. The account also made annual payments to a trust fund in Jersey that Raymond had set up for Jessica many years ago. Alex on the other hand had no interest in the complexities of investing and his numbered account was categorised 'discretionary'. Thus Rudi took all investment decisions for Alex, focussing on under-valued stocks that mostly grew extremely well.

Rudi was caught unawares by a call from Stefan Borchardt whom he had spoken to only the other day. Maybe this unusually affluent police officer simply wanted to acknowledge the code word *Capsella* that Rudi had texted. As the two million US dollars were to remain as a cash balance there was little to discuss, or so Rudi thought. After he steered Borchardt through the usual security questions he asked, 'How can I help?'

'I have urgent instructions for you, Herr Galler,' said Borchardt. His voice was husky, almost breathless.

'I'm listening.'

'I want you to transfer a quarter of a million US dollars from my account to account number seven two seven nine one three. Immediately.'

Rudi smiled. He knew the recipient who worked at a Bavarian psychiatric hospital about three hour's drive from Zurich. Rudi recalled the account number because Herr Borchardt had credited it once before, although this time it was for a much larger sum. 'I'm arranging the payment as we speak.'

'Good,' said Borchardt as Rudi tapped on his computer keyboard. 'Next I want you to set up six new numbered accounts in the names of the following people.' Borchardt gave Rudi the full names and dates of birth of six other collaborators who had been seduced into his web several times before, whose cooperation was needed again but at a much higher price to formalise Alex's committal to the best possible psychiatric facility. The six were key players from the medical profession and the public sector whose favours would earn them two hundred and fifty thousand US dollars each.

'You do understand these distributions will cut deep into the two million that's just gone into your account, Herr Borchardt?'

'Do as I say.' Borchardt's voice was desperate. 'Set up the accounts and pay a quarter of a million into each one.'

'I can set up the accounts but I can't activate them until I meet the new signatories and verify their identity,' said Rudi.

'How soon can you come to Berlin?'

'It would be a couple of weeks at least. I've got a full schedule of client meetings and fund manager briefings.'

'Not good enough. I want you in Berlin tomorrow morning.'

'What?! Why can't the six visit me here in Zurich, then I can…'

'I told you, this matter is urgent, extremely urgent,' said Borchardt. 'Cancel your engagements for tomorrow and catch an early plane to arrive in Berlin by mid-morning.'

'But how…'

'I'll cover your return fare, business class of course, and pay you ten thousand for the day's work.' Borchardt sounded frantic. 'I'll book a meeting room at a hotel near Tegel airport where you can meet your new clients at half-hourly intervals.'

'Normally I would never do this at such short notice,' said Rudi who sensed the uncharacteristic urgency. 'However just this once I'll do as you ask, but only because I know of your relationship with Dr Grishin. How is he by the way?'

'He's unwell,' said Borchardt. 'You may not hear from him for some time.'

'Give him my best wishes,' said Rudi. 'Meanwhile, I'll text you with my arrival time tomorrow. Make sure your six associates turn up with valid passports and birth certificates.'

'Excellent,' said Borchardt.

'I expect my fee of ten thousand in cash. Dollars, not deutschmarks.'

'The key points are on the list I sent you,' said Guy and the other three nodded. Seated comfortably in the Berlin Hilton, they were gathered round the meeting table laden with coffee, tea, chilled mineral water and biscuits in wrappers.

'Some of this is news to me,' said Lina. 'Are you sure of the facts?'

'I was going to ask the same thing,' said William.

'As sure as I'll ever be. Let's start with a summary of where we are now, then discuss next steps. All right?' There was no dissent so Guy began with the less palatable details.

He was not surprised by their reactions. Lina had no idea that the one hundred Spectra 6500 computers housed at Grishin Informatik GmbH were anything other than back-up sequencing machines stored at a different location for security reasons. She had mistakenly understood that if anything went wrong with the two hundred sequencers at Capsella-Biotech's Wannsee site, the back-ups would take over. Guy stunned her with news that Alex must have had a specialist team on a separate payroll at Grishin Informatik, whose function was to develop the IBEC system in order to sell it to clients such as Iraq. At this point Lina gave Samir a knowing look.

When William asked about finance Guy told him that the investment for all three hundred Spectra 6500 machines came from Herron International, while profits from the IBEC sales would be siphoned off by Alex and Raymond.

'Jesus Christ,' said William, 'what the hell was Raymond playing at?'

'He was deadly serious,' said Guy, 'although I guess his main focus always was the completion of the Human Genome. He recognised the benefit to medical science and must have reckoned that Capsella-Biotech had the edge…'

'We still do,' said Lina.

'I know but Raymond also had a personal agenda, consumed by a hatred of Huntingdon's Disease that killed his wife and caused his depression.'

'What depression?' said William.

'Raymond Herron suffered from depression. He was taking medication.'

'I never knew that.'

'What's his mental condition got to do with all of this?' said Lina.

'It means he became less rational,' said Guy, 'and thought he could justify his greed. He stood to make squillions if he and Alex ever got away with their scheme.'

'Yet it ended in tragedy,' said William. 'His brother must be gutted, like us.'

'Like his step-daughter,' said Guy.

'So how do things stand with Alex Grishin right now?'

Guy briefly summarised the events leading to Alex's imminent admission to a mental health institution, following doctors' insistence on the need for psychiatric treatment. Lina said she was the acting Chief Executive of Capsella-Biotech in Alex's absence, and Guy replied that she could remain in her new role for a long time.

'You're very quiet, Mr Samir,' said William. 'End the suspense and tell us what you can bring to the party.'

Guy cut in, 'Mr Samir was contracted by Alex to handle the IBEC sales, by association he carries weight as an ambassador for Capsella-Biotech... well, for the acting Chief Executive at any rate. Given the current security threat he's offered to act on our behalf as well. I heard this from Raymond who clearly approved of the arrangement.'

'Fair enough,' said Lina, 'it looks like I've got myself a new ambassador.' She looked straight at Samir. 'Now let's hear it from you.'

For a moment Samir looked at Guy. Then his brown eyes returned to the other two. He began to speak.

CHAPTER 37

Two months later

It was late afternoon in Starnberg, a small town south west of Munich where the Christmas Market was alight with festive decorations. Guy pressed his way towards the seasonal food, arts and crafts. The smell of warm Glühwein penetrated the cool air while he jostled with other shoppers crammed among the sparkly stalls. He never went big on the Christmas thing but chose a culinary item for someone special.

'Gift wrap?' The seller pointed at tissue paper and ribbon.

Guy nodded. His trip to Bavaria was short, to deal with a patient in the secure unit of a psychiatric hospital near the lake at Starnberger See. Conveniently diagnosed with Paranoid Personality Disorder in addition to Post-Traumatic Stress, Dr Alexander Grishin was held in the clinic against his will. It was a big achievement on the part of Polizei Kommissar Borchardt to ensnare dishonest officials to make it happen without hindrance. Desperate to avoid public humiliation and a long jail term, Stefan Borchardt also had to pay for Alex Grishin's treatment, fortunately he still had enough money on deposit in Zurich. Doctor Jan Baumann had played his part in the process by signing statutory medical declarations, and a convincing second opinion was obtained from another crooked doctor at the going rate of two hundred and fifty thousand US dollars. Such bribes were at the higher end of the scale but served their purpose - Borchardt had no difficulty bribing the director of the Bavarian psychiatric hospital to accept the new patient, neither was it difficult to have Alex struck off as a company director since when the acting Chief Executive of Capsella-Biotech GmbH, Ms Lina Rothstein, had been appointed to the permanent role.

Alex sat opposite his cousin in a consulting room while a blonde woman in nurse's uniform kept watch outside. Guy was sitting awkwardly, his right leg protruding straight. He was wearing blue cords with a red pullover while Alex was casually dressed in an open-neck shirt and slacks. His wounded hand was no longer bandaged. The room was well lit and pleasantly furnished with easy chairs, a pale green carpet with matching curtains and a side table with tea and coffee making facilities. A change in Alex's manner prompted Guy to ask about his treatment.

'It's ironic that I'm paying for it don't you think?' said Alex.

'What do you mean?'

'Borchardt pays my medical fees with the money I gave him.'

'Doesn't that mean you both lose out?'

'You could say that.' Alex smirked.

In the Zurich office of Jacob & Cie Rudi Galler was looking forward to Christmas at his alpine chalet. It would be his family's tenth winter holiday where over the years his two daughters had become accomplished downhill skiers. He and his wife were agile on the slopes too, he thought as he busily worked through his in-tray to clear the backlog before the festive holiday began. One file caught his attention because of a yellow ticket indicating that the account should be archived as dormant. He picked up the folder with an account number written on the outside cover and opened it. He had not heard from the client for quite some time. The signatory was Alexander Grishin – an expected huge deposit had not yet materialised. And talking of big deposits, Rudi asked himself, what had happened to Sir Raymond Herron's promised windfall? The alarming thought occurred that if the anticipated millions were not deposited in the Grishin and Herron numbered accounts, there would be no sumptuous commission payment from Jacob & Cie.

Apart from occasional texts Rudi never phoned, emailed or wrote to clients in case information got traced by another country's tax authorities. Hence the covert meetings at a hotel near Tegel airport where Borchardt had arranged for six corrupt professionals to present their identifications. After Rudi had transferred funds from Borchardt's account to the new ones, his commission for these client introductions was enough to buy his wife a diamond brooch for Christmas. He was unlikely to trouble Borchardt with that statistic.

Conscious of Alex's more positive air Guy repeated his original question. 'Tell me, how is your treatment going?'

Alex looked thoughtful. 'Daily sessions on how to transport my thoughts to a happier place. Powerful medication. Open discussions with other inmates…'

'You mean patients,' said Guy.

'They might be patients. I'm an inmate. But you know something Guy? I'm starting to rediscover my old self.'

'In other words you hope to convince everybody you're fit for release. Is that it?'

'You wouldn't understand. The anti-depressants gave me hell for the first two weeks,' said Alex. 'I was panicky and befuddled, disorientated, until the pills kicked in and now they work like magic. I'm gradually turning a corner and already get less wound up. I've even learned to talk more openly about my painful combat memories without actually feeling them.'

For a while they said nothing as if lost in thought, until Alex spoke. 'I was a shit, I know it, driven by greed and revenge. In the Park-Klinik you said something about losing a phenomenal sum of money if I let the Iraq deal go, but I also had another agenda to carry out a kind of reprisal for my experiences in Afghanistan. Call it retribution to even the score, or plain wrong doing for its own sake. It's so hard to explain.

'And harder to say sorry,' said Guy, but his remark was ignored.

'I'm also coming to terms with being bisexual, it didn't quite ruin my military career but it wrecked my marriage.'

Guy shifted slightly in his chair. He glanced at the door and rubbed the side of his straightened leg.

William Vinson sat at one end of the oblong oak table in the panelled Board Room of Herron International's office at Adams Court, and eyed the other five Trustees. In the centre of the table a bronze bust of Thomas Herron, founder of the business, stared benignly as if innocent of any dealings with the US eugenics movement over half a century ago. One thing was certain, the expression on the founder's face was not suicidal.

'Welcome everybody to this inaugural Trustees' meeting of The Capsella Foundation,' William said. 'Some of us have met but let's start with introductions, clockwise round the table. The late Sir Raymond's brother, Ben Herron,' he pointed at Ben, 'who will help us develop our media contacts. You're especially welcome today.'

'Thank you,' said Ben who first met William at Raymond's funeral. 'I hope to make useful introductions that'll put the Foundation on the map.'

'Next, Mr Karim Samir was the senior negotiator behind the deal for Capsella-Biotech to share data with the Human Genome Project. His job as a Trustee is to establish links with Bursary Departments of top universities.' Everyone looked at Samir who nodded. 'Next to Mr Samir is Lina Rothstein, Chief Executive of

Capsella-Biotech GmbH. The company has pledged our first five million pound endowment.' The others applauded and Lina responded by slightly raising both hands. 'Lina will also chair our panel that sifts student grant applications each year, and shortlists the candidates. Thank you for your firm's wonderful support'

'My pleasure,' said Lina.

William finally welcomed the remaining two trustees: a stern faced woman with permed grey hair, a member of the Max Planck Society's Scientific Council; and a retired Professor of Molecular Genetics from the University of London, casually dressed. Both women would sit on the grants panel chaired by Lina.

'I've received apologies from Guy Shepherd, a director at Herron International with special responsibility for CSR.'

'What's that mean?' It was Ben.

'Corporate and Social Responsibility. Call it ethics,' said William with a sideways glance at Thomas Herron's bust. 'Guy is away on business. It's a pity he's not here, the Foundation was his idea. He will head up the Foundation's fundraising.'

'And will Miss Jessica Parry become a Trustee?' said Samir.

'We approached her,' said William, 'but for personal reasons she does not wish to get involved with the Foundation's governance. We can't really complain since she's pledged to match our first five million, pound for pound, presumably from her late step-father's estate. It means we now have ten million in the pipeline to get us started.'

'Fantastic,' said Samir, 'let's hope Mr Shepherd's fundraising can top that.' The others murmured their agreement.

Alex enquired about the Human Genome sequencing at Capsella-Biotech. Guy reminded him of their conversation in the Park-Klinik. 'Since then a lot has happened. When speculation began that Capsella-Biotech may not win the genomic sequencing race, the share price collapsed. Your personal financial hit is bigger than the cancelled Iraq deal. Your shareholding has dropped by hundreds of millions.' Guy waited for an expletive from Alex, but nothing happened.

'I presume that's not the only thing you wanted to say.'

Guy took a deep breath. 'A tri-lateral deal has been brokered between the US Government, Capsella-Biotech and the Human Genome Project.'

'That's something I didn't know,' said Alex.

'Fucking listen, cousin.' Guy jabbed a finger. 'The US Government has agreed to sponsor Capsella's work to develop the IBEC system, in return for sharing all your sequenced data with the Human Genome Project. Capsella-Biotech now has new partners and its employees' jobs are safe.'

'What's the price? You can't tell me taxpayers will throw money at my gene editing system without demanding yet more in return.'

'The global scientific community will get that as well. Medical science will never be the same again. It's your legacy.'

'Legacies are for people who've passed on,' said Alex. 'I'm still here.'

'Only thanks to the Ruger pistol's safety catch. You may be sectioned in here, but don't ever expect to leave this place and stay alive. I can never forgive what you did to me in that cellar.' Guy watched Alex's face turn pale. 'In my nightmares of dad's vicious canings, you're right there, leering at me with that fucking barbed wire, then I'm drowning…'

'Perhaps you're the one who should be strapped in this bloody chair.'

'No need.' Guy glanced at the door again. He briefly wondered how Alex might react to being unexpectedly set free, then quickly brought his mind back to the job in hand. 'I've had nice dreams as well, like the Ruger's safety catch was off and your brains spattered all over the cellar.'

'There being no further business I declare this meeting closed. Thank you everybody,' said William. 'As it's Christmas I've arranged mulled wine and mince pies. Let's go to the ante-room.' There was a hum of approval.

In the ante-room the trustees stood awkwardly, no-one wished to be first to help themselves. William took charge and poured drinks. His PA passed round the mince pies.

'A successful first meeting,' said Lina.

410

'Indeed,' said the woman from the Max Planck Society, 'and wonderful to think we'll create bursaries that encourage young people into genetic science.'

'The cost of further education is prohibitive for many students,' said Lina. 'For genetics to engage with society, it makes sense to attract candidates from disadvantaged backgrounds.'

'That's exactly what we're about,' said William. 'The income from our ten million pound endowment should support at least sixty students a year. By breaking financial barriers to entry and by nurturing talent, we'll offer life-changing opportunities to aspiring young scientists who would otherwise miss out.'

'A financial lift to realise the potential of young people,' said the retired professor.

'What a good strapline,' said Ben. 'Shouldn't you be in charge of the Foundation's PR?' Everyone laughed.

William lifted his glass. 'To the Capsella Foundation.'

The others raised their glasses and said, 'The Foundation.'

Alex glowered. 'What do you want from me?'

'Even if you've changed, you should still pay for what you've done.' Guy lifted himself up keeping his right leg straight.

Alex could not move. 'Have you changed?'

'Yes. I've got my job back with Herron International provided I behave.' He loosened his belt buckle. 'I haven't told you about the new Foundation to

411

help youngsters study genetics. I'm supposed to be at the Trustees' meeting today but you know how it is, even modern science can't put me in two places at the same time.'

'So you're a Trustee.' Alex gave him a cold look. 'Doing what?'

'Fundraising.' Guy unfastened his trouser zip and limped two steps towards Alex who tensed, but did not budge. 'Ten million is already secured. I'd like to double that amount.'

'Don't approach me for funds.'

'What makes you think I would?' Guy slid his right hand down the inside of his trouser leg.

Unable to flinch, Alex tightened his grip on the arm rests of his chair as Guy suddenly produced the carving knife he had purchased at the market stall.

'Nurse!' Alex quivered. 'NURSE!!'

Guy swung around as the woman in nurse's uniform crept in. She quietly closed the door behind her and Guy turned back towards Alex, placed one hand over his mouth pressing his head against the back of the chair, knife at the ready.

'The basket's all set,' said Jessica hurriedly. 'Do it now. Make it quick for God's sake.'

* * * * * *

It was William Vinson's first day at work after the festive break. In the Chairman's office at Adams Court he stood and looked out of the window where, only a few months earlier, Raymond had observed a disgraced Guy walking in the late summer sun along the pavement below carrying his ominous sports bag. Now the cold grey sky of early January shrouded the City like a giant marquee. William had never expected his elevation to the chairmanship of Herron International, and he still felt like a new boy on his first day at school. But then Lina Rothstein probably never thought she would be propelled to the role of Capsella-Biotech's Chief Executive; he wondered how she was getting on. And then there was Guy, once discredited but now a director who, curiously, seemed to be spending rather a lot of time away from London, presumably fundraising for the Capsella Foundation.

William had a very busy time ahead of him. With strategy meetings, client visits and drinks receptions his crammed diary was more like a train timetable. He moved away from the window and went to sit at Raymond's desk - he could not bring himself to call it his own desk, yet. His email inbox had over a hundred new messages awaiting his attention and paper correspondence filled his in-tray. He was resigned to tackle it all, ignoring that morning's copy of *The Times* that his PA had placed to one side of the desk. Had he turned to the business section of the newspaper he would have found a short article about one of his firm's clients:

$100 million Contract
for Capsella-Biotech GmbH

A contract worth $100m (€112m) was signed towards the end of last year between the US government, genetic science company Capsella-Biotech GmbH and a research consortium known as the Human Genome Project. The deal includes a data-share arrangement whereby Capsella will help the consortium to fill any remaining gaps in the initial draft of sequenced human DNA.

Lina Rothstein, newly appointed Chief Executive of Capsella-Biotech commented, 'I am delighted that our future work with the Human Genome Project will provide much needed data on human DNA. Our joint goal is to finish unravelling the full code of human life itself, via a computerised technique to sequence DNA developed by Capsella's in-house research team. Our new partnership with the Human Genome Project will ensure that the entire human genomic code is sequenced by 2003 latest, which will be a fine tribute to the inspirational work of my predecessor.'

Capsella's former CEO, Dr Alexander Grishin, stepped down from his position last year amid rumours that he was seeking treatment for severe depression. In an unexpected development however, on New Year's Day his corpse was found at the water's edge of the lake at Wannsee in Berlin. An investigation is being led by Polizei Kommissar Stefan

Borchardt of Berlin Police, who has stated that all the evidence now points to a tragic case of accidental drowning and that nobody else is being sought in connection with the incident.

Due to the seasonal holiday none of the project leaders of the Human Genome Project were available for comment last week, however, on Friday Capsella-Biotech's share price was up by twelve points.

THE END

ACKNOWLEDGEMENTS

I am most grateful to many of my friends and colleagues for their encouragement and helpful feedback on various sections of this book. Particular thanks must go to Ro and Peter Wilson whose kindness enabled me to complete the manuscript on time.

For their candid editorial advice on earlier drafts I am indebted to Susan Harrison, Wanda Whiteley, Cressida Downing, Michael Thomas and Brett Hardman.

My appreciation also goes to Brigadier Charlie Calder OBE for his guidance on royal investitures; Dr Peter Jéquier and Christina Stolfo for their advice on medical matters; many of the staff at Buckingham Palace and Somerset House for their courteous help; and to numerous welcoming citizens of Berlin and New York.

My research sources included four fact-based books: *The Genome War* by James Shreeve, *Dead Silence – Fear And Terror On The Anthrax Trail* by Bob Coen and Eric Nadler, *Twin Telepathy* by Guy Lyon Playfair and *Depressive Illness: The Curse of the Strong* by Dr Tim Cantopher. Similarly I commend a fascinating exclusive feature on the CRISPR method of gene editing published in *The Independent* in November 2013.

While many excellent novels have influenced my writing, I was particularly intrigued by Ira Levin's *The Boys From Brazil* set in the fictional aftermath of Nazi eugenics.

To my family, for their forbearance and support in my quest to write fiction, thank you all.

Robin Jéquier grew up in the West Midlands of Britain and studied piano and organ at The Royal Academy of Music in London.

He then changed tack and served in the British Army for sixteen years. On completing his military service he worked in finance and fundraising consultancy.

Robin is married with three adult sons, one of whom suffers from a genetically inherited disease, an incurable condition which first triggered Robin's interest in genetics.

It was learning about the benefits and risks of gene therapy and gene editing that inspired Robin to write *The Gene Deal*, his first novel.

His home is in Wiltshire where Robin lives with his wife and dog, and where he still plays the organ.

www.robinjequier.com

Printed in Great Britain
by Amazon